Critical Fictions

THE POLITICS OF IMAGINATIVE WRITING

Dia Center for the Arts

Discussions in Contemporary Culture

Number 7

Critical Fictions

THE POLITICS OF IMAGINATIVE WRITING

Edited by

Philomena Mariani

BAY PRESS   SEATTLE   1991

Printed in the United States of America
First Printing 1991

Design by Bethany Johns with Georgie Stout
Typesetting by Strong Silent Type, New York
Printing by Malloy Lithographing

Library of Congress Number 89-650815
ISSN 1047-6806
ISBN 0-941920-24-0

Contents

III. "THAT CAPACIOUS TOPIC": GENDER POLITICS

CONFERENCE PRESENTATIONS

IV. "NO STATISTICS OF THE SOUL": SYSTEMS OF OPPRESSION AND THE STRUGGLE FOR A CULTURE

CONFERENCE PRESENTATIONS

A Note on the Series

We rely heavily on artists, critics, scholars, and others from outside Dia to sustain us in developing the "Discussions in Contemporary Culture" series of symposia and related publications. With their guidance we have ranged widely in the series, from rigorous theoretical ground in Hal Foster's *Vision and Visuality*, to new perspectives in historiography in Barbara Kruger and Phil Mariani's *Remaking History*, to the practice of art in relation to specific social and political questions in Group Material's *Democracy* and Martha Rosler's *If You Lived Here*. With this volume, *Critical Fictions* (Number 7 in the series), we look directly at literature for the first time. The contributors, all writers of fiction, each consider the critical relationship between imaginative writing and the political and social institutions that shape the writer's daily experience.

The first step toward this publication was a symposium held at Dia on May 11-12, 1990. Fifteen participants from a dozen nations met at Dia for public discussion about the politics of writing. Phil Mariani did an extraordinary job of bringing together for this event writers from all over the world and from far-ranging cultural backgrounds; she then solicited and compiled even more diverse contributions to the publication. The writers who contributed to this volume and whose struggles were the inspiration for the project have our deep respect and our gratitude for their time and efforts. I would also like to thank Bethany Johns for her work on the design of this publication and Thatcher Bailey for his help in getting the project to press.

Generous funding for this project has been provided by The Reed Foundation, Inc., the New York State Council on the Arts, and by individual members of the Dia Art Council, Dia's major annual support group.

Charles B. Wright
Executive Director
Dia Center for the Arts

Acknowledgments

Numerous friends and professional colleagues shaped this volume of essays, sharing ideas and offering practical and emotional support. Joan Duddy, Laura Fields, Karen Kelly, and Sara Rees (experts in crisis management) patiently assisted me in the organization of the symposium from start to finish; it has been a pleasure to work with such congenial and lively co-workers. Charles Wright, director of Dia Center for the Arts, has been exceedingly receptive to all my proposals for the Discussions series, and was especially enthusiastic about *Critical Fictions;* one could not ask for a more enabling work environment. Our designer, Bethany Johns, and her assistant, Georgie Stout, are always a delight to work with, and once again have produced an elegant design perfectly synchronized with the content of the volume. Thatcher Bailey and Christopher Stearns of Bay Press have been an editor's dream, and Cathy Johnson, our copyeditor, approached each essay with delicacy and discernment.

I am grateful to Homi Bhabha, Sharon Feldman, Tracy Hatton, Lynne Tillman, and Michele Wallace who, from the outset of this project, have been exceptionally generous with their time and ideas. And to the writers who attended the symposium and contributed to this volume, I hope I have done justice to the richness of their work. Finally, I am indebted to Jan Levi, a wonderful poet whose sensitivity to the complexities of the written word continually astounds me, for her artful editing and guidance in shaping the overall structure of this collection.

In the process, I have found some very dear friends. The work on this volume has been informed in indescribable ways by one of them, Arturo Islas, a kind and generous soul whose joyous energy very deeply touched all of us who knew him.

Philomena Mariani

For Chinua Achebe
whose words triggered reflections that led to this book
to wit –

For I do honestly believe that in the fat-dripping,
gummy, eat-and-let-eat regime just ended – a regime
which inspired the common saying that a man could
only be sure of what he had put away safely in his gut . . .
in such a regime, I say, you died a good death if your life
had inspired someone to come forward and shoot your
murderer in the chest – without asking to be paid.

from *A Man of the People*

I.

VISIONS AND REVISIONS

Philomena Mariani

"God Is a Man"

Consider this passage from a recent volume on the ruinous state of American manhood, Robert Bly's *Iron John*:

In the seventies I began to see all over the country a phenomenon that we might call the "soft male." Sometimes even today when I look out at an audience, perhaps half the young males are what I'd call soft. They're lovely, valuable people – I like them – they're not interested in harming the earth or starting wars. There's a gentle attitude toward life in their whole being and style of living.

But many of these young men are not happy. You quickly notice the lack of energy in them... The strong or life-giving women who graduated from the sixties, so to speak, or who have inherited an older spirit, played an important part in producing this life-preserving, but not life-giving, man... The new distribution of "yang" energy among couples didn't happen by accident. Young men for various reasons wanted their harder women, and women began to desire softer men. It seemed like a nice arrangement for a while, but we've lived with it long enough now to see that it isn't working out.[1]

As I write, *Iron John* – another installment in the offensive against the "debilitating effects" of feminism – has been on *The New York Times* best-seller list for thirty-nine weeks. Now, while it is true that attacks on feminism (in fact, all "energetic" women) have garnered an avid and grateful following, comprised primarily of right-wing intellectuals and academics, Bible-thumpers, and readers of *Soldier of Fortune*, it isn't likely that *Iron John* would be popular with that crowd (for reasons that will become apparent shortly). Clearly the book has touched a nerve. The question is: whose nerve?

Its rather high-strung language – an unstable mixture of New Age lingo, therapeutic missives, and the muscle-flexing bravado packaged by Roger Ailes to sell George Bush – may provide a clue to its appeal. *Iron John* is a kinder, gentler manifesto for rehabilitating a depleted masculinism, a nineties version of the now-defunct Moral Majority's dictum for patriarchy's grand comeback: "The father's word has to prevail."² *Iron John* is a call to arms, exhorting men to reclaim their "Zeus energy," that is, "male authority accepted for the sake of the community." Sadly, today's "soft men" have relinquished this birthright, and "Zeus energy has been steadily disintegrating decade after decade in the United States."³ Men (*all* men; race and class distinctions are elided; sexual difference ignored) have tried *too hard* to please their mothers, wives, girlfriends; and fathers have not initiated their sons into the mysteries of the "instinctive male world." Coddled in a warm fug of female sensibility, men no longer know who they are or where they are going (*Iron John*'s descriptive categories are as nebulous as this). The result: a sluggish virility crippled by too much nurturing and too little aggressiveness (nicely characterized as *softness* and *hardness*).

However, Bly is much slyer than many of his predecessors, generally avoiding the invective deployed by defenders/arousers of American masculinity. (I'm thinking specifically of Philip Wylie and Norman Mailer, but there are many more. See Wylie's tirade against American motherhood, *Generation of Vipers,* and Mailer's *Prisoner of Sex.*) Bly repeatedly denies that he is proposing a revamped machismo; rather, he claims to offer a corrective to contemporary society's misapprehension, even suppression, of masculine sensibility. He assures his female readers that his intentions are not hostile, that he is not indicting women for the miserable psychological condition in which American men find themselves. Yet the text is teeming with images of castration and impotence, thinly disguised envy of women's reproductive capacity, and paranoia that a conspiracy against men generated by feminists has now broken free of the women's movement to engulf the entire culture. Men who learn "values" from women are incomplete, come up short, are soft, faceless: "When women, even women with the best intentions, bring up a boy alone, he may in some way have no male face, or he may have no face at all." Women are not blind to their inadequacies: "One woman declared that she realized about the time her son got to high-school age that he needed more hardness than she could naturally give."⁴

But Mother can be more than benignly deficient, much, much more; she can be a menacing presence, driving a wedge between father and son: "Even when the father is living in the house there still may be a strong covert bond between mother and son to evict the father, which amounts to a conspiracy, and conspiracies are difficult to break." The son is in a bad spot: "we know that more than one man today needs a sword to cut his adult soul away from his mother-bound soul." But men/sons are no longer able to "distinguish between showing the sword and hurting someone," as our ancient friend Odysseus was able to do (mythology is treated virtually as fact). The son makes feeble attempts at separation: "If the old men haven't done their work to interrupt the mother-son unity, what else can the boys do to extricate themselves but to talk ugly?" But no matter what the son does, he is ultimately defeated, because danger lurks in even the most banal encounter with Mother: "the culture still does not take very seriously the damage caused by psychic incest between mother and son...Much sexual energy can be exchanged when the mother looks the son directly in the eyes and says, 'Here is your new T-shirt, all washed.'"[5]

Contemporary father-son relations, as well, are a confusion of murderous resentment and psychological need. The internal pandemonium caused by the mother is merely a repercussion of the father's crime: his remoteness, his *passivity*. "One could say that many young men in the sixties tried to accept initiation from women...Initiators say that boys need a second birth, this time a birth from men."[6] But fathers have rejected their ritualistic duties, leaving the son to rely on the mother for his conception of the world and everything in it, including the father. "So the son often grows up with a wounded image of his father–not brought about necessarily by the father's actions, or words, but based on the mother's observation of these words or actions."[7] One man, troubled by this long-standing emotional distance, finally confronted his father:

"I want you to understand one thing. I don't accept my mother's view of you any longer." "What happened?" [Bly] asked. "My father broke into tears, and said, 'Now I can die.'" Fathers wait. What else can they do?[8]

Yes, poor things, what else *can* they do but passively await their vindication? Their lack of vitality and a sense of self-preservation in the face of (increasingly) forceful female energy has had catastrophic effects on the male psyche, giving way to a range of destructive behaviors. Bly relies on the theories of German psychologist Alexander Mitscherlich, author of *Society Without the Father,* to frame his discussion of the negative impact of paternal neglect. According to Mitscherlich, because sons are no longer privy to the labor done by their fathers every day and throughout the year (as they apparently were during the Golden Age of preindustrialism), a "hole" develops in the son's psyche. This hole fills with "demons who tell him that his father's work is evil and that the father is evil." Bly concludes,

The son's fear that the absent father is evil contributed to student takeovers in the sixties.

Rebellious students at Columbia University took over the president's office looking for evidence of CIA involvement with the university. The students' fear that their own fathers were evil was transferred to all male figures in authority. [The son's rebellious behavior is really a way of asking] "Where is my father... why doesn't he love me? What is going on?"...

When the demons are so suspicious, how can the son later make any good connection with adult male energy, especially the energy of an adult man in a position of authority or leadership? As a musician he will smash handcrafted guitars made by old men, or as a teacher suspicious of older writers he will "deconstruct" them. As a citizen he will take part in therapy rather than politics. He will feel purer when not in authority.[9]

The mass movements of the sixties are trivialized, militant actions reduced to peevish outbursts by neglected sons, struggles for greater self-understanding and deeper social critique portrayed as pathetic resignation. This passage betrays the bitterness of the patriarch, the middle-class pique at the heart of *Iron John,* in which literally every rebellious gesture, every form of dissent or doubt is chalked up to the "hunger for the King in a time with no father." Being of the mind that most children would be better off overthrowing their parents at a very young age and raising each other, I question the assumption that boys *need* an authoritative male figure (much less a king) with which to identify. But Bly doesn't allow a dribble of ambivalence to cloud his vision of good versus bad authority, good versus bad father. Unfortunately, given contemporary social conditions, we are a little confused as to which is which, but it is out of this impasse – this bewilderment of uncertainty, of irresoluteness, of *softness* – that *Iron John* hopes to lead us.

In the same way that rule-breaking activity and psychological breakdown become synonymous, depoliticized and stripped of cultural and economic specificity, so *Iron John* levels all cultures into a vast, timeless, immutable oneness. A tangle of citations of fairy tales, ancient mythologies, modern poetry, folk narratives, New Age theory, Jungian psychology, anecdotal information, and accounts of friends' dreams is put forth as evidence that Essential Man has been lost in the conundrum of modern life. Throughout there is no discernible awareness of the ideological function of foundational narratives, literature, philosophy; no acknowledgment of their time-boundedness and contingency. Essentially a prospectus for benign paternalism with a multicultural gloss, *Iron John's* message seems to be: What's good enough for the ancient Greeks – or the Seneca Indians, or the Celts – should be good enough for us. Needless to say, there is no critique of the concept of male entitlement ("Zeus energy") authorized by these narratives.

Instead, there is Bly's prescriptive. Men may ultimately refuse the burden of guilt imposed by the mother and retrieve the image of the King by reclaiming their Zeus energy: "Every modern male has, lying at the bottom of his psyche, a large, primitive being covered with hair down to his feet. Making contact with this Wild Man is the step the Eighties male or the Nineties male has yet to take."[10] The apotheosis of the Nineties Man lies in his rediscovery of the ancient narratives and their message for men. (Apparently this message has nothing to do with masculine anxiety.) To redistribute "yang" energy properly, men must plunge into that "wet, dark region" some call *soul* (yes) to rediscover the warrior inside them (to be distinguished from the killer inside the warrior). This entails submitting to a number of trials by fire that involve blindly accepting the authority of others. Here the language of *Iron John* becomes a militaristic hodgepodge of Reaganese, Spielbergian juvenilia, and video game parlance:

> ... *we have linked warriorhood to self-sacrifice and service to the King, to intellectual combat, to clean fighting in marriage, and to the sharpness of the Vajra sword. The Vajra sword should move in such a way as to cut apart what has been inappropriately joined. When the sword has done its work and the Logos-Knife has cut well, we will find ourselves less needy and more ready to enter the pairs of opposites. We recall the pairs of opposites that Pythagoras named: light and dark, limited and unlimited, male and female, the resting and the moving...* [11]

Iron John invites absurd associations. One imagines its audience composed of retired Trekkies and Tolkienites, but also a younger, more conservative generation lapping up its contempt for dissent and love of authority, its reassuringly backward sexual politics. How comforting it must be to ignore the last twenty years of critical theory in favor of embracing old myths as if they represented ahistorical, transcendent truths. "Myth deals in false universals, to dull the pain of particular circumstances," as Angela Carter aptly notes. "Its savage denial of the complexity of human relations is also a consolatory nonsense."[12] (Carter understands well the sexual anxiety hidden behind fairy tales and folk narratives and has rewritten a number of them from a feminist perspective.) In this sense, *Iron John* must be understood as one practice among many that, taken together, represent an imposing reaffirmation of "traditional" narratives across economic, cultural, and political spheres.

> Imagine a society in which everybody was either a cynic
> or a masochist, or both. In such a situation there would be
> no need for ideology, in the sense of a set of discourses
> concealing or legitimating injustice, because the maso-
> chists would not mind their suffering and the cynics
> would feel no unease about inhabiting an exploitative
> social order.
> – Terry Eagleton, *Ideology*

Just a few weeks after Pope John Paul II endorsed capitalism in the first papal
document on social issues in a century, *The New York Post* reported that Cardinal
O'Connor (who has applied his unique logic to many a social brain twister) announced that God is indeed a man. The *Post* thoughtfully provided its readers with
front-page coverage of the event, and even included a representation of God himself, from Michelangelo's *Last Judgment* in the Sistine Chapel (note that he's white,
too), as incontrovertible proof of O'Connor's assertion. The *Post* hailed O'Connor's "Father's Day blast from the pulpit" as a direct hit on radical feminists.
(Curiously enough, alongside the headline is a photo of a beleaguered George
Bush inelegantly rubbing his eyes while divulging that he may not run for president in 1992 for reasons of health.) The next day, O'Connor corrected the *Post*
story, maintaining that he had not in fact precisely fixed God's gender, but merely
pointed out the deficiencies of female *representations* of the Lord.

These events – the religious sanctioning of an exploitive economic system, the
divine certification of patriarchy – have in common with Bly's text the appeal to
unreason, fear, and resentment typical of the elite bid to maintain control of the
representational arena. The challenge to the old order begun in the sixties has
frightened corporate and intellectual elites, who have responded, appropriately
enough, by attempting to recuperate their exclusive authority over the production
of knowledge. This has not been easy, given the multiplicity of voices speaking
with ever-greater urgency and power from heterogeneous perspectives. Elite
prestige will be assured only through the reacculturation – the redomestication – of
feminists, people of color, gays, lesbians, the working class, the poor, to a world in
which the political is narrowly defined as electoral participation, hierarchical economic and social structures are perceived as organic and immutable, patriarchal
power is restored for "the good of the community," race and gender differences
are negatively defined – a world in which is reinscribed a history cleansed of Others.

Elite reaction has been given concrete form by the cultural ruminations of con-servative intellectuals like Roger Kimball, Shelby Steele, Dinesh D'Souza, and Allan Bloom. Culture-of-poverty theorists Lawrence Mead, Glenn Loury, and George Gilder, and right-wing think-tanks such as the Manhattan Institute, the Heritage Foundation, and the American Enterprise Institute have made heroic at-tempts to unburden the State of social responsibility. Highly placed doctrinaire re-ligious representatives have inspired thousands of "Bible-believing Americans" to political action against feminist and gay liberationist advances. "Masculinists" like Robert Bly and Michael Novak have contributed their singular observations to the growing body of work on heterosexual "male culture." And disgruntled women-who-claim-to-be-feminists like Camille Paglia have been eager to strip feminist theory and practice of both its scope and subtlety in order to police the "inappro-priate" behavior of other women.[13] Often appealing to racism, misogyny, and ho-mophobia and purportedly dodging the club of political correctness, the arbiters of the return to "tradition" invoke a Western world rapidly losing ground to the moral and intellectual degeneracy of feminism, gay/lesbian liberation, and multiculturalism.

Thus, in the name of rescuing "our society," the banners of *Western Civilization, cultural standards, laissez-faire, family, humanism, paternalism, privatization* have been unfurled. This last concept has been especially flexible in its applications. Way back in 1980, at the beginning of Moral Majority fervor, reproductive rights activ-ist and legal scholar Rosalind Pollack Petchesky observed that "although the lan-guage of New Right ideology evokes the sentiment of personal freedom from state interference, what distinguishes that ideology from classical conservatism is that it is spoken on behalf of *corporate* bodies rather than individuals. It is, in other words, corporate privatism – in the service of business, church, private school, and patriarchal family – that is intended, not individual privacy."[14] Conservative ideo-logues, then, have mobilized to protect the sanctity of *institutions,* and, not surpris-ingly, those institutions that guarantee their continued dominance. Thus, the cohe-siveness of American culture (and upper-class white male intellectual privilege) must be protected from the fragmenting tendencies of "barbaric" multiculturalism (Kimball's term). The public (defined as suburban, white, middle-class, hetero-sexual) must be protected from the incursions of the homeless, the poor, the *alien,* and other dangers lurking in the urban space. The church must be defended against "blasphemous" assaults by artists and writers. The integrity of academic scholar-ship and the educational system must be preserved in the face of the ideologically motivated intolerance of "special interest groups" such as feminists, Marxists, Afrocentrists, and so on (thereby limiting the possibility of another generation of college students developing the capacity to criticize the social and economic order). Traditional virtues – self-sufficiency, sacrifice – must be safeguarded against the culture of dependency threatening to consume the nation. And, most fragile institution of all, the family ("as historically defined") must be shielded from attempts to reconstitute its traditional arrangement (thereby leaving intact male prerogative over women and children).

But it is important to remember that if Gilder and Company feel compelled to rewrite the history of the social welfare state to justify the further disenfranchisement of the poor and working class in the United States, it is because an imposing body of theoretical and empirical work has contested the "natural law" of the free market and other mythic conceptions of the capitalist order. Likewise, if legislators avidly pursue means to separate public and private, it is because feminists, gays, and lesbians have challenged the socioeconomic privilege sustained by the artificial divide between domestic and public and exposed the connections between oppressive economic structures and the patriarchal family. And if D'Souza et al. frantically defend the Western canon against the blight of politics and ideology, it is certainly because artists, writers, theorists, poets, novelists, and filmmakers of every color and sexual orientation are advancing radically different images and scenarios of our past, present, and future.

I do not mean to imply by this focus on the ideological that the current political struggles are being waged at a discursive level alone. The human suffering caused by economic restructuring and the abandonment of the public sector, the texture of violence governing so many communities of color, the indifference of the State to the death of thousands from AIDS or to battered, raped, and murdered women, the destruction of the public education system, which has circumscribed the future of millions of low-income children: all of this tends to put academic theorizing and cultural production into perspective. But if only because the right understands "proofs" in the representational sphere to mean justification for the cruelest forms of political and social disenfranchisement, it must also continually deny that anything better could be imagined. Hence its hostility to oppositional culture, of which critical fictions – imaginative writing – are a part.

> As far as most people are concerned, I have been invited
> here because I have written some books and some people
> have read them. In fact, that is only part of the reason.
> The whole reason is that . . . some black children got their
> brains shot out in streets all over this country, and, having
> the "good fortune" to be televised, slowly, slowly forced
> the State to pay attention . . . I am a read writer (as op-
> posed to an unread one) because of those children. I am
> clear on that point. For had I lived the life the State
> planned for me from the beginning . . . I would have lived
> and died in somebody else's kitchen, on somebody else's
> land, and never written a word.
>
> — Toni Morrison, statement made at the 1986 PEN
> congress, "The Writer's Imagination and the
> Imagination of the State"

This is a book of essays by novelists. They speak from diverse geographic locations and cultural perspectives about the politics of literary production, about
what it means to be writing from specific race, class, and gender positions at a particular historical moment. All the writers in this volume are linked by the understanding that a critical imagination is forged in struggle. By *struggle* I mean not
only the writer's psychic wrestlings with speech and silence, but the intersection
of that private task and its public context. As Toni Morrison so eloquently suggests, writers of critical fiction understand that bodies – if not *their* bodies – are laid
on the line for the right to imagine freely.

There are many other points of contact and also of disagreement among the
contributors to this volume. Some contest universalist paradigms of literature,
others discuss ways of transforming the canon. Still others argue against the
notion of the canon itself. Many discuss the deadening effects of authoritarian/
colonialist regimes or patriarchal structures, sexual repression or racist violence,
others the impact of exile as one negotiates a new geographic or linguistic terrain.
Most agree, implicitly or explicitly, that a critical culture is produced through
struggle against dominant discourses, but some note also the need for vigilance
against the institutionalization of a formerly oppressed culture, or the relapse into
nativist or essentialist practices.

Almost all are tacitly engaged in a project of unmasking the interested nature of claims to universal truth, and through their fiction uncover alternative realities (political, psychological, cultural), unearthing what was previously unseen by the God's-eye-view of the modernist gaze. The realities of critical fiction are multiple, chaotic, inclusive, hybridized, undomesticated, unpurified; often polemical, anti-universal. The writers make no apologies for creating this disorder.

The interrogation of unitary narratives, the naming of manifold identities, the exploration of multiple subjectivities – that is, this creation of disorder, has earned the malice of not only conservative critics but also many on the left, who resent the "centrifugal tendencies" generated by drawing attention to difference and away from class struggle. But nostalgia for the surety of master narratives – Family, Nation, God, Progress, or even Class Struggle – veils a desire to escape the complexity of historical and cultural realities exposed by oppositional postmodern practices. The awareness of the shifting ground of reality and of the need to continually rethink strategies of resistance is the conceptual location of the writer of critical literature. It is to this space that critical fictions draw the reader – to be, finally, stripped of the familiar – compelling a process of self-critique.

Although often accused of mindlessly celebrating difference for its own sake, multiculturalists, lesbians, gays, feminists – the political and cultural location of many contributors to this volume – in fact call upon the traditional left to reexamine its most fundamental precepts. This confrontation within the left represents a struggle to redefine left theory and practice, the challenge posed by an oppositional postmodernism to conceive of difference in other than negative terms, to incorporate ambivalence and ambiguity as elements of resistance, to encourage nothing less than a radical transformation in subjectivity.

Zoë Wicomb

An Author's Agenda

Having had little success in coming to terms with the topic – "an author's agenda" – or positioning myself in relation to it, this essay is more exploration than statement, an exploration that does not get very far beyond problematizing the title and that is not free of contradictions.

If an agenda is a list of items to be attended to, then what could an author's agenda possibly be? In the light of current debates, it would probably be imperatives like: the writer must address the political reality, or – what is commonly seen as its opposite – the writer's first concern should be aesthetics, that is, she should focus on writing well rather than on the "correct" subject matter.

My response to any such agenda-dictating would undoubtedly be a bad-tempered one, but I am also struck by the redundancy of these particular prescriptions. First of all, to argue for the politicization of writing is surely unnecessary. All writing, whether it deals directly with the revolution or not, occupies a political position. Similarly, the injunction to write well is, as I have argued elsewhere, nonsensical, since no one perversely sets out to write badly. Revolutionaries surely recognize that the aesthetics-politics opposition is itself a construct that places readers in a menial relation to writers. The fixing of any agenda, then, seems to ignore a crucial fact about writing – that as an act of communication it is of no consequence without a reader.

Along with all sensible people, I agree that the writer has a social responsibility, but I argue for responsibility in the broadest sense, based on the belief that all signifying systems affect the ways in which we perceive the world. Having for many years imbibed questionable values put about by "the great men" like Shakespeare, Wordsworth, or William Golding, it occurs to me that veneration of the author had prevented me from being a resistant reader. Had my education offered the possibility of revolutionary reading, I would have done what I do with any commodity produced in the culture that I am told is good for me: sift out what I consider valuable from that which I find objectionable. As resistant readers, we do not have to accept the values promoted in the work of authors, whether canonized or not. If our concern then is the social and political impact of writing, it might be more fruitful to focus on what Catherine Belsey calls "post-Copernican readers" who will reject the authority of the author. At this point I'd like to amend my title, to erase the word *author* and replace it with the word *writer*.

As a writer, I do not have an agenda. But, like everyone else, I write from a political position – as, amongst other things, a black South African and feminist. This position informs my writing just as my material situation as teacher, mother, or member of a nuclear family affects my practice. I would like to think that my writing does not support or reproduce the inequities of a reprehensible system, although I do not, of course, have total control over meaning. (A story I wrote about an abortion has to my dismay, for instance, been read as having an anti-abortion message.)

But to think in terms of fixing an agenda seems both hopelessly reductive and dangerous. For me, the validity of discussing this topic lies in rewriting it. In other words, as a creative reader I can resist the topic of a writer's agenda. The process is instructive, for I believe that our role as readers of the term *agenda*, our attempts at interpreting it, could mean a reinscription of the term. So I would once again like to amend the title to include the reader's agenda. This is not to evade responsibility: as a response to the concern about writing as a conductor of ideology, the rubric of this paper can be extended to foreground the role of the reader, whose activity is of equal significance.

As a *reader*, I might be more amenable to the idea of an agenda, and so draw up a list of the kind of things I deem correct or revolutionary or pleasurable to read. This spawns new questions: Do we then need the writer at all? What would the writer's function be? To flesh out an agenda, that is, to serve the tautological role of telling us what we have told her to tell us? Or telling people what they already know, for example, about their oppression? The demands of so-called relevant literature hardly accord with my notion of revolution, which includes bringing new or fresh insights to a situation. Can telling people what they expect to hear provide them with a more stimulating environment than the restrictive social and political environment of Apartheid? The writer with an agenda can surely not offer us the experience of discontinuity, ambiguity, violation of our expectations, or irony – the stock and trade of contradictory interpretations.

A writer's agenda implies a disregard for writing as a process of discovery, as well as a disregard for the materiality of language, which resists the implied separation of form and content. There may be consensus that we should promote the democratic struggle, but precisely because writing deals with the slippery stuff of language, there is likely to be disagreement about meaning. How would we know whether such work in fact promotes the democratic struggle? How valid is the term *revolutionary writing* for material that deals directly with the political struggle, when we have no evidence that such work moves people to political action more than, say, writing about hair-straightening? In any case, is there not something unpleasant about the writer who persuades others to take up arms while she writes poetry? We could argue that that's not what the worker-poets do, but we're not all workers and to call ourselves cultural workers is on one level disingenuous when our material conditions have nothing in common with the working class.

It seems to me that we can produce an agenda only if we think in terms of an adamic language, that is, a language before corruption, an innocent system of nomenclature that corresponds directly with things in the world. Precisely because the very term *Writer's Agenda* is not innocent, however, we are able to contextualize it, to probe its origins and evolution. Why is the "Writer's Agenda" on the agenda? It is precisely because of the debate on revolutionary versus aesthetic or good versus bad writing in South Africa. We are discussing agendas because Albie Sachs, speaking from the legitimized platform of the African National Congress, has shocked the faithful by an attack on the lackluster work produced in the name of relevance and the revolution. Sachs's tongue-in-cheek solution to the crisis in writing is to ban the statement that has loaded the pens of our writers – that culture is a weapon of the struggle. Sachs argues that the production of so much "bad writing" can be remedied only by banning the idea of committed writing.

I find this concern about so-called bad work paranoiac and puzzling. If we did not have such normative categories as "literature," this issue would not appear on the agenda. And precisely because I do not think that moral, political, or aesthetic value lies in subject matter, I do not think it helpful to ban the notion of committed writing. It *is* possible to write an interesting novel about hippos in the street *or* about the armed struggle; the problem lies with prescription. Setting an agenda that bans certain subjects and prescribes others seems foolish, since it can generate only two categories of writers: the obedient, who will slavishly follow the agenda, and the disobedient, who will avoid it as a matter of principle.

Now if we were to view writing from another perspective, that is to say, simply as a depository of the culture, then we would arrive at a different set of statements. Then, instead of value judgments, we would say that South African writing shows a preoccupation with the liberation struggle. But we can also infer from this writing a number of other things about the culture: for one, unease about the use of standard dialects, reflected in the reclaiming by some of nonstandard varieties as a literary language. We could also explore how the question of gender relations is either suppressed or subsumed under the national liberation struggle.

If we stop thinking of literature, which is to say, of writing, in hegemonic terms, if we secularize it and consider writing simply as language-in-use, and think of the struggle as something that moves people to find their voices or teaches them to be comfortable in their use of language, then would it matter whether we call such products poems, or whether we assess them to be good or bad poems? Literacy skills, as any teacher knows, are best acquired when the learner is affectively involved with his or her material. If people who start off without the linguistic capital necessary to communicate effectively or produce good poetry find on the activists' platform a space where they are moved to use language, where they manage to overcome linguistic insecurity, it seems churlish to complain that the poetry is not good, and silly to infer that the doctrine of relevance is responsible for the production of bad poetry.

What I consider to be of importance is to find one's voice and to value writing as a process of discovery, rather than focusing on the product. Political oppression invariably means linguistic oppression, and for marginalized groups like black women who are doubly bound, it is difficult to break through the silence. Having found her voice, the new writer will, through practice, improve her skills, or she may well abandon creative writing and put her language skills to other use. But if the ineffective writer wants to continue producing poems, I fail to see why anyone should object.

My final amendment of the topic, then, is to erase the word *agenda* and replace it with *education*. Thinking about a more learner-centered, democratic education system, of how confidence in language use can be instilled, and of how pupils' personal language histories can be validated – these are the issues implicated in the kind of writing produced by a culture. An understanding of language as a site of struggle or as a conductor of ideology will empower us as both readers and writers. The right to claim linguistic space is a basic human right. Rather than set agendas for various kinds of writing, we can do no more than ask of our education system that it encourage the writer to think about how she positions herself in that political space. Reactionary positions may well be reduced, or may not. But readers will have to be prepared for both possibilities.

Gary Indiana

Identity Check

Few memories of starting to write, precious few memories of the kinds of stories that came into my head, but I recognize, in the trick ending of a play I wrote on the train between Paris and Berlin, *Phantoms of Louisiana*, echoes of an infantile wish for affairs to be neatly tied up, disasters reversed, the dead revived in their coffins. "Everything will be explained."

Here is a story that seems, looking back, paradigmatic of one kind of American childhood: Mary Ellen and I are playing in the woods, sliding down pine needle slopes on metal saucers designed for snow sledding. We climb to the crest of a little hill and see flames crackling in the underbrush, clouds of smoke rolling into the pine trees. We run for the house, go rushing into the kitchen, where Mary Ellen's mother, at that time a dipso, is ironing and carrying on a desultory phone conversation, the vodka bottle handy under the sink. "The woods are on fire, the woods are on fire!" "These damned kids," her mother mutters with educated irony, giving us a glassy stare. "They're always making up stories. Now they think the woods are on fire." Meanwhile, hundreds of acres of forest burn to the ground.

My creative efforts, once they take on a certain edge, are greeted with nervous mistrust. Quiet, brooding, spends too much time by himself... nose always buried in a book... As children, my brother and I had the run of the town, as most kids did, it being the crime-free, undercrowded 1950s; we fell easily and deliciously into bad company. The little town was a vast, inexhaustibly mysterious world. Nothing prepared me to ever leave it, and perhaps if I had been "normal," gifted with the indigenous lack of curiosity, I would be there even today. Writing spoiled me, warped my perspective.

At twelve, weekly appointments with a child psychologist in Concord, a Mrs. Riggs, who gives me good advice that I fail to follow through on: I should get out of the house during the summer, paint billboards, get some fresh air. The unspoken: my parents are suffocating me with their constant dramas, always the same, my father's drunken rages, my mother's silent seething anger, a psychotic theater played out with my brother and myself a captive audience. I keep a secret notebook. In it I record a sexual fantasy about a Portuguese teenager, a friend of my brother's, who lives, literally, on the wrong side of the tracks. Eugene's family's poverty disturbs my mother, raises suspicions about that whole tribe... Eugene (is he still alive?) is a bad influence. He has never even shown me his penis, but I have imagined it in monumental detail. My diary describes a torrid scene of fellatio, for which I have Eugene paying me thirteen dollars (I do not yet grasp the mechanics of the client-hustler relation). Like the witch in a fairy tale, my mother discovers the notebook, reads it, brandishes it in my face when I come home from school one afternoon. She refuses to believe that Eugene's big, stiff cock is a little boy's fantasy. She grills me for days, an avenging cop: Where did it happen? How many times? Eager to blame an outsider for "corrupting" me, she cites this episode years later, still convinced of its reality, as the likely "cause" of my homosexuality.

That might have been my first intimation of the power of the word. If the evidence of my senses was dismissed as fantasy in the case of the fire (and many other cases, too), this writing was able to cause an eruption of violent feelings. My imagination altered the state of things in the real world. For years after this incident I wrote "for the drawer," hiding even the most perfunctory and innocent written observation, as if any record of my thought process on paper comprised an act of extreme provocation. Possession of a subjectivity, an "I" attaching its own interpretation to events and passing time, seemed a de facto invitation to an onslaught of shame and guilt. I see now that Eugene, the dark proletarian lover of my erotic mental life, stood for much of what my family dreaded. My parents had scrabbled their way out of the class Eugene belonged to. It was awful enough that I wanted to suck a man's cock, but that I wanted to suck a *guinea* was an inassimilable nightmare.

So, quite precociously, I came by my "subject," or at least one of the themes that would haunt my work years later. I came to associate writing with secrecy and exposure; the most innocuous sequence of words, I believed, would reveal the deformity inside me. My plays would be about freaks: incest-riddled Southern families, alligator girls, werewolves, Roman Polanski. I would always be most comfortable describing acute discomfort, the feelings of being out-of-place, awkward, unwanted, grotesque—the feelings I knew best.

I read prodigiously. Especially "forbidden" paperbacks, novels about sex. I stole them from the well-stocked local newspaper store: *Our Lady of the Flowers, Totem-*

pole, Lady Chatterley's Lover, Naked Lunch, a curious novel called *Night* that described a love affair between a prisoner of war and his captor in North Korea – and anything, everything else I could carry off, purchase, borrow from the library. It seemed to me that I read everything, but in fact I didn't, much of classic literature I skimmed and had to burrow through years later. A lot of what I did read I didn't understand at all, though I pretended to. I was aware of a special connection between myself and the people who wrote books. Unlike them, however, I had nothing to say. I was full of vague longings and an increasingly desperate desire to please. Did I have the right to make something from nothing? The brains? The will? Life conspired to destroy my confidence.

I was having the bad experiences that I would, much later, put to good use.

Miserable at Boston University, I write a long letter home, confessing my sexual "orientation," mail it off, the next day realize I've made a ridiculous mistake, jump on a bus for New Hampshire hoping to arrive ahead of my letter, walk into the kitchen ten minutes after they've both read it. A few days later, I'm in a Boston mental clinic – once again, my writing has provoked disaster out of thin air – attended by a Dr. Bigwood, a bald British refugee from socialized medicine and all-round quack, who gets me addicted to valium for seven years and informs me that I'm not a homosexual at all, that I have "an adolescent adjustment problem," that my desire to write books is absurd because I'm not bright enough, that "my only hope" is to return to school, finish my studies, find a job. I remain in his long-distance care while at Berkeley, where I have another nervous breakdown, and so on.

By the time my formal education sputters to an undistinguished stop, I'm sufficiently pulverized by psychiatry and antidepressants to be ripe for the work force and devoid of all ambition. I do, periodically, write, alternately muzzy with dreams of best-sellerdom and squashed by the complete worthlessness of everything I do. I drift, pulled here and there by strange currents. I have not yet found a reason to write. Others, perhaps, don't need one, assured from the start that every scribble is worthwhile. But I have had the idea of writing as an end in itself pressed out of me. I don't have a strong ego, or what you would call a world view. In the gay ghetto of backwater Boston, I cultivate a more genteel, campy version of my father's alcoholism, whore around, consume "relationships" like potato chips. I find jobs in offices, edit manuscripts for neurologists and plastic surgeons, pick up odd bits of data, indulge my "creative" side by making little Super8 movies, painting, taking pictures. In my head, it's a question of *when* rather than *if* I will write.

The obscure embarrassment of being loveless, of having less than others.

In Boston I am "comfortable." I earn more than I need. I am surrounded by people with no plans for the future and people who have given up their plans in favor of a comfy, sodden muddle. I publish some short stories in a Marxist gay magazine, some movie reviews, book reviews, little pieces that get wide attention in the tiny microcosm I inhabit, and which therefore give me an illusion of importance. In Boston I content myself with the praise of people even less ambitious than myself. I know, at most, two other people who want to be "real" writers. I meet plenty of writers who don't care about "art," who write strictly about politics – in the Boston gay community, I have several brushes with the custodians of official reality, for whom what I write is insufficiently informed by gay history, gay mannerisms, gay rectitude. I am anti-utopian. Years later, I hear that certain erstwhile opponents have "forgiven me" my early errors. My later work, under a different name, has redeemed the previous lack of political smarts. I can't help believing that what's really happened is, the people involved have all aged twenty years.

Boston life assumed an almost idyllic uneventfulness. Boston is a town where you can hole up and rot for thirty years without even thinking about it: in those days, people rented crumbling four-story houses in the South End or Cambridge and lived with eight or ten people in enchanted desuetude. My day job at Cambridge Legal Aid was effortless. I shared a ground floor flat in Brookline with an easygoing, forty-five-year-old lesbian drunkard; we disintegrated in close synchronization for almost two years, and then, quite suddenly, I was offered a job in Los Angeles. I had no good reason to accept it. Life was easy. But I was drowning. The stasis of that awful town, the feeling that next year would be an exact copy of this year...I needed to burn it all down.

Watts changes me. Watts changes everything. I spend twelve-hour days working on hopeless cases. Children attacked by rats. Women assaulted by drugged ex-husbands, boyfriends with switchblades. Vampire landlords, gun-totin' sheriff's department goons, families locked out of their houses, families defrauded by used car dealers and roving aluminum siding salesmen, myriad ingenious and often pathetically trivial forms of exploitation. Our clients live in a slough of total despair, on minimum disability and welfare payments, with stunning handicaps, many of them illiterate and heartbreakingly gullible, gouged by Beverly Hills landlords who own vast tracts of slum property, bungalows with collapsing ceilings, rotting doors, ratholes the size of dormers. *While serving papers on Mr. Levinsky in Century City*, I could write, the vast mosaic of America shrank into deep focus, it suddenly all made sense. The richest made their money off the poorest. There was nothing gradual or ameliorative about capitalism, *capitalism in its pure form exploits an area's resources, sucks it dry, and puts nothing back in.* It came to me one afternoon, standing in an office of smoked Plexiglas and glossy plants, where the attorney for the other side in a housing dispute was ordering a Lear jet at the Burbank airport for his ski weekend in Aspen, that Levinsky on Doheny Drive has his $2 million house and his Rolls and his condo in Palm Springs *because* Queen Elizabeth Jones down on Manchester Avenue has rats falling into her children's hair, that this is not a side-effect or a "flaw" in an otherwise benign system, but a direct and calculated result.

Between Watts and Westwood (where I eventually took a late-night second job, selling popcorn at a movie theater), a constellation of Hollywood and Silverlake gay bars offered the most varied and accessible sexual provender. The Spike, The Stud, The One-Way, The Detour. At that time it was easy to connect, simple to score. The key to this facile exchange of body fluids was Youth: a young face, a young body. It is strange to see the traditional revulsion of gay youth against faces and bodies over thirty institutionalized, today, in spurious polemical terms, with the older generation cast in the role of the doddering NAACP, the younger set comparing itself to the Black Panthers. In 1977, there was no rhetorical cosmetic: if you looked okay you could probably get laid by someone else who looked okay, after a few drinks at any of the bars I have mentioned. I looked more than okay in 1977, and thanks to Eskatrol spansules, I had plenty of leftover energy after working my two jobs. Intergenerational tension, class differences between the loved and the lover, the prerogatives of "beauty" as opposed to "goodness" – the real-politik of sexuality – are the features of homosexuality that have always jumped out at me as *literary*, rather than the smarmier aspects of love, which are boring. The "gay literature" that had come into existence by the late seventies was already qualitatively different from the work of Genêt, for example, or Pasolini, or even Gore Vidal. An acceptable sort of fag writer was emerging, with staunch, middle-class values, liberal condescension toward blacks and other minorities, in certain ways the kind of homosexual heterosexuals had always felt comfortable with – the kind who cries himself to sleep over how much discomfort his difference is causing other members of the family, who dreams of "acceptance" by the society around him. These writers were, are, writers of formally unadventurous books stamped with the dead poetic boilerplate of *The New Yorker*. Their token acceptance within the literary establishment underscores the basic homogeneity of the power base – writers, editors, publishers, and reviewers who all went to the same schools, own property in the same communities, and pass the baton to others like themselves when they're ready to retire.

The more dangerous possibilities of sexual difference – that one kind of difference leads to another, that the perspective of difference provides a judgment of society, a rejection of bourgeois mentality – have been widely rejected in the backlash atmosphere of the AIDS epidemic. It seems that within the world of AIDS activism, libertarian elements struggle against the draconian effusions of the usual will to power. Forms of rhetoric are jumbled together, utopian intentions are attached to sleazy public pilloryings ("outing"), a kind of empowerment that comes from slinging mud at homosexuals who decline to "get with the program" has come into existence. These may all be negative, chaotic effects of oppression, for which there is no obvious remedy. A sense of humor would help, though.

In 1977, America was, or so it seemed, preparing to "buy" homosexuality – a right-wing, Orange County, Gay Republicans brand of homosexuality, founded on strong property values and passionate racism. Political power, in cities like San Francisco, was defined by economic power, by (white) gays owning businesses and houses – a systemic critique of capitalism was something for the extreme fringes of the gay movement. By ingratiating themselves with the business ethic, the work ethic, gays would win acceptance for an expanded sense of the sexually permissible. This new sexuality (widely touted as "bisexuality," doubling the sexual options of white males) would become a commodity the culture could sell back to us in the form of products. Sex had become a taste, an entertainment, an innocuous leisure-time activity that large numbers of people indulged in with many partners, inevitably becoming jaded and hungry for variation. As a taste, sex could be freely exploited in the urban zones of America. Eleven years into the AIDS epidemic, the seventies look like a time of hope and innocence. But they weren't, really.

In the seventies I discovered who I wasn't going to be and the kind of writer I probably would be.

"Don't you love writing?" Because it is the romantic myth of "creativity" that you continue to love something once it is responsible for your salary, but the fact is, however pleasurable the actual process of writing, everything around it is poisoned. A book, once finished, makes the rounds of editors, who everyone agrees are stupid, commercial hacks (including the editors themselves), and unless the book is truly a pile of ordure, the publisher won't trouble himself to sell it. Even though homosexuality is not my real subject, and "gay literature," like most parochial manifestations of group thought, makes me feel like a secular Jew trapped at Grossinger's during an especially shtick-heavy lounge act, I have been out of the closet for twenty years, and if your work treats homosexual subjects without moralism, in other words, matter-of-factly, the Sulzberger empire will make you pay for it, one way or another. When the novel *Horse Crazy* was published, I was already an established writer in New York; nevertheless, *The New York Times* assigned the book to a homophobic nonentity for review. This (straight) woman concluded that "in the age of AIDS," the book's indulgence of sexual fantasy was almost criminally inappropriate. The reviewer didn't simply distort the content of the book (something one automatically expects of the *Times*), she quite flagrantly lied about it, in language which, if used to describe a work by a black or a Jew, would have been instantly rejected as inflammatory, even by the oblivious, incompetent *oncle-thomas* who edits the "In Brief" section.

On the other hand, reviews in the gay press were almost insanely fixated on the "gay content" of the book, blissfully unaware that its author might have been trying to do something of a literary nature. A hilarious attack in a Washington paper, by a writer whose bio note announced his authorship of an unseemly vast number of "gay" theater plays, attributed the protagonist's neuroticism to the absence of a single "gay book" in a long inventory of his bookshelves; apparently, a heartfelt reading of the works of Edmund White and Armistead Maupin is a sure-fire remedy for romantic disaster, financial depression, and the host of other problems besetting the narrator of *Horse Crazy*.

These kinds of attack are inevitable and have nothing to do with any reputable form of literary criticism; they're simply meant to obliterate the author's work from discussion and, in the case of the *Times* review, to assassinate the author's character, in the interests of ideological conformity. What's interesting in the case of the gay reviewer is a utilitarian view of literature not unrelated to certain denunciations of "harmful" Hollywood movies. In a country with a large totalitarian capacity, perhaps only now being fully tapped by the institutions of the State, it is not hard to raise a consensus *against* the notion of a plurality of consciousnesses. Within groups targeted for further removal to the margins, *how we present ourselves to our executioners* becomes a key concern to those who've elected themselves spokespersons for our existential condition.

Bharati Mukherjee

A Four-Hundred-Year-Old Woman

I was born into a class that did not live in its native language. I was born into a city
that feared its future, and trained me for emigration. I attended a school run by
Irish nuns, who regarded our walled-off school compound in Calcutta as a corner
(forever green and tropical) of England. My "country" – called in Bengali *desh*, and
suggesting more a homeland than a nation of which one is a citizen – I have never
seen. It is the ancestral home of my father and is now in Bangladesh. Nevertheless,
I speak his dialect of Bengali, and think of myself as "belonging" to Faridpur,
the tiny green-gold village that was his birthplace. I was born into a religion that
placed me, a Brahmin, at the top of its hierarchy while condemning me, as a
woman, to a role of subservience. The larger political entity to which I gave my
first allegiance – India – was not even a sovereign nation when I was born.

My horoscope, cast by a neighborhood astrologer when I was a week-old infant, predicted that I would be a writer, that I would win some prizes, that I would
cross "the black waters" of oceans and make my home among aliens. Brought up
in a culture that places its faith in horoscopes, it never occurred to me to doubt it.
The astrologer meant to offer me a melancholy future; to be destined to leave
India was to be banished from the sources of true culture. The nuns at school, on
the other hand, insinuated that India had long outlived its glories, and that if we
wanted to be educated, modern women and make something of our lives, we'd
better hit the trail westward. All my girlhood, I straddled the seesaw of contradictions. *Bilayat*, meaning the scary, unknown "abroad," was both boom time and
desperate loss.

I have found my way to the United States after many transit stops. The un-
glimpsed phantom Faridpur and the all too real Manhattan have merged as "desh."
I am an American. I am an American writer, in the American mainstream, trying to
extend it. This is a vitally important statement for me – I am not an Indian writer,
not an exile, not an expatriate. I am an immigrant; my investment is in the American reality, not the Indian. I look on ghettoization – whether as a Bengali in India

or as a hyphenated Indo-American in North America – as a temptation to be surmounted.

It took me ten painful years, from the early seventies to the early eighties, to overthrow the mothering tyranny of nostalgia. The remaining struggle for me is to make the American readership, meaning the editorial and publishing industries as well, acknowledge the same fact. (As the reception of such films as *Gandhi* and *A Passage to India* as well as *The Far Pavilions* and *The Jewel in the Crown* shows, nostalgia is a two-way street. Americans can feel nostalgic for a world they never knew.) The foreign-born, the exotically raised Third World immigrant with a non-Western religion and non-European language and appearance, can be as American as any steerage passenger from Ireland, Italy, or the Russian Pale. As I have written in another context (a review article in *The Nation* on books by Studs Terkel and Al Santoli), we are probably only a few years away from a Korean *What Makes Choon-li Run?* or a Hmong *Call It Sleep*. In other words, my literary agenda begins by acknowledging that America has transformed *me*. It does not end until I show how I (and the hundreds of thousands like me) have transformed America.

The agenda is simply stated, but in the long run revolutionary. Make the familiar exotic, the exotic familiar.

I have had to create an audience. I cannot rely on shorthand references to my community, my religion, my class, my region, or my old school tie. I've had to sensitize editors as well as readers to the richness of the lives I'm writing about. The most moving form of praise I receive from readers can be summed up in three words: *I never knew*. Meaning, I see these people (call them Indian, Filipino, Korean, Chinese) around me all the time and I never knew they had an inner life. I never knew they schemed and cheated, suffered, felt so strongly, cared so passionately. When even the forms of praise are so rudimentary, the writer knows she has an inexhaustible fictional population to enumerate. Perhaps even a mission, to appropriate a good colonial word.

I have been blessed with an enormity of material. I can be Chekhovian and Tolstoyan – with melancholic and philosophical perspectives on the breaking of hearts as well as the fall of civilizations – and I can be a brash and raucous homesteader, Huck Finn and Woman Warrior, on the unclaimed plains of American literature. My material, reduced to jacket-flap copy, is the rapid and dramatic transformation of the United States since the early 1970s. Within that perceived perimeter, however, I hope to wring surprises.

Yet (I am a writer much given to "yet") my imaginative home is also in the tales told by my mother and grandmother, the world of the Hindu epics. For all the hope and energy I have placed in the process of immigration and accommodation – I'm a person who couldn't ride a public bus when she first arrived, and now I'm someone who watches tractor pulls on obscure cable channels – there are parts of me that remain Indian, parts that slide against the masks of newer selves. The form that my stories and novels take inevitably reflects the resources of Indian mythology – shape-changing, miracles, godly perspectives. My characters can, I hope, transcend the straitjacket of simple psychologizing. The people I write about are culturally and politically several hundred years old: consider the history they have witnessed (colonialism, technology, education, liberation, civil war, up-rooting). They have shed old identities, taken on new ones, and learned to hide the scars. They may sell you newspapers, or clean your offices at night.

Writers (especially American writers, weaned on the luxury of affluence and freedom) often disavow the notion of a "literary duty" or "political conscious-ness," citing the all-too-frequent examples of writers ruined by their shrill com-mitments. Glibness abounds on both sides of the argument, but finally I have to side with my "Third World" compatriots: I do have a duty, beyond telling a good story or drawing a convincing character. My duty is to give voice to continents, but also to redefine the nature of *American* and what makes an American. In the process, work like this by myself and others will open up the canon of American literature.

It has not been an easy transition, from graduate student to citizen, from natural-born expatriate to the hurly-burly of immigration. My husband Clark Blaise and I spent fifteen years in his *desh* of Canada, and Canada was a country that discouraged the very process of assimilation. Eventually, it also discouraged the very presence of "Pakis" in its midst, and in 1980, a low point in our lives, we left, gave up our tenured, full-professor lives for the free-lancing life in the United States.

We were living in Iowa City in 1983 when Emory University called me to be writer-in-residence for the winter semester. My name, apparently, had been sug-gested to them by an old friend. I hadn't published a book in six years (two earlier novels, *The Tiger's Daughter* and *Wife*, as well as our joint nonfiction study, *Days and Nights in Calcutta*, were out of print), but somehow Emory didn't hold that against me.

Atlanta turned out to be the luckiest writing break of my life. For one of those mysterious reasons, stories that had been gathering in me suddenly exploded. I wrote nearly all the stories in *Darkness* (1985) in those three months. I finally had a glimpse of my true material, and that is immigration. In other words, transformation – not preservation. I saw myself and my own experience refracted through a dozen separate lives. Clark, who remained in Iowa City until our younger son finished high school, sent me newspaper accounts, and I turned them into stories. Indian friends in Atlanta took me to dinners, and table gossip became stories. Suddenly, I had begun appropriating the American language. My stories were about the hurly-burly of the unsettled magma between two worlds.

Eventually – inevitably – we made our way to New York. My next batch of stories (*The Middleman and Other Stories*, 1988) appropriates the American language in ways that are personally most satisfying to me (one Chicago reviewer likened it to Nabokov's *Lolita*), and my characters are now as likely to be American as immigrant, and Chinese, Filipino, or Middle Eastern as much as Indian. That book has enjoyed widespread support both critically and commercially, and empowered me to write a new novel, *Jasmine*, and to contract for a major work, historical in nature, that nevertheless incorporates a much earlier version of my basic theme, due for completion in the next three years. *Days and Nights in Calcutta* is being made into a feature film.

My theme is the making of new Americans. Wherever I travel in the (very) Old World, I find "Americans" in the making, whether or not they ever make it to these shores. I see them as dreamers and conquerors, not afraid of transforming themselves, not afraid of abandoning some of their principles along the way. In *Jasmine*, my "American" is born in a Punjabi village, marries at fourteen, and is widowed at sixteen. Nevertheless, she is an American and will enter the book as an Iowa banker's wife.

Ancestral habits of mind can be constricting; they also confer one's individuality. I know I can appropriate the American language, but I can never be a minimalist. I have too many stories to tell. I am aware of myself as a four-hundred-year-old woman, born in the captivity of a colonial, preindustrial, oral culture and living now as a contemporary New Yorker.

My image of artistic structure and artistic excellence is Moghul miniature painting, with its crazy foreshortening of vanishing point, its insistence that everything happens simultaneously, bound only by shape and color. In the miniature paintings of India, there are a dozen separate foci, the most complicated stories can be rendered on a grain of rice, the corners are as elaborated as the centers. There is a sense of the interpenetration of all things. In the Moghul miniature of my life, there would be women investigating their bodies with mirrors, but they would be doing it on a distant balcony under fans wielded by bored serving girls; there would be a small girl listening to a bent old woman; there would be a white man eating popcorn and watching a baseball game; there would be cocktail parties and cornfields and a village set among rice paddies and skyscrapers. In a sense, I wrote that story, "Courtly Vision," at the end of *Darkness*. And in a dozen other ways I'm writing it today, and I will be writing, in the Moghul style, till I get it right.

James Baldwin

Notes of a Native Son

I

On the 29th of July, in 1943, my father died. On the same day, a few hours later, his last child was born. Over a month before this, while all our energies were concentrated in waiting for these events, there had been, in Detroit, one of the bloodiest race riots of the century. A few hours after my father's funeral, while he lay in state in the undertaker's chapel, a race riot broke out in Harlem. On the morning of the 3rd of August, we drove my father to the graveyard through a wilderness of smashed plate glass.

The day of my father's funeral had also been my nineteenth birthday. As we drove to the graveyard, the spoils of injustice, anarchy, discontent, and hatred were all around us. It seemed to me that God himself had devised, to mark my father's end, the most sustained and brutally dissonant of codas. And it seemed to me, too, that the violence which rose all about us as my father left the world had been devised as a corrective for the pride of his eldest son. I had declined to believe in that apocalypse which had been central to my father's vision; very well, life seemed to be saying, here is something that will certainly pass for an apocalypse until the real thing comes along. I had inclined to be contemptuous of my father for the conditions of his life, for the conditions of our lives. When his life had ended I began to wonder about that life and also, in a new way, to be apprehensive about my own.

I had not known my father very well. We had got on badly, partly because we shared, in our different fashions, the vice of stubborn pride. When he was dead I realized that I had hardly ever spoken to him. When he had been dead a long time I began to wish I had. It seems to be typical of life in America, where opportunities, real and fancied, are thicker than anywhere else on the globe, that the second generation has no time to talk to the first. No one, including my father, seems to have known exactly how old he was, but his mother had been born during slavery. He was of the first generation of free men. He, along with thousands of other

Negroes, came North after 1919 and I was part of that generation which had never seen the landscape of what Negroes sometimes call the Old Country.

He had been born in New Orleans and had been a quite young man there during the time that Louis Armstrong, a boy, was running errands for the dives and honky-tonks of what was always presented to me as one of the most wicked of cities – to this day, whenever I think of New Orleans, I also helplessly think of Sodom and Gomorrah. My father never mentioned Louis Armstrong, except to forbid us to play his records; but there was a picture of him on our wall for a long time. One of my father's strong-willed female relatives had placed it there and forbade my father to take it down. He never did, but he eventually maneuvered her out of the house and when, some years later, she was in trouble and near death, he refused to do anything to help her.

He was, I think, very handsome. I gather this from photographs and from my own memories of him, dressed in his Sunday best and on his way to preach a sermon somewhere, when I was little. Handsome, proud, and ingrown, "like a toenail," somebody said. But he looked to me, as I grew older, like pictures I had seen of African tribal chieftains: he really should have been naked, with war paint on and barbaric mementos, standing among spears. He could be chilling in the pulpit and indescribably cruel in his personal life and he was certainly the most bitter man I have ever met; yet it must be said that there was something else in him, buried in him, which lent him his tremendous power and, even, a rather crushing charm. It had something to do with his blackness, I think – he was very black – with his blackness and his beauty, and with the fact that he knew that he was black but did not know that he was beautiful. He claimed to be proud of his blackness but it had also been the cause of much humiliation and it had fixed bleak boundaries to his life. He was not a young man when we were growing up and he had already suffered many kinds of ruin; in his outrageously demanding and protective way he loved his children, who were black like him and menaced, like him; and all these things sometimes showed in his face when he tried, never to my knowledge with any success, to establish contact with any of us. When he took one of his children on his knee to play, the child always became fretful and began to cry; when he tried to help one of us with our homework the absolutely unabating tension which emanated from him caused our minds and our tongues to become paralyzed, so that he, scarcely knowing why, flew into a rage and the child, not knowing why, was punished. If it ever entered his head to bring a surprise home for his children, it was, almost unfailingly, the wrong surprise and even the big watermelons he often brought home on his back in the summertime led to the most appalling scenes. I do not remember, in all those years, that one of his children was ever glad to see him come home. From what I was able to gather of his early life, it seemed that his inability to establish contact with other people had always marked him and had been one of the things which had driven him out of New Orleans. There was something in him, therefore, groping and tentative, which was never expressed and which was buried with him. One saw it most clearly when he was facing new people and hoping to impress them. But he never did, not for long. We went from church to smaller and more improbable church, he found himself in less and less demand as a minister, and by the time he died none of his friends had come to see him for a long time. He had lived and died in an intolerable bitterness of spirit and it frightened me, as we drove him to the graveyard through those unquiet, ruined streets, to see how powerful and overflowing this bitterness could be and to realize that this bitterness now was mine.

When he died I had been away from home for a little over a year. In that year I had had time to become aware of the meaning of all my father's bitter warnings, had discovered the secret of his proudly pursed lips and rigid carriage: I had discovered the weight of white people in the world. I saw that this had been for my ancestors and now would be for me an awful thing to live with and that the bitterness which had helped to kill my father could also kill me.

He had been ill a long time – in the mind, as we now realized, reliving instances of his fantastic intransigence in the new light of his affliction and endeavoring to feel a sorrow for him which never, quite, came true. We had not known that he was being eaten up by paranoia, and the discovery that his cruelty, to our bodies and our minds, had been one of the symptoms of his illness was not, then, enough to enable us to forgive him. The younger children felt, quite simply, relief that he would not be coming home anymore. My mother's observation that it was he, after all, who had kept them alive all these years meant nothing because the problems of keeping alive are not real for children. The older children felt, with my father gone, that they could invite their friends to the house without fear that their friends would be insulted or, as had sometimes happened with me, being told that their friends were in league with the devil and intended to rob our family of everything we owned. (I didn't fail to wonder, and it made me hate him, what on earth we owned that anybody would want.)

His illness was beyond all hope of healing before anyone realized that he was ill. He had always been so strange and had lived, like a prophet, in such unimaginably close communion with the Lord that his long silences which were punctuated by moans and hallelujahs and snatches of old songs while he sat at the living-room window never seemed odd to us. It was not until he refused to eat because, he said, his family was trying to poison him that my mother was forced to accept as a fact what had, until then, been only an unwilling suspicion. When he was committed, it was discovered that he had tuberculosis and, as it turned out, the disease of his mind allowed the disease of his body to destroy him. For the doctors could not force him to eat, either, and, though he was fed intravenously, it was clear from the beginning that there was no hope for him.

In my mind's eye I could see him, sitting at the window, locked up in his terrors; hating and fearing every living soul including his children who had betrayed him, too, by reaching toward the world which had despised him. There were nine of us. I began to wonder what it could have felt like for such a man to have had nine children whom he could barely feed. He used to make little jokes about our poverty, which never, of course, seemed very funny to us; they could not have seemed very funny to him, either, or else our all too feeble response to them would never have caused such rages. He spent great energy and achieved, to our chagrin, no small amount of success in keeping us away from the people who surrounded us, people who had all-night rent parties to which we listened when we should have been sleeping, people who cursed and drank and flashed razor blades on Lenox Avenue. He could not understand why, if they had so much energy to spare, they could not use it to make their lives better. He treated almost everybody on our block with a most uncharitable asperity and neither they, nor, of course, their children were slow to reciprocate.

The only white people who came to our house were welfare workers and bill collectors. It was almost always my mother who dealt with them, for my father's temper, which was at the mercy of his pride, was never to be trusted. It was clear that he felt their very presence in his home to be a violation: this was conveyed by his carriage, almost ludicrously stiff, and by his voice, harsh and vindictively polite. When I was around nine or ten I wrote a play which was directed by a young, white schoolteacher, a woman, who then took an interest in me, and gave me books to read and, in order to corroborate my theatrical bent, decided to take me to see what she somewhat tactlessly referred to as "real" plays. Theatergoing was forbidden in our house, but, with the really cruel intuitiveness of a child, I suspected that the color of this woman's skin would carry the day for me. When, at school, she suggested taking me to the theater, I did not, as I might have done if she had been a Negro, find a way of discouraging her, but agreed that she should pick me up at my house one evening. I then, very cleverly, left all the rest to my mother, who suggested to my father, as I knew she would, that it would not be very nice to let such a kind woman make the trip for nothing. Also, since it was a schoolteacher, I imagine that my mother countered the idea of sin with the idea of "education," which word, even with my father, carried a kind of bitter weight.

Before the teacher came my father took me aside to ask *why* she was coming, what *interest* she could possibly have in our house, in a boy like me. I said I didn't know but I, too, suggested that it had something to do with education. And I understood that my father was waiting for me to say something—I didn't quite know what; perhaps that I wanted his protection against this teacher and her "education." I said none of these things and the teacher came and we went out. It was clear, during the brief interview in our living room, that my father was agreeing very much against his will and that he would have refused permission if he had dared. The fact that he did not dare caused me to despise him: I had no way of knowing that he was facing in that living room a wholly unprecedented and frightening situation.

Later, when my father had been laid off from his job, this woman became very important to us. She was really a very sweet and generous woman and went to a great deal of trouble to be of help to us, particularly during one awful winter. My mother called her by the highest name she knew: she said she was a "christian." My father could scarcely disagree but during the four or five years of our relatively close association he never trusted her and was always trying to surprise in her open, Midwestern face the genuine, cunningly hidden, and hideous motivation. In later years, particularly when it began to be clear that this "education" of mine was going to lead me to perdition, he became more explicit and warned me that my white friends in high school were not really my friends and that I would see, when I was older, how white people would do anything to keep a Negro down. Some of them could be nice, he admitted, but none of them were to be trusted and most of them were not even nice. The best thing was to have as little to do with them as possible. I did not feel this way and I was certain, in my innocence, that I never would.

But the year which preceded my father's death had made a great change in my life. I had been living in New Jersey, working in defense plants, working and living among southerners, white and black. I knew about the South, of course, and about how southerners treated Negroes and how they expected them to behave, but it had never entered my mind that anyone would look at me and expect *me* to behave that way. I learned in New Jersey that to be a Negro meant, precisely, that one was never looked at but was simply at the mercy of the reflexes the color of one's skin caused in other people. I acted in New Jersey as I had always acted, that is as though I thought a great deal of myself – I had to *act* that way – with results that were, simply, unbelievable. I had scarcely arrived before I had earned the enmity, which was extraordinarily ingenious, of all my superiors and nearly all of my co-workers. In the beginning, to make matters worse, I simply did not know what was happening. I did not know what I had done, and I shortly began to wonder what *anyone* could possibly do, to bring about such unanimous, active, and un-bearably vocal hostility. I knew about jim-crow but I had never experienced it. I went to the same self-service restaurant three times and stood with all the Princeton boys before the counter, waiting for a hamburger and coffee; it was always an extraordinarily long time before anything was set before me; but it was not until the fourth visit that I learned that, in fact, nothing had ever been set before me: I had simply picked something up. Negroes were not served there, I was told, and they had been waiting for me to realize that I was always the only Negro present. Once I was told this, I determined to go there all the time. But now they were ready for me and, though some dreadful scenes were subsequently enacted in that restaurant, I never ate there again.

It was the same story all over New Jersey, in bars, bowling alleys, diners, places to live. I was always being forced to leave, silently, or with mutual imprecations. I very shortly became notorious and children giggled behind me when I passed and their elders whispered or shouted – they really believed that I was mad. And it did begin to work on my mind, of course; I began to be afraid to go anywhere and to compensate for this I went places to which I really should not have gone and where, God knows, I had no desire to be. My reputation in town naturally en-hanced my reputation at work and my working day became one long series of ac-robatics designed to keep me out of trouble. I cannot say that these acrobatics succeeded. It began to seem that the machinery of the organization I worked for was turning over, day and night, with but one aim: to eject me. I was fired once, and contrived, with the aid of a friend from New York, to get back on the payroll; was fired again, and bounced back again. It took a while to fire me for the third time, but the third time took. There were no loopholes anywhere. There was not even any way of getting back inside the gates.

That year in New Jersey lives in my mind as though it were the year during which, having an unsuspected predilection for it, I first contracted some dread, chronic disease, the unfailing symptom of which is a kind of blind fever, a pounding in the skull and fire in the bowels. Once this disease is contracted, one can never be really carefree again, for the fever, without an instant's warning, can recur at any moment. It can wreck more important things than race relations. There is not a Negro alive who does not have this rage in his blood – one has the choice, merely, of living with it consciously or surrendering to it. As for me, this fever has recurred in me, and does, and will until the day I die.

My last night in New Jersey, a white friend from New York took me to the nearest big town, Trenton, to go to the movies and have a few drinks. As it turned out, he also saved me from, at the very least, a violent whipping. Almost every detail of that night stands out very clearly in my memory. I even remember the name of the movie we saw because its title impressed me as being so patly ironical. It was a movie about the German occupation of France, starring Maureen O'Hara and Charles Laughton and called *This Land Is Mine*. I remember the name of the diner we walked into when the movie ended: it was the "American Diner." When we walked in the counterman asked what we wanted and I remember answering with the casual sharpness which had become my habit: "We want a hamburger and a cup of coffee, what do you think we want?" I do not know why, after a year of such rebuffs, I so completely failed to anticipate his answer, which was, of course, "We don't serve Negroes here." This reply failed to discompose me, at least for the moment. I made some sardonic comment about the name of the diner and we walked out into the streets.

This was the time of what was called the "brown-out," when the lights in all American cities were very dim. When we re-entered the streets something happened to me which had the force of an optical illusion, or a nightmare. The streets were very crowded and I was facing north. People were moving in every direction but it seemed to me, in that instant, that all of the people I could see, and many more than that, were moving toward me, against me, and that everyone was white. I remember how their faces gleamed. And I felt, like a physical sensation, a *click* at the nape of my neck as though some interior string connecting my head to my body had been cut. I began to walk. I heard my friend call after me, but I ignored him. Heaven only knows what was going on in his mind, but he had the good sense not to touch me – I don't know what would have happened if he had – and to keep me in sight. I don't know what was going on in my mind, either; I certainly had no conscious plan. I wanted to do something to crush these white faces, which were crushing me. I walked for perhaps a block or two until I came to an enormous, glittering, and fashionable restaurant in which I knew not even the intercession of the Virgin would cause me to be served. I pushed through the doors and took the first vacant seat I saw, at a table for two, and waited.

I do not know how long I waited and I rather wonder, until today, what I could possibly have looked like. Whatever I looked like, I frightened the waitress who shortly appeared, and the moment she appeared all of my fury flowed toward her. I hated her for her white face, and for her great, astounded, frightened eyes. I felt that if she found a black man so frightening I would make her fright worthwhile.

She did not ask me what I wanted, but repeated, as though she had learned it somewhere, "We don't serve Negroes here." She did not say it with the blunt, derisive hostility to which I had grown accustomed, but, rather, with a note of apology in her voice, and fear. This made me colder and more murderous than ever. I felt I had to do something with my hands. I wanted her to come close enough for me to get her neck between my hands.

So I pretended not to have understood her, hoping to draw her closer. And she did step a very short step closer, with her pencil poised incongruously over her pad, and repeated the formula: "...don't serve Negroes here."

Somehow, with the repetition of that phrase, which was already ringing in my head like a thousand bells of a nightmare, I realized that she would never come any closer and that I would have to strike from a distance. There was nothing on the table but an ordinary water-mug half full of water, and I picked this up and hurled it with all my strength at her. She ducked and it missed her and shattered against the mirror behind the bar. And, with that sound, my frozen blood abruptly thawed, I returned from wherever I had been, I *saw*, for the first time, the restaurant, the people with their mouths open, already, as it seemed to me, rising as one man, and I realized what I had done, and where I was, and I was frightened. I rose and began running for the door. A round, potbellied man grabbed me by the nape of the neck just as I reached the doors and began to beat me about the face. I kicked him and got loose and ran into the streets. My friend whispered, "*Run!*" and I ran.

My friend stayed outside the restaurant long enough to misdirect my pursuers and the police, who arrived, he told me, at once. I do not know what I said to him when he came to my room that night. I could not have said much. I felt, in the oddest, most awful way, that I had somehow betrayed him. I lived it over and over and over again, the way one relives an automobile accident after it has happened and one finds oneself alone and safe. I could not get over two facts, both equally difficult for the imagination to grasp, and one was that I could have been murdered. But the other was that I had been ready to commit murder. I saw nothing very clearly but I did see this: that my life, my *real* life, was in danger, and not from anything other people might do but from the hatred I carried in my own heart.

II

I had returned home around the second week in June – in great haste because it seemed that my father's death and my mother's confinement were both but a matter of hours. In the case of my mother, it soon became clear that she had simply made a miscalculation. This had always been her tendency and I don't believe that a single one of us arrived in the world, or has since arrived anywhere else, on time. But none of us dawdled so intolerably about the business of being born as did my baby sister. We sometimes amused ourselves, during those endless, stifling weeks, by picturing the baby sitting within in the safe, warm dark, bitterly regretting the necessity of becoming a part of our chaos and stubbornly putting it off as long as possible. I understood her perfectly and congratulated her on showing such good sense so soon. Death, however, sat as purposefully at my father's bedside as life stirred within my mother's womb and it was harder to understand why he so lingered in that long shadow. It seemed that he had bent, and for a long time, too, all of his energies toward dying. Now death was ready for him but my father held back.

All of Harlem, indeed, seemed to be infected by waiting. I had never before known it to be so violently still. Racial tensions throughout this country were exacerbated during the early years of the war, partly because the labor market brought together hundreds of thousands of ill-prepared people and partly because Negro soldiers, regardless of where they were born, received their military training in the South. What happened in defense plants and army camps had repercussions, naturally, in every Negro ghetto. The situation in Harlem had grown bad enough for clergymen, policemen, educators, politicians, and social workers to assert in one breath that there was no "crime wave" and to offer, in the very next breath, suggestions as to how to combat it. These suggestions always seemed to involve playgrounds, despite the fact that racial skirmishes were occurring in the playgrounds, too. Playground or not, crime wave or not, the Harlem police force had been augmented in March, and the unrest grew – perhaps, in fact, partly as a result of the ghetto's instinctive hatred of policemen. Perhaps the most revealing news item, out of the steady parade of reports of muggings, stabbings, shootings, assaults, gang wars, and accusations of police brutality, is the item concerning six Negro girls who set upon a white girl in the subway because, as they all too accurately put it, she was stepping on their toes. Indeed she was, all over the nation.

I had never before been so aware of policemen, on foot, on horseback, on corners, everywhere, always two by two. Nor had I ever been so aware of small knots of people. They were on stoops and on corners and in doorways, and what was striking about them, I think, was that they did not seem to be talking. Never, when I passed these groups, did the usual sound of a curse or a laugh ring out and neither did there seem to be any hum of gossip. There was certainly, on the other hand, occurring between them communication extraordinarily intense. Another thing that was striking was the unexpected diversity of the people who made up these groups. Usually, for example, one would see a group of sharpies standing on the street corner, jiving the passing chicks; or a group of older men, usually, for some reason, in the vicinity of a barber shop, discussing baseball scores, or the numbers, or making rather chilling observations about women they had known. Women, in a general way, tended to be seen less often together – unless they were church women, or very young girls, or prostitutes met together for an unprofessional instant. But that summer I saw the strangest combinations: large, respectable, churchly matrons standing on the stoops or the corners with their hair tied up, together with a girl in sleazy satin whose face bore the marks of gin and the razor, or heavy-set, abrupt, no-nonsense older men, in company with the most disreputable and fanatical "race" men, or these same "race" men with the sharpies, or these sharpies with the churchly women. Seventh Day Adventists and Methodists and Spiritualists seemed to be hobnobbing with Holyrollers and they were all, alike, entangled with the most flagrant disbelievers; something heavy in their stance seemed to indicate that they had all, incredibly, seen a common vision, and on each face there seemed to be the same strange, bitter shadow.

The churchly women and the matter-of-fact, no-nonsense men had children in the Army. The sleazy girls they talked to had lovers there, the sharpies and the "race" men had friends and brothers there. It would have demanded an unquestioning patriotism, happily as uncommon in this country as it is undesirable, for these people not to have been disturbed by the bitter letters they received, by the newspaper stories they read, not to have been enraged by the posters, then to be found all over New York, which described the Japanese as "yellow-bellied Japs." It was only the "race" men, to be sure, who spoke ceaselessly of being revenged – how this vengeance was to be exacted was not clear – for the indignities and dangers suffered by Negro boys in uniform; but everybody felt a directionless, hope-less bitterness, as well as that panic which can scarcely be suppressed when one knows that a human being one loves is beyond one's reach, and in danger. This helplessness and this gnawing uneasiness does something, at length, to even the toughest mind. Perhaps the best way to sum all this up is to say that the people I know felt, mainly, a peculiar kind of relief when they knew that their boys were being shipped out of the South, to do battle overseas. It was, perhaps, like feeling that the most dangerous part of a dangerous journey had been passed and that now, even if death should come, it would come with honor and without the com-plicity of their countrymen. Such a death would be, in short, a fact with which one could hope to live.

It was on the 28th of July, which I believe was a Wednesday, that I visited my fa-ther for the first time during his illness and for the last time in his life. The moment I saw him I knew why I had put off this visit so long. I had told my mother that I did not want to see him because I hated him. But this was not true. It was only that I *had* hated him and I wanted to hold on to this hatred. I did not want to look on him as a ruin: it was not a ruin I had hated. I imagine that one of the reasons people cling to their hates so stubbornly is because they sense, once hate is gone, that they will be forced to deal with pain.

We traveled out to him, his older sister and myself, to what seemed to be the very end of a very Long Island. It was hot and dusty and we wrangled, my aunt and I, all the way out, over the fact that I had recently begun to smoke and, as she said, to give myself airs. But I knew that she wrangled with me because she could not bear to face the fact of her brother's dying. Neither could I endure the reality of her despair, her unstated bafflement as to what had happened to her brother's life, and her own. So we wrangled and I smoked and from time to time she fell into a heavy reverie. Covertly, I watched her face, which was the face of an old woman; it had fallen in, the eyes were sunken and lightless; soon she would be dying, too.

In my childhood—it had not been so long ago—I had thought her beautiful. She had been quick-witted and quick-moving and very generous with all the children and each of her visits had been an event. At one time one of my brothers and myself had thought of running away to live with her. Now she could no longer produce out of her handbag some unexpected and yet familiar delight. She made me feel pity and revulsion and fear. It was awful to realize that she no longer caused me to feel affection. The closer we came to the hospital the more querulous she became and at the same time, naturally, grew more dependent on me. Between pity and guilt and fear I began to feel that there was another me trapped in my skull like a jack-in-the-box who might escape my control at any moment and fill the air with screaming.

She began to cry the moment we entered the room and she saw him lying there, all shriveled and still, like a little black monkey. The great, gleaming apparatus which fed him and would have compelled him to be still even if he had been able to move brought to mind, not beneficence, but torture; the tubes entering his arm made me think of pictures I had seen when a child, of Gulliver, tied down by the pygmies on that island. My aunt wept and wept, there was a whistling sound in my father's throat; nothing was said; he could not speak. I wanted to take his hand, to say something. But I do not know what I could have said, even if he could have heard me. He was not really in that room with us, he had at last really embarked on his journey; and though my aunt told me that he said he was going to meet Jesus, I did not hear anything except that whistling in his throat. The doctor came back and we left, into that unbearable train again, and home. In the morning came the telegram saying that he was dead. Then the house was suddenly full of relatives, friends, hysteria, and confusion and I quickly left my mother and the children to the care of those impressive women, who, in Negro communities at least, automatically appear at times of bereavement armed with lotions, proverbs, and patience, and an ability to cook. I went downtown. By the time I returned, later the same day, my mother had been carried to the hospital and the baby had been born.

III

For my father's funeral I had nothing black to wear and this posed a nagging problem all day long. It was one of those problems, simple, or impossible of solution, to which the mind insanely clings in order to avoid the mind's real trouble. I spent most of that day at the downtown apartment of a girl I knew, celebrating my birthday with whiskey and wondering what to wear that night. When planning a birthday celebration one naturally does not expect that it will be up against competition from a funeral and this girl had anticipated taking me out that night, for a big dinner and a nightclub afterwards. Sometime during the course of that long day we decided that we would go out anyway, when my father's funeral service was over. I imagine *I* decided it, since, as the funeral hour approached, it became clearer and clearer to me that I would not know what to do with myself when it was over. The girl, stifling her very lively concern as to the possible effects of the whiskey on one of my father's chief mourners, concentrated on being conciliatory and practically helpful. She found a black shirt for me somewhere and ironed it and, dressed in the darkest pants and jacket I owned, and slightly drunk, I made my way to my father's funeral.

The chapel was full, but not packed, and very quiet. There were, mainly, my father's relatives, and his children, and here and there I saw faces I had not seen since childhood, the faces of my father's one-time friends. They were very dark and solemn now, seeming somehow to suggest that they had known all along that something like this would happen. Chief among the mourners was my aunt, who had quarreled with my father all his life; by which I do not mean to suggest that her mourning was insincere or that she had not loved him. I suppose that she was one of the few people in the world who had, and their incessant quarreling proved precisely the strength of the tie that bound them. The only other person in the world, as far as I knew, whose relationship to my father rivaled my aunt's in depth was my mother, who was not there.

It seemed to me, of course, that it was a very long funeral. But it was, if anything, a rather shorter funeral than most, nor, since there were no overwhelming, uncontrollable expressions of grief, could it be called – if I dare to use the word – successful. The minister who preached my father's funeral sermon was one of the few my father had still been seeing as he neared his end. He presented to us in his sermon a man whom none of us had ever seen – a man thoughtful, patient, and forbearing, a Christian inspiration to all who knew him, and a model for his children. And no doubt the children, in their disturbed and guilty state, were almost ready to believe this; he had been remote enough to be anything and, anyway, the shock of the incontrovertible, that it was really our father lying up there in that casket, prepared the mind for anything. His sister moaned and this grief-stricken moaning was taken as corroboration. The other faces held a dark, noncommittal thoughtfulness. This was not the man they had known, but they had scarcely expected to be confronted with *him*; this was, in a sense, deeper than questions of fact, the man they had known; and the man they had not known may have been the real one. The real man, whoever he had been, had suffered and now he was dead: this was all that was sure and all that mattered now. Every man in the chapel hoped that when his hour came he, too, would be eulogized, which is to say forgiven, and that all of his lapses, greeds, errors, and strayings from the truth would be invested with coherence and looked upon with charity. This was perhaps the last thing human beings could give each other and it was what they demanded, after all, of the Lord. Only the Lord saw the midnight tears, only He was present when one of His children, moaning and wringing hands, paced up and down the room. When one slapped one's child in anger the recoil in the heart reverberated through heaven and became part of the pain of the universe. And when the children were hungry and sullen and distrustful and one watched them, daily, growing wilder, and further away, and running headlong into danger, it was the Lord who knew what the charged heart endured as the strap was laid to the backside; the Lord alone who knew what one *would* have said if one had had, like the Lord, the gift of the living word. It was the Lord who knew of the impossibility every parent in that room faced: how to prepare the child for the day when the child would be despised and how to *create* in the child—by what means?—a stronger antidote to this poison than one had found for oneself. The avenues, side streets, bars, billiard halls, hospitals, police stations, and even the playgrounds of Harlem—not to mention the houses of correction, the jails, and the morgue—testified to the potency of the poison while remaining silent as to the efficacy of whatever antidote, irresistibly raising the question of whether or not such an antidote existed; raising, which was worse, the question of whether or not an antidote was desirable; perhaps poison should be fought with poison. With these several schisms in the mind and with more terrors in the heart than could be named, it was better not to judge the man who had gone down under an impossible burden. It was better to remember: *Thou knowest this man's fall; but thou knowest not his wrassling.*

While the preacher talked and I watched the children—years of changing their diapers, scrubbing them, slapping them, taking them to school, and scolding them had had the perhaps inevitable result of making me love them, though I am not sure I knew this then—my mind was busily breaking out with a rash of disconnected impressions. Snatches of popular songs, indecent jokes, bits of books I had read, movie sequences, faces, voices, political issues—I thought I was going mad; all these impressions suspended, as it were, in the solution of the faint nausea produced in me by the heat and liquor. For a moment I had the impression that my alcoholic breath, inefficiently disguised with chewing gum, filled the entire chapel. Then someone began singing one of my father's favorite songs and, abruptly, I was with him, sitting on his knee, in the hot, enormous, crowded church which was the first church we attended. It was the Abyssinian Baptist Church on 138th Street. We had not gone there long. With this image, a host of others came. I had forgotten, in the rage of my growing up, how proud my father had been of me when I was little. Apparently, I had had a voice and my father had liked to show me off before the members of the church. I had forgotten what he had looked like when he was pleased but now I remembered that he had always been grinning with pleasure when my solos ended. I even remembered certain expressions on his face when he teased my mother – had he loved her? I would never know. And when had it all begun to change? For now it seemed that he had not always been cruel. I remembered being taken for a haircut and scraping my knee on the foot-rest of the barber's chair and I remembered my father's face as he soothed my crying and applied the stinging iodine. Then I remembered our fights, fights which had been of the worst possible kind because my technique had been silence.

I remembered the one time in all our life together when we had really spoken to each other.

It was on a Sunday and it must have been shortly before I left home. We were walking, just the two of us, in our usual silence, to or from church. I was in high school and had been doing a lot of writing and I was, at about this time, the editor of the high school magazine. But I had also been a Young Minister and had been preaching from the pulpit. Lately, I had been taking fewer engagements and preached as rarely as possible. It was said in the church, quite truthfully, that I was "cooling off."

My father asked me abruptly, "You'd rather write than preach, wouldn't you?"

I was astonished at his question – because it was a real question. I answered, "Yes."

That was all we said. It was awful to remember that that was all we had *ever* said.

The casket now was opened and the mourners were being led up the aisle to look for the last time on the deceased. The assumption was that the family was too overcome with grief to be allowed to make this journey alone and I watched while my aunt was led to the casket and, muffled in black, and shaking, led back to her seat. I disapproved of forcing the children to look on their dead father, considering that the shock of his death, or, more truthfully, the shock of death as a reality, was already a little more than a child could bear, but my judgment on this matter had been overruled and there they were, bewildered and frightened and very small, being led, one by one, to the casket. But there is also something very gallant about children at such moments. It has something to do with their silence and gravity and with the fact that one cannot help them. Their legs, somehow, seem *exposed*, so that it is at once incredible and terribly clear that their legs are all they have to hold them up.

I had not wanted to go to the casket myself and I certainly had not wished to be led there, but there was no way of avoiding either of these forms. One of the deacons led me up and I looked on my father's face. I cannot say that I looked like him at all. His blackness had been equivocated by powder and there was no suggestion in that casket of what his power had or could have been. He was simply an old man dead, and it was hard to believe that he had ever given anyone either joy or pain. Yet, his life filled that room. Further up the avenue his wife was holding his newborn child. Life and death so close together, and love and hatred, and right and wrong, said something to me which I did not want to hear concerning man, concerning the life of man.

After the funeral, while I was downtown desperately celebrating my birthday, a Negro soldier, in the lobby of the Hotel Braddock, got into a fight with a white policeman over a Negro girl. Negro girls, white policemen, in or out of uniform, and Negro males – in or out of uniform – were part of the furniture of the lobby of the Hotel Braddock and this was certainly not the first time such an incident had occurred. It was destined, however, to receive an unprecedented publicity, for the fight between the policeman and the soldier ended with the shooting of the soldier. Rumor, flowing immediately to the streets outside, stated that the soldier had been shot in the back, an instantaneous and revealing invention, and that the soldier had died protecting a Negro woman. The facts were somewhat different – for example, the soldier had not been shot in the back, and was not dead, and the girl seems to have been as dubious a symbol of womanhood as her white counterpart in Georgia usually is, but no one was interested in the facts. They preferred the invention because this invention expressed and corroborated their hates and fears so perfectly. It is just as well to remember that people are always doing this. Perhaps many of those legends, including Christianity, to which the world clings began their conquest of the world with just some such concerted surrender to distortion. The effect, in Harlem, of this particular legend was like the effect of a lit match in a tin of gasoline. The mob gathered before the doors of the Hotel Braddock simply began to swell and to spread in every direction, and Harlem exploded.

The mob did not cross the ghetto lines. It would have been easy, for example, to have gone over Morningside Park on the west side or to have crossed the Grand Central railroad tracks at 125th Street on the east side, to wreak havoc in white neighborhoods. The mob seems to have been mainly interested in something more potent and real than the white face, that is, in white power, and the principal damage done during the riot of the summer of 1943 was to white business establishments in Harlem. It might have been a far bloodier story, of course, if, at the hour the riot began, these establishments had still been open. From the Hotel Braddock the mob fanned out, east and west along 125th Street, and for the entire length of Lenox, Seventh, and Eighth avenues. Along each of these avenues, and along each major side street—116th, 125th, 135th, and so on—bars, stores, pawn-shops, restaurants, even little luncheonettes had been smashed open and entered and looted—looted, it might be added, with more haste than efficiency. The shelves really looked as though a bomb had struck them. Cans of beans and soup and dog food, along with toilet paper, corn flakes, sardines, and milk tumbled every which way, and abandoned cash registers and cases of beer leaned crazily out of the splintered windows and were strewn along the avenues. Sheets, blankets, and clothing of every description formed a kind of path, as though people had dropped them while running. I truly had not realized that Harlem *had* so many stores until I saw them all smashed open; the first time the word *wealth* ever entered my mind in relation to Harlem was when I saw it scattered in the streets. But one's first, incongruous impression of plenty was countered immediately by an impression of waste. None of this was doing anybody any good. It would have been better to have left the plate glass as it had been and the goods lying in the stores.

It would have been better, but it would also have been intolerable, for Harlem had needed something to smash. To smash something is the ghetto's chronic need. Most of the time it is the members of the ghetto who smash each other, and themselves. But as long as the ghetto walls are standing there will always come a moment when these outlets do not work. That summer, for example, it was not enough to get into a fight on Lenox Avenue, or curse out one's cronies in the barber shops. If ever, indeed, the violence which fills Harlem's churches, pool halls, and bars erupts outward in a more direct fashion, Harlem and its citizens are likely to vanish in an apocalyptic flood. That this is not likely to happen is due to a great many reasons, most hidden and powerful among them the Negro's real relation to the white American. This relation prohibits, simply, anything as uncomplicated and satisfactory as pure hatred. In order really to hate white people, one has to blot so much out of the mind—and the heart—that this hatred itself becomes an exhausting and self-destructive pose. But this does not mean, on the other hand, that love comes easily: the white world is too powerful, too complacent, too ready with gratuitous humiliation, and above all, too ignorant and too innocent for that. One is absolutely forced to make perpetual qualifications and one's own reactions are always canceling each other out. It is this, really, which has driven so many

people mad, both white and black. One is always in the position of having to decide between amputation and gangrene. Amputation is swift but time may prove
that the amputation was not necessary – or one may delay the amputation too
long. Gangrene is slow, but it is impossible to be sure that one is reading one's
symptoms right. The idea of going through life as a cripple is more than one
can bear, and equally unbearable is the risk of swelling up slowly, in agony, with
poison. And the trouble, finally, is that the risks are real even if the choices do
not exist.

"But as for me and my house," my father had said, "we will serve the Lord." I
wondered, as we drove him to his resting place, what this line had meant for him. I
had heard him preach it many times. I had preached it once myself, proudly giving
it an interpretation different from my father's. Now the whole thing came back to
me, as though my father and I were on our way to Sunday school and I were
memorizing the golden text: *And if it seem evil unto you to serve the Lord, choose you this
day whom you will serve; whether the gods which your fathers served that were on the other
side of the flood, or the gods of the Amorites, in whose land ye dwell: but as for me and my
house, we will serve the Lord.* I suspected in these familiar lines a meaning which had
never been there for me before. All of my father's texts and songs, which I had decided were meaningless, were arranged before me at his death like empty bottles,
waiting to hold the meaning which life would give them for me. This was his
legacy: nothing is ever escaped. That bleakly memorable morning I hated the unbelievable streets and the Negroes and whites who had, equally, made them that
way. But I knew that it was folly, as my father would have said, this bitterness was
folly. It was necessary to hold on to the things that mattered. The dead man mattered, the new life mattered; blackness and whiteness did not matter; to believe
that they did was to acquiesce in one's own destruction. Hatred, which would destroy so much, never failed to destroy the man who hated and this was an immutable law.

It began to seem that one would have to hold in the mind forever two ideas
which seemed to be in opposition. The first idea was acceptance, the acceptance,
totally without rancor, of life as it is, and men as they are: in the light of this idea,
it goes without saying that injustice is a commonplace. But this did not mean that
one could be complacent, for the second idea was of equal power: that one must
never, in one's own life, accept these injustices as commonplace but must fight
them with all one's strength. The fight begins, however, in the heart and it now
had been laid to my charge to keep my own heart free of hatred and despair. This

intimation made my heart heavy and, now that my father was irrecoverable, I wished that he had been beside me so that I could have searched his face for the answers which only the future would give me now.

II.

"CALIBAN SPEAKS TO PROSPERO": CULTURAL IDENTITY AND THE CRISIS OF REPRESENTATION

CONFERENCE PRESENTATIONS

MAY 11, 1990

bell hooks

Homi K. Bhabha

Michelle Cliff

Arturo Islas

Anton Shammas

Luisa Valenzuela

Narratives of Struggle

> My mother used to say that through her life, through her
> living testimony, she tried to tell women that they too had
> to participate, so that when the repression comes and
> with it a lot of suffering, it's not only the men who suffer.
> Women must join the struggle in their own way. My
> mother's words told them that any evolution, any change,
> in which women had not participated, would not be a
> change, and there would be no victory. She was as clear
> about this as if she were a woman of all sorts of theories
> and a lot of practice.
> — *I, Rigoberta Menchú*

> If it is true that a revolution can fail, even though it be
> nurtured on perfectly conceived theories, nobody has yet
> successfully practiced Revolution without a revolution-
> ary theory.
> — Amilcar Cabral, *Unity and Struggle*

Each time I begin work on a new piece of writing, a theoretical essay, a critical
book, fiction, autobiography, I confront within myself extreme dread that the subjectivity that I have fought so hard to claim will not assert itself. Paralyzed by the
fear that I will not be able to name or speak words that fully articulate my experience or the collective reality of struggling black people, I am tempted to be silent.
The persistence of this dread has intensified my awareness that wounds inflicted
by oppressive structures of racism, class exploitation, and sexist domination mark
me/us; that political self-recovery, the development of revolutionary consciousness
heals but does not erase. This dread surfaces as a forgotten scar, permanently inscribed on the body, a sign of past terror and torture, aggressively demanding
recognition.

The production of terror, unmediated dread, in the minds and hearts of the exploited and oppressed, binds us to a politics of domination, keeps us in place, unable to resist, afraid to resist. On all levels, confronting this dread, breaking its hold on our lives, is a joyous gesture of resistance. That remnants of the dread remain in individuals, like myself, who believe our political self-recovery to be complete, unsettles, but it need not disenable. This dread returns me to memory, to places and situations I often want to forget. It forces me to remember, to hold close the knowledge that for people globally who fight for liberation, resistance is also "a struggle of memory against forgetting." Remembering makes us subjects in history. It is dangerous to forget.

I do not forget the poverty of our childhood, the weight of patriarchy's heavy hand in our household, the apartheid social structure which slapped us in the face each time we walked out the door. Everywhere so little has changed – in that place of childhood, and that familiar world of home. In that hostile space outside, nothing has changed: racism, class exploitation, and sexist domination prevail. Deprivation intensifies, despair abounds, and suffering lingers. Being an intellectual does not separate or estrange me from this reality. I became an intellectual in resistance, responding consciously, critically, to conditions of suffering in my life and the lives of family and community. I wanted knowledge only to the degree that it would enable that suffering to end. I wanted education to offer the critical guidance that would provoke, stimulate awareness and the will to change. I learned about the importance of critical reflection, cultivating strategies that would ensure survival in the face of abuse and open up the possibility of a transformed future for us, the black poor, the underclass, the disinherited.

Coming to consciousness in the context of a concrete experiential struggle for self-actualization and collective black self-determination, I began to see clearly the mutual, reciprocal relationship between theory and practice. In the process of transformation, of moving from object to subject, I learned how to use knowledge in the service of liberation. Poetry and novels brought me close to myself, helped me to overcome the estrangement that domination breeds between psyche and self. Reading, I could vicariously experience, dare to know and feel, without threat of repression, retaliation, silencing. My mind became a place of refuge, a sanctuary, a room I could enter with no fear of invasion. My mind became a site of resistance.

I chose to be a writer in my girlhood because books rescued me. They were the places where I could bring the broken bits and pieces of myself and put them together again, the places where I could dream about alternative realities, possible futures. They let me know firsthand that if the mind was to be the site of resistance, only the imagination could make it so. To imagine, then, was a way to begin the process of transforming reality. All that we cannot imagine will never come into being.

Critical fictions emerge when the imagination is free to wander, explore, question, transgress. Years ago, I heard Ivan Van Sertima speak about *They Came Before Columbus*, his work documenting the presence of Africans in the "New World."[1] Commenting on black liberation struggles globally, he asserted that it is not just our minds that have been colonized, but our imaginations. Thinking about the imagination in a subversive way, not seeing it as a pure, uncorrupted terrain, we can ask ourselves under what conditions and in what ways can the imagination be decolonized. Globally, literature that enriches resistance struggles speaks about the way the individuals in repressive, dehumanizing situations use imagination to sustain life and maintain critical awareness. In oppressive settings the ability to construct images imaginatively of a reality not present to the senses or perceived may be the only means to hope. How many of us in our daily life think about the connection between our capacity to imagine and resistance struggle? Often in radical circles, the imaginative mind is perceived as threatening, as though it will obstruct and disrupt progressive action. Certainly it is useful in a culture of domination to project the sense that the imagination is primarily useful as a means to produce fantasy. In this country, the work of Gabriel García Márquez is often read and talked about as though his fictions are fantasy, narratives of escape, works that invite readers to forget, to lose themselves in the exotic world of the Other. In *The Fragrance of Guava*, García Márquez critiques this emphasis on fantasy and speaks instead about the primacy of the imagination: "I believe the imagination is just an instrument for producing reality and that the source of creation is always, in the last instance, reality. Fantasy, in the sense of pure and simple Walt Disney–style invention without any basis in reality, is the most loathsome thing of all."[2]

All too often the colonized mind thinks of the imagination as the realm of the psyche that, if fully explored, will lead one into madness, away from reality. Consequently, it is feared. For the colonized mind to think of the imagination as the instrument that does not estrange us from reality, but returns us to the real more fully, in ways that help us to confront and cope, is a liberatory gesture. In El Salvadoran writer Manlio Argueta's novel, *One Day of Life*, Lupe's emergent critical consciousness is consistently linked to the gradual expansion of her imaginative abilities. Free to imagine, she can invent rituals of remembrance that sustain her revolutionary spirit when Chepe, her husband and *compañero*, has been assassinated. Recalling his presence, she imaginatively constructs a redemptive heterosexual paradigm to stand as testimony of their union, love, and struggle:

The odor of Chepe lingers, the same odor that he brings everyday from work, the clean and agreeable odor of the sweat of a real man. It is like the perfume of our life. One becomes accustomed to it and the pleasure is in conserving the moistness of the body. The body itself absorbs it. Maybe deep within it nourishes us with that same sweat.[3]

Characters in *One Day of Life* walk a tightrope of the imagination, wherein the possibility of courageous critical awakening coexists with the dangerous forgetfulness that breeds complicity and betrayal. Everyone must choose, imagine, and act accordingly. As the novel concludes, Adolfina, with prophetic insight, assures Grandma Lupe that justice will prevail, telling her that this knowledge of the future appeared "in my imagination, it came upon me like a revelation."[4]

Many new critical fictions disrupt conventional ways of thinking about the imagination and imaginative work, offering fictions that demand careful scrutiny, that resist passive readership. Consciously opposing the notion of literature as escapist entertainment, these fictions confront and challenge. Often language is the central field of contestation. The way writers use language often determines whether or not oppositional critical approaches in fiction or theory subvert, decenter, or challenge existing hegemonic discourses. Styles of language pointedly identify specific audiences both as subjects of the text and as that audience one addresses more intimately. If I choose to write using black vernacular speech, this creative decision will make a work appear more familiar to readers who use that patois. Yet to address more intimately is not to exclude; rather, it alters the terms of inclusion. To fully experience Michelle Cliff's novel, *No Telephone to Heaven*, readers must shift locations and grapple with language. Readers unfamiliar with Jamaican patois must be ever vigilant to keep the sense of the text, to experience its pleasure. I chose to read *No Telephone to Heaven* without turning to the glossary at the end of the novel, seeking instead the contextualized meaning of words I did not understand. After the first reading, I read the glossary and began again. The writer of critical fictions is necessarily concerned with using languages in ways that open up a text to multiple audiences. Many new works by writers of color in the United States contain passages or chapters that can be read orally to audiences with varying degrees of literacy. In this way, the boundaries separating oral story-telling and written work can be traversed.

Writers in exile speak about the struggle to come to voice in alien tongues. Those writers who hold to the language that most connects them with home, work to maintain ties. Turkish writer Nedim Gürsel writes:

Although I continue to write in Turkish, my syntax is being distorted. To resist the impact of the present which this daily practice of French unleashes in me, I must bind myself to the words of my childhood. In describing this painful yet enriching experience, I want to show how reality can sometimes sustain the literary language without being reflected by it.[5]

Readers of critical fiction cannot approach work assuming that they already possess a language of access, or that the text will mirror realities they already know and understand. Much critical fiction dynamically seeks to deconstruct conventional ways of knowing. It effectively critically intervenes and challenges dominant/hegemonic narratives by compelling audiences to actually transform the way they read and think. Toni Morrison's revolutionary novel, *The Bluest Eye*, begins with the disruption of that way of learning to read and think that teaches white bourgeois notions of reality as though they represent a social norm. Indeed, by beginning her novel with a passage taken from a reading primer, she reminds readers that art is socially constructed, that there is no realm of the imagination that is not acted upon by reality. Changes in typography force the reader to be conscious of the evolution of printing and the development of a publishing industry. Morrison places the writer within a social and historical framework. The way *The Bluest Eye* is constructed forces the reader to confront the reality that the critical apparatus necessary to understand this fiction cannot be reached by conventional ways of knowing. Readers must learn to "see" the world differently if they want to understand this work. This is the fundamental challenge of critical fictions. They require that the reader shift her paradigms and practice empathy as a conscious gesture of solidarity with the work.

Critical fictions effectively intervene and challenge dominant reading practices when they compel the uncritical reader to put aside set notions of what literature should be or do and enthusiastically grasp new and different approaches. Anyone can be an audience for a particular work if they engage willingly and empathetically. This may indeed require them to relinquish privilege and their acceptance of dominant ways of knowing as preparation for hearing different voices. The ability to be empathetic is rooted in our capacity to imagine. Imagination can enable us to understand fictive realities that in no way resemble where we are coming from. By calling on the reader to enter realms of the unknown with no will to colonize or possess, critical fictions offer alternatives to an imperialist paradigm which constructs the text as territory to be conquered, taken over, irrevocably altered. Concurrently, writers of critical fiction do not mask their self-conscious engagement with the work. Expecting to be held accountable for their fictions, they acknowledge that imaginative work does not emerge in a realm outside history. It is precisely the writer's longing to participate in the transformation of history that fosters the artistic vigilance necessary for the production of a critical fiction.

Significantly, the writer of critical fiction makes the conscious decision to locate her work in the realm of oppositional cultural production. That choice is most often informed by a desire to intervene critically in the status quo, to participate in cultural revolution. In the United States it is often assumed that any work by indigenous folks of color or individuals from the Third World is necessarily "a critical fiction," one that will radically subvert and challenge dominant discourses. Informed by narrow essentialist notions of "otherness," such thinking has to be critically interrogated. Often a writer may do one work that is critically subversive, and other fictions by the same author may simply reinscribe the status quo. Even though the individual writer may perceive a work to be oppositional, in the end reader response will determine the power of the text to challenge and transform.

Unfortunately, audience response may also influence whether an oppositional work will be accorded that status. Certainly many feminist readers were and are unable to fully appreciate the oppositional nature of Angela Carter's *The Sadeian Woman*, as critical meditation on ideology, as insightful commentary on the social construction of female sexuality, and as a transgressive reading of Marquis de Sade's writing. To feminist thinkers who want to maintain a discursive space within feminist politics for discussions of sexuality, of varied and diverse sexual practices, Carter's work continues to provide insight and critical direction. Reflecting on the unwillingness of writers and readers of pornographic fiction to take it seriously, Carter poses a critique that can easily apply to the production of critical fictions. Often such work is seen – particularly in academic and/or intellectual circles – as simply propaganda, especially if it enriches and promotes resistance struggle, as though canonized works of art do not serve the interests of specific political concerns. Carter comments, "Fine art, that exists for itself alone, is art in the final state of impotence. If nobody, including the artist, acknowledges art as a means of knowing the world, then art is relegated to a kind of rumpus room of the mind and the irresponsibility of the artist and the irrelevance of art to actual living become part and parcel of the practice of art."[6]

Critical fictions work to connect art with lived practices of struggle. Constituting a genealogy of subjugated knowledges, they provide a cultural location for the construction of alternative readings of history told from the standpoint of the oppressed, the disinherited, or those who are open to seeing the world from this perspective. Concurrently they enable the articulation of cultural practices that are part of the reality of marginalized groups, not forged in the context of struggle. The assertion of a decolonized subjectivity allows us to emphasize resistance, as well as other aspects of our experience. A work like *I, Rigoberta Menchú* seeks to call attention to the oppression of the Guatemalan peasant, while contextualizing that reality so that it is evident that the people are more than their pain. Literature emerging from marginalized groups that is only a chronicle of pain can easily act to keep in place the existing structures of domination. The writer producing work in a revolutionary context may specifically call attention to particular forms of oppression, graphically depicting suffering to document and inform. Writers working in a nonrevolutionary context must be careful not to appropriate narratives of struggle in ways that reduce them to colorful spectacle.

Certainly it is difficult for the writer in the United States to find publishers for critical fictions. Again it must be reiterated that a growing interest on the part of publishers and consumers in works by writers of color does not mean that the works that are published and most talked about are necessarily critical fictions. Although work by black women writers seems to be receiving unprecedented attention at this historical moment in this society, much of that work is in no way subversive. Perhaps it is a bitter commentary to think that writers may strategically include passages or chapters in work so that it appears to be a critical intervention even as the overall work in no way breaks with prevailing oppressive and repressive norms. Such moments may merely reflect contradictions. Interest in works by black women writers should not blind us to the reality that this society does not support or affirm the production of critical fictions by black women.

Militancy, akin to that one finds in Ama Ata Aidoo's *Our Sister Killjoy* or Nawal El Saadawi's *Woman at Point Zero*, is not a characteristic trademark of black women writers here or globally. *Our Sister Killjoy* was first published in 1977. Written before an established body of feminist writing by black women had been produced, it was a fictive foretelling of the way the words of militant black women – opposing gender, race, class, and imperialist oppression – would be received: Sister Killjoy's militant speech is greeted with silence. She remains unrelenting in her critique of colonization, internalized racism, and complicity throughout the novel, making her critical observations with humor and wit. Identifying the way knowledge is produced to mask imperialism, she also identifies the enemy: "The academic-pseudo-intellectual ... who in the face of reality that is more tangible than the massive walls of the slave forts standing along our beaches, still talks of universal truth, universal art, universal literature and the Gross National Product."[7]

El Saadawi published *Woman at Point Zero* in 1975. Identifying her location in the introduction, naming her solidarity with the disinherited, the prisoner, the exile, she wrote of this narrative that it is "the story of a woman driven by despair to the darkest of ends. This woman, despite her misery and despair, evoked in all those, like me, who witnessed the final moments of life, a need to challenge and to overcome those forces that deprive human beings of their right to live, to love and to real freedom."[8] These words pose a radical challenge to writers of critical fiction. If we ally ourselves in the struggle with the oppressed (and especially if we are working and living in the context of privilege), how will our fictions, our theory, name this solidarity? Fundamentally, this gesture of commitment to radical change will inform our fictions, so that they become both sign and expression that society is undergoing a transformation, that a new history is emerging. Peruvian liberation theologian Gustavo Gutiérrez, in his critical interpretation of the Book of Job, urges recognition that it is radical communion with the suffering of human beings which brings us to the deepest level of history.[9] Without reducing artistic practice to mere propagandistic function, in a manner that censors and represses the imagination, revolutionary critical fictions prophetically construct and name the transformed future.

A shared history in struggle allows politically committed revolutionary individuals to form communities of resistance, locations that sustain those who fear they will be defeated by despair and alienation. Palestinian writer Anton Shammas evokes a politics of exile that sees in that location a potential space of empowerment. Responding to Somalian writer Nuruddin Farah's assertion that we are "driven from Paradise," Shammas offers the playful yet serious oppositional response: "Nuruddin, the Garden of Eden is a masterpiece of boredom, who wants to go there? Exile is far more interesting. I would support expulsion from the Garden of Eden, because it makes life and literature more interesting."[10] Brazilian educator Paulo Freire, in conversation with the Chilean critical thinker Antonio

Faundez, also problematizes the question of exile:

Wherever exiles finally settle, they tend to experience from the moment they arrive the ambiguous feeling of freedom on the one hand, freedom at having escaped from something threatening them, and on the other of having suffered a tragic break in their history. Learning to live with that ambiguity is difficult but it has to be done ... If they do succeed in doing so, then their time of waiting in exile, actively waiting, will become for them a time of hope.[11]

It is this hope that African Americans as an exilic people have sustained throughout our history in the United States. It is hope rooted in struggle, a hope that forms the basis of resistance. Vietnamese Buddhist Thich Nhat Hanh reminds us in *The Raft Is Not the Shore* that: "The purpose of resistance, here, is to seek the healing of yourself in order to be able to see clearly ... I think that communities of resistance should be places where people can return to themselves more easily, where the conditions are such that they can heal themselves and recover their wholeness."[12] Such clarity must inform revolutionary critical fictions, theory, and practice.

Within communities of resistance, narratives of struggle are testimony. Writing about the place of testimony in black religious experience in *My Soul Looks Back*, James Cone states that "the purpose of testimony is not only to strengthen an individual's faith but also to build the faith of the community."[13] As writers and readers of critical fictions, we rejoice in the power of community, because it renews our hope, intensifies awareness, and invites us to imagine together.

Homi K. Bhabha

When the demonic dimensions of fiction are acted out in the psycho-mythology of everyday life, then perhaps it is time to turn to that baggy monster, "the novel," to learn what forms of language are appropriate for this "neurasthenic hour." That phrase – neurasthenic hour – comes from Tom Wolfe's most recent literary manifesto, "The New Social Novel," published in *Harper's*, November 1989. He uses it to describe the anxiety-producing reality of the American city – chaotic, random, and discontinuous – in the wake of what he calls the fourth great wave of immigration, which brought Asians, North Africans, Latin Americans, and Caribbeans to the United States, and which, Wolfe predicts, will result in political power passing to those nonwhite majorities within the decade. Now, faced with this Armageddon, Wolfe calls for a return to the linear and liberal traditions of literary realism. A fairly simple story, he says, is what we need to understand the present situation.

In *The Satanic Verses*, Salman Rushdie celebrates what Wolfe abhors, the hybrid hodgepodge of the mongrel postmodern world, with black, brown, and white leaking into one another in tropicalized London. Despite their literary and political differences, both Rushdie and Wolfe mark out an agenda for the metropolitan novel in the nineties. The historical experience of the Western metropolis cannot now be fictionalized without the marginal oblique gaze of its postcolonial migrant populations cutting cross the imaginative geography of territory and community, tradition and culture.

In the high noon of Wolfe's *Bonfire of the Vanities*, you might recall, the racist mayor of New York taunts the general partners and merger lawyers, daring them to step outside their Upper East Side co-ops. "Do you really think this is *your* city any longer?" he says in fear and loathing. "It's the Third World down there! Puerto Ricans, West Indians, Haitians, Dominicans ... Go visit the frontiers, you gutless wonders! Morningside Heights, St. Nicholas Park, Washington Heights ..."[1] In an essay in *The Independent* (London), Rushdie turned such fear and loathing into a text for our times, writing, "If *The Satanic Verses* is anything, it is the migrant's view of the world. It is written from the very experience of uprooting, disjuncture, metamorphosis, that is the migrant condition from which I believe can be derived a metaphor for all humanity." To think of migration as metaphor suggests that the very language of the novel, its form and rhetoric, must be open to meanings that are ambivalent, doubling, and dissembling. Metaphors produce hybrid realities by yoking together unlikely traditions of thought. Singularities are explained through differences. Similarity is often plural. The metaphor of migrancy suggests that metropolitan histories cannot be conceived without invoking savage colonial antecedents. It also implies that the language of rights and obligations so central to the modern myth of democratic people must be questioned on the basis of the legal and cultural disenfranchisement experienced by migrant and refugee populations. The postcolonial perspective forces us to rethink the profound limitations of a consensual and collusive liberal sense of community. The time for assimilating minorities to totalizing and organic notions of cultural value has passed. In this "neurasthenic hour," the very language of cultural community needs to be rethought, with an energy as powerful as that deployed by feminists, as well as gay activists, in re-examining the language of sexuality, self, and society.

Deprived and excluded minorities must feel sure that participating in the reinscription of their traditions and values will lead to a more equal distribution of power and influence in the cultural conversation among the contentious and competing languages that form the metropolitan canon. They seek new forms of authority and autonomy, not assimilation, as the basis for integration in a global community. What is needed is, first, a new interpretive community to bear witness to this experience. If this sounds like a pious and utopian vision in these vicious times, let us take heart from history. A migrant or postcolonial public sphere would, I suggest, resemble the kind of interpretive community established by women's movements in the seventies. Fiercely anti-assimilationist, women's movements not only generated conversations across political and cultural minorities but also, more significantly, sought to establish a sense of community that could tolerate difference and dissent. The metaphor of migration, its hybridity and hodgepodge, can only be properly written and read within such a community.

The term *postcolonial* is increasingly used to describe that form of social criticism that bears witness to those unequal and uneven processes of representation by which the historical experience of the once-colonized Third World comes to be framed in the West. The postcolonial perspective, as it has been more recently developed by cultural and social historians and theorists, departs from the traditions of the sociology of underdevelopment or dependency theory. As a mode of analysis, it disavows any nationalist or nativist pedagogy that sets up the relations of Third World and First World in a binary structure of opposition, recognizing that the social boundaries between First and Third Worlds are far more complex.

It is from the experience of a productive hybridization of cultural influence and national determination that the postcolonial attempts to elaborate the historical and literary project.

Such a project will not allow cultural and historical differences to be transcended in a scale of universalism, or a relativism that assumes, as the philosopher Ernest Gellner put it, "a public and symmetrical world." The possibilities of a differential history have recently led Fredric Jameson to recognize the internationalization of the national situation in the work of Roberto Fernández Retamar, which, Jameson argues, calls *us* into question as much as it acknowledges the Other, neither reducing the Third World to some homogeneous Other of the West, nor vacuously celebrating the astonishing pluralism of human cultures.

We have, already, the foundations for our work. I shall talk about only three postcolonial thinkers very briefly. C.L.R. James, the great Caribbean visionary, once remarked that the postcolonial prerogative consisted in reinterpreting and rewriting the forms and effects of an older colonial consciousness from the later experience of migration, diaspora, and cultural displacement. It is the return of the gaze of the Other that serves simultaneously as the conceptual imperative and the political constituency of the postcolonial intellectual. In this spirit, Jean-Paul Sartre, in his preface to Frantz Fanon's *The Wretched of the Earth*, also stands as a postcolonial intellectual, in that moment in which he writes of Fanon, "For we in Europe too are being decolonized: that is to say that the settler which is in every one of us is being savagely rooted out...First, we must face that unexpected revelation, the strip tease of our humanism."[2] Finally, in the work of Edward Said, we find a brilliant assessment of the response of disparate postcolonial regions, what he calls "a tremendously energetic attempt to engage in the metropolitan world in a common effort at reinscribing and reinterpreting and expanding the sites of intensity and the cultural terrain contested within Europe."

Our major task now is to probe further the cunning of Western modernity, its historical ironies, its disjunctive temporalities, its much-vaunted crisis of representation. It is important to say that it would change the values of all critical work if the emergence of modernity were given a colonial and postcolonial genealogy. We must never forget that the establishment of colonized space profoundly informs and historically contests the emergence of those so-called post-Enlightenment values associated with the notion of modern stability.

In concluding I would just like to suggest that many of the narrative traditions that are read as postmodern in contemporary critical fictions, emerging from colonized areas that were once seen as culturally peripheral, come to contest the division between the public and the private. What is interesting is that the notion of the public sphere is very often now being *feminized*. And I find it very strange that, with all the hullabaloo over Rushdie's renaming of the prophets' wives and the offending secularism in the chapter in *The Satanic Verses* of the return to Galilee, that no one – or no one I know of – has actually discussed that chapter in relation to a much earlier chapter in the book in which the writer-narrator returns home to confront the death of his mother. In that kind of *trompe l'oeil* moment, Rushdie is quite strongly suggesting that it is around this problem of sexuality and "femininity" that he first becomes secularized. So what I want to suggest is that the public sphere, posited as a feminized body of memory and imagination, may allow us to think of the social contract not merely as part of a kind of "visibility and rationality of traditions," as Hannah Arendt puts it. But that through this feminization, we might actually be able to explore other forms of social affiliation – those that come to us through pleasure, eroticism, friendship, and a profound political rearticulation of private values and public virtues.

Michelle Cliff

I want to begin by quoting the "coloured" South African writer Zoë Wicomb, author of the novel *You Can't Get Lost in Cape Town*, who speaks of the use of language as it seems to her. Her words move me; they are connected at base with how I have felt about language and writing. She says:

When I think about my own process of writing, the fact that I did not write for years and years, though I wanted to, it has to do with a sense of confidence. Unless your daily trans- action with words is successful, unless words work for you, unless when you speak there are re- sults, you're not going to have the confidence to use language.[1]

She speaks for me, another "coloured," from another end of the Empire.

• • •

The first piece of writing I produced, beyond a dissertation on intellectual game- playing in the Italian Renaissance (which I negotiated through six Western lan- guages – five living; one dead – validating my intellect all the while), was entitled "Notes on Speechlessness." In these notes, I talked about my identification with Victor, the wild child of Aveyron. After his "rescue" from the forest and wildness – and, presumably, from the she-wolf who nourished him, the aboriginal mother – by a well-meaning doctor of Enlightenment Europe, Victor became tame, civilized, but never came to speech.

I empathized with Victor: my wildness had been tamed, a wildness that em- braced imagination, emotions, spontaneity, history, memory, revolution, flights of fancy, the forest. Flesh was replaced by air, Caliban by Ariel. For as Roberto Fernández Retamar, in his essay "Caliban: Notes Toward a Discussion of Culture in Our America," has observed: "There is no real Ariel-Caliban polarity; both are slaves in the hands of Prospero, the foreign magician. But Caliban is the rude and unconquerable master of the island, while Ariel, a creature of the air, although also a child of the isle, is the intellectual."[2]

Victor's name, given him by Dr. Itard, lives in odd juxtaposition to his fate. The victory is not his, it belongs to his civilizer, his tamer, his Prospero – he who would erase Victor's history, his identity, prior to his indoctrination, assume the mere brutishness of the forest, as he tells the tale, the life of Victor, from his own view-point, as history has usually been written.

Then, too, Victor is speechless. His inability to speak is charged to the forest or life before abandonment – in either case, it is the female who is charged – I remember the scar on his throat. But I use Victor here for the metaphor of the colonized child, of myself as a Jamaican child, subject to the privilege of the colonizer, and wonder further about his speechlessness. Is it self-erasure? Rebellion? How would I categorize my own?

There are several versions of the colonized child. There is the child who is chosen, as was I, to represent the colonizer's world, peddle the colonizer's values, ideas, notions of what is real, alien, other, normal, supreme. To apotheosize his success as civilizer.

There are of course different brands of colonization. Some children will turn a profit for the colonizer, others perish in defense of his boundaries; some may one day slit his throat. But all are awash in the notion that life prior to the Middle Passage, civilization, represents only brutishness and is best forgotten. That child cannot become whole under such stringent taming; but wholeness is not desired.

This is by way of explaining that part of my purpose as a writer of Afro-Caribbean – Indian, African, European – experience and heritage and Western experience and education has been to reject speechlessness, a process which has taken years, and to invent my own peculiar speech, with which to describe my own peculiar self, to draw together everything I am and have been, both Caliban and Ariel. At times, Miranda too. And the great-granddaughter of Sycorax.

Caliban speaks to Prospero, saying, "You taught me language, and my profit on't/ Is, I know how to curse."

Yes. And this declaration immediately brings to my mind the character of Bertha Rochester, wild and raving *ragoût* as Charlotte Brontë describes her, more beast than human, as Brontë envisions her: "Oh, sir, I never saw a face like it! It was a discoloured face – it was a savage face."

It took a Caribbean novelist, Jean Rhys, to describe Bertha from the inside, using the lens of the colonized female questioning colonization, keeping Bertha's "humanity, indeed her sanity as a critic of imperialism, intact," in Gayatri Spivak's words, feminist Marxist deconstructivist, wild colonial girl. As was Jean Rhys, as am I, the latter, not the former.[3] What a fine phrase, *critic of imperialism*, to describe the character we all encountered as girls – our hair plaited, our bodies uniformed, our minds trained on the mother (*sic*) country – as the madwoman in the attic, uncontrolled and uncontrollable, the worst thing a woman could become. Jean Rhys once said, speaking of Bertha and *Wide Sargasso Sea*, "I thought I'd try to write her a life." It is a statement at once moving and sensible.[4]

The protagonist of my two novels is Clare Savage. She is not exactly an autobiographical character, but one who is an amalgam of myself and others. Eventually she becomes herself alone. Bertha Rochester is her ancestor.

As is Heathcliff.

Nelly Dean, narrator of *Wuthering Heights*, describes the child Heathcliff: "It's as dark almost as if it came from the devil." Then: "It only stared round, and repeated over and over again some gibberish [African language? Mother tongue?] that nobody could understand." Finally: "The master tried to explain . . . a tale of his seeing it starving, and houseless, and as good as dumb, in the streets of Liverpool, where he enquired for its owner."

Owner? What does this suggest?

It helps to know that at the time of the novel, Liverpool was the absolute center of the Atlantic slave trade, where "free or discarded blacks swelled the ranks of the poor and destitute . . . [And] the gruesome accessories of the slave trade were on display in shop windows: 'chains and manacles, devices for forcing open Negroes' mouths . . . thumbscrews and all other instruments of oppression.'"[5]

Yes, *owner*.

There's much more to say; perhaps some day someone will finally decode *Wuthering Heights*; at least, write Heathcliff "a life."

• • •

Clare Savage's first name signifies light-skinned, which she is; and in the worlds she knows light skin stands for privilege, civilization, erasure, proximity to the colonizer. Light skin – in the world in which Clare originates, the island of Jamaica in the period of British hegemony; and to which she is transported, the United States in the sixties; and to which she transports herself, Britain in the seventies – is meant to ordain her behavior. She is not meant to curse or rave or be a critic of imperialism; were she to do so, she would be considered at least deviant, possessed perhaps by a rogue gene. She is meant to speak softly and to keep to her place. And to keep others to their places – that is, of course, key.

Clare Savage's surname is self-explanatory. It is meant to invoke the wildness that has been bleached from her skin – understanding that my use of the word *wildness* is ironic, mocking the master's meaning, evoking non-Western values that are empowering and essential to survival, and wholeness – her wholeness. A knowledge of history, the past that has been bleached from her mind, just as the rapes of her grandmothers bleached her skin. And this bleached skin is the source of her privilege and her power, too, she thinks, for she is a colonized child. She is a light-skinned female who has been removed from her homeland in a variety of ways and whose life is a movement back – ragged, interrupted, uncertain – to that place. She is fragmented, damaged, incomplete.

By the end of *No Telephone to Heaven*, Clare Savage has cast her lot, quietly and somewhat tentatively, but most definitely. She ends life literally burned into the landscape of Jamaica, as one of a small band of guerrillas engaged in a symbolic act of revolution. While essentially tragic, I see it and envisioned it as an ending that completes the circle, actually the triangle of the character's life. In her death she has achieved complete identification with her homeland. Soon enough she will be indistinguishable from the ground. Her bones will turn to potash as did her ancestors' bones. Her grandmother's relics will be unable to distinguish her from her darker-skinned sister.

This ending, and the sense it conveys, is connected to the work of the Cuban artist Ana Mendieta. Like Clare Savage, like me, a child exile. The art critic Elizabeth Hess has described Mendieta's work:

Mendieta's art took shape in performance, earthworks, sculptures and photographs … Again and again, she carved a haunting, iconic female figure into the ground, onto the side of a cave, or even into a stream of water – by defining the form with ripples and rocks. On occasion the figure was born in flames, literally exploding into existence – then burning up. All that was left of these pieces, called the "Silueta Series," was a scar, or a shadow-image … The earth owns these works, which eventually will disappear over time.[6]

Some of Mendieta's etched landscapes exist today in Cuba, where she worked in 1981. Her work, like mine, has been a movement back, to homeland and identity. She represents this homeland, this landscape of identity, as female, the contours of a female body, at times filling the contours with blood, at other times fixing the silhouette to the earth by gunpowder.

At the end of *No Telephone to Heaven*, Clare Savage is burned into the landscape with gunfire, but she is also enveloped in the deep green of the hills and the delicate intricacy of birdsong. Her death occurs at the moment she forgets human language. Both Mendieta and I understand the landscapes of our islands as female.

For me, the land is redolent of my grandmother and mother. The same could be said of Clare Savage, who seeks out the landscape of her grandmother's farm as she would seek out her grandmother or mother. There is nothing left at that point but the land, and it is infused with the spirit of passion of these two women.[7]

• • •

Looking back over *Abeng* and *No Telephone to Heaven*, I find the theme of the grandmother repeated. I try in both of these novels to show the authority of the grandmother as well as her victimization. Hers is a power directly related to landscape, gardens, planting when the heavenly signs are right, burying the placenta and umbilical cord, preparing the dead for burial.

This powerful aspect of the grandmother originates in Nanny, the African warrior and Maroon leader. At her most powerful, the grandmother is the source of knowledge, magic, ancestors, healing, food. She assists in rites of passage, protects, and teaches. She is the inheritor of African belief systems, African languages. She is informed with *àshe*, the power-to-make-things-happen, which carries with it the responsibility to mete justice. She appears in several places in my work. Most prominently, she is Miss Mattie, the grandmother of Clare Savage. With her brown arms furiously, sensuously working as she pounds coffee beans into dust in her carved mortar, with her smoothed pestle, she embodies power, the life-force she represents. When she appears as the grandmother of Christopher, a character in *No Telephone to Heaven*, she inhabits the Dungle, literally a garbage heap on which people lived. Here, the grandmother is all but bereft of power, except for the power to judge, to assess the worthiness or unworthiness of others. The vestige of her African power-source, its symbol, is the thunderstone that sits in her enamel water jug, purifying the water she draws from a dripping standpipe. The theme of the grandmother, specifically the Jamaican grandmother, her tradition, her history, embraces both these women. Finally, it is her death(s) in the almshouse fire in Kingston in 1985 that impels Clare to Jamaica once and for all.

There is one grandmother who stands apart from the others in *No Telephone to Heaven*. She is the woman that Hart Crane envisioned as the flesh of America, Powhatan's daughter, Pocahontas. She becomes grandmother in death, while in life she was daughter, mother. Pocahontas is buried in Gravesend, having died on the Thames at the start of her journey home in 1616, in her twentieth year. Her son and husband returned to Virginia. Her name has been synonymous with collaborator, traitor, consort of the enemy. The truth is not so. Pocahontas was kidnapped by colonists and held against her will, forced to abandon the belief system of her people and to memorize the Apostle's Creed, the Lord's Prayer, and the Ten Commandments. She was taken to England and there displayed, a tame Indian, supposedly cleansed of aboriginal longing, the forest behind her. She became known as the "friend of the earliest struggling colonists, whom she boldly rescued, protected, and helped," as it is written on her memorial tablet in St. George's Church. She is memorialized there as Rebecca Wrolfe, her real name, which translates as "getting joy from the spirits," erased. She exists in history like Victor—speechless. When Clare Savage recognizes Pocahontas in that graveyard at Gravesend, she makes a choice, begins a series of choices, that will take her from the mother country back to the grandmother country, which is, in the end, her own.

Arturo Islas

My grandparents were from Mexico, and my parents are first-generation North American citizens. My first language was Spanish, taught to me by the only grandmother I knew, who had been a teacher in northern Mexico and had come northward during the revolution of 1910. Her husband, a grandfather I never knew, died en route, and my father, the youngest of ten children, was born en route. Before migrating to Northern California, where I have lived half of my life, I was brought up and educated in English, weaned and disciplined away from Spanish in the public schools of a town on the Mexico-Texas border. My hometown, El Paso, has many more ties to northern Mexico and southern New Mexico than to the rest of Texas, which ignores that little border town except during statewide elections.

Now – and for the past twenty years – people of Mexican ancestry like myself make up the majority group. Still, their political and cultural status remains patently second class. When I lived on the Border in the forties and fifties, Mexican people, American citizens of Mexican heritage, constituted 40 percent of the population, and in order to vote, my parents had to pay a poll tax. I have returned often to this southwestern desert country because I love it and consider myself still a child of the Border, which has a cultural identity all its own.

That landscape and its people are what I write about in my fictions, and, like some of my characters, I have led a double life, between cultures, between languages, between sexes, between nations, between two very compelling and different ways of looking at the world and its people. Now, because of the very peculiar circumstances of my personal life and education, I find myself between my profession as a teacher of literature and my vocation as a novelist. The novelist part of myself always feels very uncomfortable at conferences and discussions such as this. When I write, I have the privilege of being on the bridge between these disparate entities, and in my imagination I can walk from one side of the Border to the other with ease. Some of my characters are not so fortunate.

When I look at my own work through professorial eyes, I suppose I agree that it falls between the North American and Latin American literary traditions. With those eyes, let me look briefly at the crisis of representation for Chicano and Mexican-American writers in this country.

At the first annual Latin American writers conference, held in Long Beach, California, in April 1990, Peruvian poet Antonio Cisneros described the political situation in his country with humor and despair, and wondered aloud whether Peru would even exist when he returned to it and to his family. Fernando Alegría, Chilean novelist and *don* of Latin American letters in this country, told us about his recent visit to Chile. After many years of not being allowed to see his family and his native land, his return included a triumphant celebration of the publication of his biography of Salvador Allende. In a deadpan voice, he described how his Chilean brothers and sisters forget all about history in the summer months and lie side by side on the beaches of the Hispanic-Pacific coast rim.

From Mexico, the wondrous Elena Poniatowska noted that the talk of the writers of the Latin American conference somehow always gets back to politics and that, like it or not, writers are political figures in Latin America. She chided her Peruvian brother Cisneros for speaking about his wife as if she were a possession and said she wished she had a wife to take care of the business of living while she wrote her essays and novels. Antonio Scármeta, from Argentina, revealed that Mr. Fujimori, most probably the next president of Peru, was in reality a fictional invention of Gabriel García Márquez, created for the purpose of driving fellow novelist Mario Vargas Llosa out of his mind. And later, during the question-and-answer period when I was asked about the connection and communication between Mexican and Chicano/Mexican-American writers, I took the opportunity to say in an aside that I would gladly be Elena Poniatowska's wife. (She accepted, by the way.) Before then, I was struck by the privilege of being treated as an equal by these fine writers, known and revered in their respected countries, who took my work and words seriously, and were eager to listen to my descriptions of my place as a Chicano/Mexican-American writer in the cultural life of the United States. What could I tell them but the truth?

I see my presence here at this conference as recognition of me as a writer from an immensely rich culture that has been ignored by its own country for far too long. I am grateful for such recognition in the name of the many from my background who came before and who are with me now in the trenches, and whose work and contributions to not only the political and economic but the cultural life as well of North America have not been acknowledged. Happily the literary establishment of the Northeast does recognize the works of some Latin American writers. It discusses them with respect and admiration in the periodicals that are considered worthy and that decide what the rest of the country reads. We see the names of these writers alongside the names of those writers, young and old, who are revered in Anglo-America.

But, alas, except for two notable and instructive exceptions, we have not seen the names of any writers from the Chicano and Mexican-American tradition in any of these esteemed journals. In the eighties, much attention was given to two writers of Mexican heritage born and educated in this country. Both received front-page coverage and lengthy reviews in northeastern literary journals and periodicals and throughout the country. One of them, at thirty-five, wrote an auto-biography in which he excoriates any teacher who favors affirmative action or bilingual education, even though he himself reaped the benefits of such programs for his own education. The other, who wrote a novel told in the first person by a young Chicano gang member in East Los Angeles, turned out not to be Hispanic at all, but an upper-class, Yale-educated older member of the literary establishment who had been blacklisted for his political views and could write only when he imagined himself to be an underprivileged Chicano from the *barrio*. The angels weep. And that is all. They are the only two writers who have made their way as Mexican-Americans and Chicanos and Chicanas into the dominant cultural life of the nation. Now that, I think, can be called a crisis of representation. We writers from Mexican-American culture remain *un*listed.

Anton Shammas

Last year, when I was invited for some outlandish reason to attend this symposium, I went out hunting for the works of those participants that I hadn't known before for various reasons. I know one can always find excuses and pretexts to make one's ignorance seem potentially rigorous, like a pensive silkworm. However, I am not going to indulge in such cocoons: I hereby publicly and immediately denounce my past ignorance. Still, there is a wily Third Worlder inside me trying to talk me into finding some mitigating circumstances for this, but perhaps some other time. So in my defense, I would say only that, unlike most of the participants, English is my third language. I had known most of the authors' names, but was not familiar with their work. So for somebody like myself who was living as a nonresident alien in the pure-American-buttered-popcorn-belt of the Midwest for a while now, but otherwise is a resident of the battered Middle East, this is really a treat for me. For one of our problems is that we, the writers here, sometimes hardly know of each other until some kind, generous people invite us to a symposium.

Speaking of ignorance, let me first enlighten you about my ignorant self. I am a Palestinian citizen of Israel, a contradiction in terms, which means I am a walking cave inside of which there are (on a good day) at least two trapped, puffing dragons consistently, but as benignly as possible, arguing about cultural identity and the crisis of representation. I can show you in afterwards, if you like. My mother tongue is Arabic, the language in which I count, sometimes dream, sometimes whisper a curse, and sometimes remember phone numbers, but above all the language in which I remember tales. I also used to write poetry in it, until my stepmother tongue snatched me "like a child from the crib" in order to write my first novel in Hebrew, a novel whose subject was the vicissitudes of Palestinian life. Hebrew and Arabic, as you probably know, share Semitic origins, something you cannot say about Urdu and English (and you know who I mean). They share Semitic origins, but that is all. Otherwise, for a century now, Hebrew and Arabic have been in a state of fierce war. And to cap it all, I find myself every now and then being lured by, shall we say, an anti-Semitic language, the *lingua franca* of the colonized, Her Majesty's English, as if I needed a highbrow dragon for my collection.

I come from a region that has been for centuries in a state of (among other things) cultural siege. As were all the colonized regions of the world. "Our" colonizing powers were too many, and the countries of the Near East were exposed over the ages to too many counting systems, shifting rules of grammar and gender in too many languages of the earth. At the beginning of the sixteenth century, the Ottoman Empire took over and in the name of religion – Islam, in this case – kept the region in total darkness for four hundred years until the British stepped in after World War I. The cross supplanted the crescent, and darkness – darkness. Among the great achievements of the Ottoman Empire in the Middle East, one can always single out the perpetuation of the absence of narrative art. Storytelling, as the subversive oral art, for centuries kept the line of narrative alive while the written tradition was outlawed. This might to some extent explain the fact that the first Arabic novel was written only eighty years ago by an Egyptian writer who was at the time living in Paris. So it took Arab literature some thirteen hundred years to come to terms with narrative (note: in Paris, not in Cairo), bearing in mind that this is the same literature that had produced the oral and "uncanonical" narrative tradition of the *Book of the Thousand and One Nights*, but failed to translate this achievement into its literate culture.

In November 1987, again in Paris, there was what *The New York Times* called at the time a major political as well as literary event. Tahar Ben Jelloun, the then forty-three-year-old Moroccan novelist, won France's most prestigious literary award, the Prix Goncourt, for his novel *The Sacred Night*, an exotic tale of an Arab woman raised as a boy but finally freed of the bondage of her false identity. Although six non-French novelists have won the Goncourt since the prize was established in 1903, Ben Jelloun was the first writer from one of France's former North African colonies to be chosen for the prize. Critics were saying that the Moroccan novelist, writing in French, was bringing "a whiff of youth into French writing by reviving the ancient tradition of Arab storytelling." Tahar Ben Jelloun was quoted as saying that he approves of polygamy with languages, not women. He said, "My wife is Arabic and my mistress is French and I maintain a relationship of betrayal with both of them."[1] When it comes to writing novels and poetry, the *Times* reporter observed, Ben Jelloun has been more faithful to his mistress than his wife. Now, let me say that I find Ben Jelloun's attitude toward Arabic and French, as being his wife and mistress respectively, utterly indecorous and sexist. Male writers of the Third World should be more cautious and extremely non-chauvinistic in their dealings with both women and languages. In any case, they should respect women more than languages.

Be that as it may, the Moroccan novelist Tahar Ben Jelloun lives in Paris and writes in French and, like some of his peers, brought – and I repeat – "a whiff of youth into French writing by reviving the ancient tradition of Arab storytelling." Now, Derek Walcott would have talked here about the "language of the torturer mastered by the victim." And if we wish to add another touch to this definition from yet another French angle, we could use Gilles Deleuze and Félix Guattari's definition of minor literature and say that what Ben Jelloun has been doing, indeed what even Salman Rushdie has been doing in this respect, has been to let Caliban deterritorialize the language of Prospero. Minor literature, Deleuze and Guattari say in their book on Kafka, "does not come from a minor language; it is rather that which a minority constructs within a major language."[2] There are three character-istics of a minor literature. The first is that in it, language is affected with a high coefficient of deterritorialization. Kafka's Prague German is a deterritorialized language appropriate for strange and minor uses. Salman Rushdie once said that he is trying to liberate the English language from the rule of the British Empire.

In my humble case, as a Palestinian who was ungracefully deterritorialized by the Hebrew language (which Dante had described in the fourteenth century as the language of Grace) – what I am trying to do is deterritorialize the Hebrew lan-guage, or, more bluntly, to un-Jew the Hebrew language and make it a language of personal narrative discourse. In a certain sense, that is what most of the writers of the Third World are doing these days: undoing the culture of the majority from within. The deterritorialization of the colonizers' language is the only way to claim their own territory, and it is the only territory left to them as writers to de-clare as an independent state – the only one they can afford to call a homeland. "I had no nation now but the imagination." I can hear this line almost humming around, Walcott's overquoted line from his overquoted poem, which I have come across in Michelle Cliff's *The Land of Look Behind*. Cliff writes in her introduction to this book, "It is Jamaica that forms my writing for the most part, and which has formed for the most part, myself. Even though I often feel what Derek Walcott expresses in his poem, 'The Schooner *Flight*': 'I had no nation now but the imagination.' It is a complicated business."[3] Well, my sentiments exactly: it is a complicated business.

That is why the second characteristic of a minor literature is that everything in it is political. Minor literature's "cramped space" forces each individual intrigue to connect immediately to politics. The third characteristic is that in minor literature everything takes on a collective value. "It is literature," Deleuze and Guattari write, "that produces an active solidarity in spite of skepticism; and if the writer is in the margins or completely outside his or her fragile community, this situation allows the writer all the more possibility to express another possible community and to forge the means for another consciousness and another sensibility." Deleuze and Guattari ask, "How many people today live in a language that is not their own? Or no longer, or not yet, even know their own and know poorly the major language that they are forced to serve?"[4]

Imagination has been mentioned here quite often in its political context. There are certain moments in the history of cultures when the internalized alphabetic literacy clashes head-on with orality. Such a moment occurs, for instance, in Plato's *Republic*, when poets are excluded, among other reasons, because they stand for orality, for the formulaic style, for memory. In the West, such a moment occurred, in my opinion, when the novel was introduced as a genre. In his reflections on the works of Nikolai Leskov, published in 1936 under the title "The Storyteller," Walter Benjamin laments that the art of storytelling is coming to an end.[5] We encounter with less and less frequency people with the ability to tell a tale properly. The reason, as Benjamin contends, is that experience has fallen in value (remember, we are talking about 1936), and our ability to exchange experiences is ebbing away. The rise of the novel and the invention of print triggered the decline of storytelling. For what distinguishes the novel from the story, or more exactly, from the tale, is its essential dependence on the book. While the birthplace of the novel is the solitary individual, and while the novel has isolated itself, the storyteller depends on the listeners and he has what Benjamin calls a counsel for them, something useful—a moral, practical advice, a maxim. The uncounseled novelist, on the other hand, cannot counsel others. His alleged wisdom comes from the information, as opposed to the intelligence, of the storyteller. In short, and to make a vulgar paraphrase of Benjamin's essay, it comes down to memory and imagination being the respective tools of the storyteller and the novelist.

Now those who have interiorized the alphabets feel so privileged that they won't let us storytellers in. They practice their ownership over imagination. They would tell writers like Salman Rushdie to go back to their reality, their memory, their storytelling. That is how I understand the decolonization of the novel. It is the liberation movement of the literate storytellers against the monopoly over imagination of those who "invented" the novel. On the other hand, the death sentence against Rushdie is, in a way, against his attempt to decolonize the novel. It is blasphemous to make the transition from memory into imagination. This is the crisis of representation. But this is a crisis that carries with it its own solution.

Luisa Valenzuela

The Writer, the Crisis, and a Form of Representation

When Phil Mariani began dreaming about a writers' conference on the crisis of representation, Salman Rushdie's name was one of the first to be mentioned. That was some years ago—little could she have guessed that the Rushdie controversy would become, in a sense, the epitome of such a crisis.

It is true that when dogma interferes with the necessary ambiguity of the symbol, freezing it, we are in serious trouble. For just like Kurt Vonnegut's "Ice Nine," the freezing can easily contaminate others. In *La transparence du mal*, Jean Baudrillard alludes to the great feat of Khomeini, who managed to make Rushdie the hostage of the Western World and thus turn the Western World into a kind of hostage of itself, so giving "spectacular proof of the possibility of a reversal of all the relations of power through the symbolic force of the word."[1]

It was precisely by the power of the word (as well as the literal application of the verb *to kill*), by the appropriation and distortion of the word—slogans promising power to the Nation, twists of the double bind by which the people were humiliated when the de facto government was criticized—that military dictatorships, as we know them all too well throughout Latin America, managed to turn some writers into hostages of their own countries.

"Silence is health," announced a gigantic banner that appeared smack in the center of Buenos Aires in the early seventies. We thought then that it was a government campaign against noise pollution, but soon we learned to read better. Silence was the ransom price for the Argentine people, and as state terrorism progressed, it was paid to the extent of obliterating memory.

Many writers silenced themselves purposefully: internal exile, some called it, trying to soften the wound. But those who could afford it, materially and spiritually, opted for real exile and abandoned the country, leaving their hearts behind. They left—we left—in order to avoid being silenced, and later we learned that distance and a certain perspective were helpful in gaining understanding of the incomprehensible terror being implemented in our countries.

The discourse of power exacerbated the breach, the separation. There will be two Argentine literatures, they said: the literature of the writers who remained in the country, thus keeping in touch with the language; and the literature of those who left, which will drift farther and farther away from its original roots. Divide and conquer; it was an easy maneuver and its effects quite insidious.

The writers who stayed behind said – and may keep on saying, now, long after the horrors are over – that those who left lost touch with local reality and were never able to sense the deep truth. On the other hand, those who left said – and will keep on saying – that those who stayed behind were not only gagged but blindfolded to the possibility of acknowledging a reality too painful to be easily accepted on a conscious level.

A crisis of representation, yes, implemented as usual by the hegemonic power that will always benefit from the confusion.

It is never the writer who takes fact for fiction or vice versa. Writers can detect and enhance or even detonate the metaphor, as if it were a bomb. But those who are not used to the metaphor's duplicity, to its underlying layers of meanings and contradictions, can easily get caught in the trap of the literal.

Nowadays the coin is showing its other side: no more silence. Now everything is named, perversions of power and corruption are out in the open, but the magical possibility of the word (the act of naming, conveyor of reality) is not enough to change the situation. Excessive representation can also constitute a crisis, but the show must go on.

Literality goes against the grain of the writer. It fixes meaning into people like the pin fixes a butterfly, and no more questions are asked. Anyway, there is nobody to answer them. Questions are forbidden, doubt is banned, uncertainty is only a principle acknowledged in subatomic levels of nonentity. What you see is what you get. And one is supposed to see only what benefits the powers to be.

For the Latin American writer, for the Argentine writer – because of the frequency of dictatorships – the real crisis is one of *self*-representation, perhaps even of self-justification. What is one doing in this solitary confinement called *writing fiction* when all around you people are being tortured and killed and "disappeared" and the twists of grammar and imagination go beyond human comprehension? One is trying to see through imposed lies. Trying to understand, to find some logic in the chaos. One is aware that somewhere out there, in perverse authoritarian structures, there must be some underlying metaphors that it would be important to deconstruct – out of a need to know a little more of the workings of the human mind and its will to power, its need to be right, its desperately mad belief in being sole owner of the truth.

My country, Argentina, has its share of owners of the truth. They don't all wear uniforms. But a particularly favored one does – or did. He has been defrocked of late, even though he maintains a loyal group of followers. His name is Aldo Rico, ex-lieutenant colonel, now in open rebellion against the present military establishment. Rico knows exactly what he meant when he said, "Doubt is a conceit of intellectuals; we military don't doubt, we act."

Rico's phrase gives me a great sense of relief, for it tells me that writers are correct in writing, if only because we *bask* in the luxury of doubt, the experience of which allows us to see far beyond our shortsighted certainties. I want to know what this madness of power is all about, and I write a book, trying to get under the skin of those who covet power, who have it, or who believe in it. I give them power over words, and suddenly, with language, they begin overwhelming even I who created them. It is exciting and terrifying at the same time. It is language that conveys power, and those who manage to freeze it master others.

Was it Vargas Llosa's sense of mastery over language that convinced him he could rule his country? So close to the master, so close to the colonizer? And what were those other intellectuals thinking when they wrote their letters congratulating Vargas Llosa and celebrating his probable triumph, while lamenting the loss of a great writer who vowed himself to fictional silence while in power? What power? What will fictional silence do to a fictional writer-president when writing is his only access to understanding and knowledge?

As I create, I discover, said Martin Buber. For me, this is the attitude of a real work of art, always one step beyond the artist, or two steps, or more. The metaphor will speak for us, in spite of us, and through us, and perhaps we may attain some wisdom or at least de-block the word, allow its flow, restore it to whom it belongs.

"Argentina, arise and walk," exhorted our president on the day of his inauguration. The madness of power resides in its idea that it can control fiction, that is to say, the imaginary expression of desire. The madness of fiction is to believe that it doesn't.

Leslie Marmon Silko

Language and Literature from a Pueblo Indian Perspective

Where I come from, the words most highly valued are those spoken from the heart, unpremeditated and unrehearsed. Among the Pueblo people, a written speech or statement is highly suspect because the true feelings of the speaker remain hidden as she reads words that are detached from the occasion and the audience. I have intentionally not written a formal paper because I want you to *hear* and to experience English in a structure that follows patterns from the oral tradition. For those of you accustomed to being taken from point A to point B to point C, this presentation may be somewhat difficult to follow. Pueblo expression resembles something like a spider's web – with many little threads radiating from the center, crisscrossing each other. As with the web, the structure emerges as it is made and you must simply listen and trust, as the Pueblo people do, that meaning will be made.

My task is a formidable one: I ask you to set aside a number of basic approaches that you have been using, and probably will continue to use, and instead, to approach language from the Pueblo perspective, one that embraces the whole of creation and the whole of history and time.

What changes would Pueblo writers make to English as a language for literature? I have some examples of stories in English that I will use to address this question. At the same time, I would like to explain the importance of storytelling and how it relates to a Pueblo theory of language.

So, I will begin, appropriately enough, with the Pueblo Creation story, an all-inclusive story of how life began. In this story, Tséitsínako, Thought Woman, by thinking of her sisters, and together with her sisters, thought of everything that is. In this way, the world was created. Everything in this world was a part of the original creation; the people at home understood that far away there were other human beings, also a part of this world. The Creation story even includes a prophecy, which describes the origin of European and African peoples and also refers to Asians.

This story, I think, suggests something about why the Pueblo people are more concerned with story and communication and less concerned with a particular language. There are at least six, possibly seven, distinct languages among the twenty pueblos of the southwestern United States, for example, Zuñi and Hopi. And from mesa to mesa there are subtle differences in language. But the particular language being spoken isn't as important as what a speaker is trying to say, and this emphasis on the story itself stems, I believe, from a view of narrative particular to the Pueblo and other Native American peoples – that is, that language *is* story.

I will try to clarify this statement. At Laguna Pueblo, for example, many individual words have their own stories. So when one is telling a story, and one is using words to tell the story, each word that one is speaking has a story of its own, too. Often the speakers or tellers will go into these word-stories, creating an elaborate structure of stories-within-stories. This structure, which becomes very apparent in the actual telling of a story, informs contemporary Pueblo writing and storytelling as well as the traditional narratives. This perspective on narrative – of story within story, the idea that one story is only the beginning of many stories, and the sense that stories never truly end – represents an important contribution of Native American cultures to the English language.

Many people think of storytelling as something that is done at bedtime, that it is something done for small children. But when I use the term *storytelling*, I'm talking about something much bigger than that. I'm talking about something that comes out of an experience and an understanding of that original view of creation – that we are all part of a whole; we do not differentiate or fragment stories and experiences. In the beginning, Tséitsínako, Thought Woman, thought of all things, and all of these things are held together as one holds many things together in a single thought.

So in the telling (and you will hear a few of the dimensions of this telling) first of all, as mentioned earlier, the storytelling always includes the audience, the listeners. In fact, a great deal of the story is believed to be inside the listener; the storyteller's role is to draw the story out of the listeners. The storytelling continues from generation to generation.

Basically, the origin story constructs our identity – with this story, we know who we are. We are the Lagunas. This is where we come from. We came this way. We came by this place. And so from the time we are very young, we hear these stories, so that when we go out into the world, when one asks who we are, or where we are from, we immediately know: we are the people who came from the north. We are the people of these stories.

In the Creation story, Antelope says that he will help knock a hole in the earth so that the people can come up, out into the next world. Antelope tries and tries; he uses his hooves, but is unable to break through. It is then that Badger says, "Let me help you." And Badger very patiently uses his claws and digs a way through, bringing the people into the world. When the Badger clan people think of themselves, or when the Antelope people think of themselves, it is as people who are of *this* story, and this is *our* place, and we fit into the very beginning when the people first came, before we began our journey south.

Within the clans there are stories that identify the clan. One moves, then, from the idea of one's identity as a tribal person into clan identity, then to one's identity as a member of an extended family. And it is the notion of "extended family" that has produced a kind of story that some distinguish from other Pueblo stories, though Pueblo people do not. Anthropologists and ethnologists have, for a long time, differentiated the types of stories the Pueblos tell. They tended to elevate the old, sacred, and traditional stories and to brush aside family stories, the family's account of itself. But in Pueblo culture, these family stories are given equal recognition. There is no definite, preset pattern for the way one will hear the stories of one's own family, but it is a very critical part of one's childhood, and the storytelling continues throughout one's life. One will hear stories of importance to the family – sometimes wonderful stories – stories about the time a maternal uncle got the biggest deer that was ever seen and brought it back from the mountains. And so an individual's identity will extend from the identity constructed around the family – "I am from the family of my uncle who brought in this wonderful deer and it was a wonderful hunt."

Family accounts include negative stories, too; perhaps an uncle did something unacceptable. It is very important that one keep track of all these stories – both positive and not so positive – about one's own family and other families. Because even when there is no way around it – old Uncle Pete *did* do a terrible thing – by knowing the stories that originate in other families, one is able to deal with terrible sorts of things that might happen within one's own family. If a member of the family does something that cannot be excused, one always knows stories about similarly inexcusable things done by a member of another family. But this knowledge is not communicated for malicious reasons. It is very important to understand this.

Keeping track of all the stories within the community gives us all a certain distance, a useful perspective, that brings incidents down to a level we can deal with. If others have done it before, it cannot be so terrible. If others have endured, so can we.

The stories are always bringing us together, keeping this whole together, keeping this family together, keeping this clan together. "Don't go away, don't isolate yourself, but come here, because we have all had these kinds of experiences." And so there is this constant pulling together to resist the tendency to run or hide or separate oneself during a traumatic emotional experience. This separation not only endangers the group but the individual as well – one does not recover by oneself.

Because storytelling lies at the heart of Pueblo culture, it is absurd to attempt to fix the stories in time. "When did they tell the stories?" or "What time of day does the storytelling take place?" – these questions are nonsensical from a Pueblo perspective, because our storytelling goes on constantly: as some old grandmother puts on the shoes of a child and tells her the story of a little girl who didn't wear her shoes, for instance, or someone comes into the house for coffee to talk with a teenage boy who has just been in a lot of trouble, to reassure him that someone else's son has been in that kind of trouble, too. Storytelling is an ongoing process, working on many different levels.

Here's one story that is often told at a time of individual crisis (and I want to remind you that we make no distinctions between types of story – historical, sacred, plain gossip – because these distinctions are not useful when discussing the Pueblo *experience* of language). There was a young man who, when he came back from the war in Vietnam, had saved up his army pay and bought a beautiful red Volkswagen. He was very proud of it. One night he drove up to a place called the King's Bar right across the reservation line. The bar is notorious for many reasons, particularly for the deep *arroyo* located behind it. The young man ran in to pick up a cold six-pack, but he forgot to put on his emergency brake. And his little red Volkswagen rolled back into the *arroyo* and was all smashed up. He felt very bad about it, but within a few days everybody had come to him with stories about other people who had lost cars and family members to that *arroyo*, for instance, George Day's station wagon, with his mother-in-law and kids inside. So everybody was saying, "Well, at least your mother-in-law and kids weren't in the car when it rolled in," and one can't argue with that kind of story. The story of the young man and his smashed-up Volkswagen was now joined with all the other stories of cars that fell into that *arroyo.*

Now I want to tell you a very beautiful little story. It is a very old story that is sometimes told to people who suffer great family or personal loss. This story was told by my Aunt Susie. She is one of the first generation of people at Laguna who began experimenting with English – who began working to make English speak for us – that is, to speak from the heart. (I come from a family intent on getting the stories told.) As you read the story, I think you will hear that. And here and there, I think, you will also hear the influence of the Indian school at Carlisle, Pennsylvania, where my Aunt Susie was sent (like being sent to prison) for six years.

This scene is set partly in Acoma, partly in Laguna. Waithea was a little girl living in Acoma and one day she said, "Mother, I would like to have some *yashtoah* to eat." *Yashtoah* is the hardened crust of corn mush that curls up. *Yashtoah* literally means "curled up." She said, "I would like to have some *yashtoah,*" and her mother said, "My dear little girl, I can't make you any *yashtoah* because we haven't any wood, but if you will go down off the mesa, down below, and pick up some pieces of wood and bring them home, I will make you some *yashtoah.*" So Waithea was glad and ran down the precipitous cliff of Acoma mesa. Down below, just as her mother had told her, there were pieces of wood, some curled, some crooked in shape, that she was to pick up and take home. She found just such wood as these.

She brought them home in a little wicker basket. First she called to her mother as she got home, "*Nayah, deeni!* Mother, upstairs!" The Pueblo people always called "upstairs" because long ago their homes were two, three stories, and they entered from the top. She said, "*Deeni!* UPSTAIRS!" and her mother came. The little girl said, "I have brought the wood you wanted me to bring." And she opened her little wicker basket to lay out the pieces of wood but here they were snakes. They were snakes instead of the crooked sticks of wood. And her mother said, "Oh my dear child, you have brought snakes instead!" She said, "Go take them back and put them back just where you got them." And the little girl ran down the mesa again, down below to the flats. And she put those snakes back just where she got them. They were snakes instead and she was very hurt about this and so she said, "I'm not going home. I'm going to *Kawaik,* the beautiful lake place, *Kawaik,* and drown myself in that lake, *byn'yah'nah* [the "west lake"]. I will go there and drown myself."

So she started off, and as she passed by the Enchanted Mesa near Acoma she met an old man, very aged, and he saw her running, and he said, "My dear child, where are you going?" "I'm going to *Kawaik* and jump into the lake there."

"Why?" "Well, because," she said, "my mother didn't want to make any *yashtoah* for me." The old man said, "Oh, no! You must not go my child. Come with me and I will take you home." He tried to catch her, but she was very light and skipped along. And every time he would try to grab her she would skip faster away from him.

The old man was coming home with some wood strapped to his back and tied with yucca. He just let that strap go and let the wood drop. He went as fast as he could up the cliff to the little girl's home. When he got to the place where she lived, he called to her mother. "*Deeni!*" "Come on up!" And he said, "I can't. I just came to bring you a message. Your little daughter is running away. She is going to *Kawaik* to drown herself in the lake there." "Oh my dear little girl!" the mother said. So she busied herself with making the *yashtoah* her little girl liked so much. Corn mush curled at the top. (She must have found enough wood to boil the corn meal and make the *yashtoah*.)

While the mush was cooling off, she got the little girl's clothing, her *manta* dress and buckskin moccasins and all her other garments, and put them in a bundle – probably a yucca bag. And she started down as fast as she could on the east side of Acoma. (There used to be a trail there, you know. It's gone now, but it was accessible in those days.) She saw her daughter way at a distance and she kept calling: "Stsamaku! My daughter! Come back! I've got your *yashtoah* for you." But the little girl would not turn. She kept on ahead and she cried: "My mother, my mother, she didn't want me to have any *yashtoah*. So now I'm going to *Kawaik* and drown myself." Her mother heard her cry and said, "My little daughter, come back here!" "No," and she kept a distance away from her. And they came nearer and nearer to the lake. And she could see her daughter now, very plain. "Come back, my daughter! I have your *yashtoah*." But no, she kept on, and finally she reached the lake and she stood on the edge.

She had tied a little feather in her hair, which is traditional (in death they tie this feather on the head). She carried a feather, the little girl did, and she tied it in her hair with a piece of string, right on top of her head she put the feather. Just as her mother was about to reach her, she jumped into the lake. The little feather was whirling around and around in the depths below. Of course the mother was very sad. She went, grieved, back to Acoma and climbed her mesa home. She stood on the edge of the mesa and scattered her daughter's clothing, the little moccasins, the *yashtoah*. She scattered them to the east, to the west, to the north, to the south. And the pieces of clothing and the moccasins and *yashtoah*, all turned into butterflies. And today they say that Acoma has more beautiful butterflies: red ones, white ones, blue ones, yellow ones. They came from this little girl's clothing.[1]

Now this is a story anthropologists would consider very old. The version I have given you is just as Aunt Susie tells it. You can occasionally hear some English she picked up at Carlisle – words like "precipitous." You will also notice that there is a great deal of repetition, and a little reminder about *yashtoah*, and how it is made. There is a remark about the cliff trail at Acoma – that it was once there, but is there no longer. This story may be told at a time of sadness or loss, but within this story many other elements are brought together. Things are not separated out and categorized; all things are brought together. So that the reminder about the *yashtoah* is valuable information that is repeated – a recipe, if you will. The information about the old trail at Acoma reveals that stories are, in a sense, maps, since even to this day there is little information or material about trails that is passed around with writing. In the structure of this story the repetitions are, of course, designed to help you remember. It is repeated again and again, and then it moves on.

The next story I would like to tell is by Simon Ortiz, from Acoma Pueblo. He is a wonderful poet who also works in narrative. One of the things I find very interesting in this short story is that if you listen very closely, you begin to hear what I was talking about in terms of a story never beginning at the beginning, and certainly never ending. As the Hopis sometimes say, "Well, it has gone this far for a while." There is always that implication of a continuing. The other thing I want you to listen for is the many stories within one story. Listen to the kinds of stories contained within the main story – stories that give one a family identity and an individual identity, for example. This story is called "Home Country":

"Well, it's been a while. I think in 1947 was when I left. My husband had been killed in Okinawa some years before. And so I had no more husband. And I had to make a living. O I guess I could have looked for another man but I didn't want to. It looked like the war had made some of them into a bad way anyway. I saw some of them come home like that. They either got drunk or just stayed around a while or couldn't seem to be satisfied anymore with what was there. I guess now that I think about it, that happened to me too although I wasn't in the war not in the Army or even much off the reservation just that several years at the Indian School. Well there was that feeling things were changing not only the men the boys, but things were changing.

"One day the home nurse the nurse that came from the Indian health service was at my mother's home my mother was getting near the end real sick and she said that she had been meaning to ask me a question. I said what is the question. And the home nurse said well your mother is getting real sick and after she is no longer around for you to take care of, what will you be doing you and her are the only ones here. And I said I don't know. But I was thinking about it what she said made me think about it. And then the next time she came she said to me Eloise the government is hiring Indians now in the Indian schools to take care of the boys and girls I heard one of the supervisors saying that Indians are hard workers but you have to supervise them a lot and I thought of you well because you've been taking care of your mother real good and you follow all my instructions. She said I thought of you because you're a good Indian girl and you would be the kind of person for that job. I didn't say anything I had not ever really thought about a job but I kept thinking about it.

"Well my mother she died and we buried her up at the old place the cemetery there it's real nice on the east side of the hill where the sun shines warm and the wind doesn't blow too much sand around right there. Well I was sad we were all sad for a while but you know how things are. One of my aunties came over and she advised me and warned me about being too sorry about it and all that she wished me that I would not worry too much about it because old folks they go along pretty soon life is that way and then she said that maybe I ought to take in one of my aunties kids or two because there was a lot of them kids and I was all by myself now. But I was so young and I thought that I might do that you know take care of someone but I had been thinking too of what the home nurse said to me about working. Hardly anybody at our home was working at something like that no woman anyway. And I would have to move away.

"Well I did just that. I remember that day very well. I told my aunties and they were all crying and we all went up to the old highway where the bus to town passed by everyday. I was wearing an old kind of bluish sweater that was kind of big that one of my cousins who was older had got from a white person a tourist one summer in trade for something she had made a real pretty basket. She gave me that and I used to have a picture of me with it on it's kind of real ugly. Yeah that was the day I left wearing a baggy sweater and carrying a suitcase that someone gave me too I think or maybe it was the home nurse there wasn't much in it anyway either. I was scared and everybody seemed to be sad I was so young and skinny then. My aunties said one of them who was real fat you make sure you eat now make your own tortillas drink the milk and stuff like candies is no good she learned that from the nurse. Make sure you got your letter my auntie said. I had it folded into my purse. Yes I had one too a brown one that my husband when he was still alive one time on furlough he brought it on my birthday it was a nice purse and still looked new because I never used it.

"The letter said that I had a job at Keams Canyon the boarding school there but I would have to go to the Agency first for some papers to be filled and that's where I was going first. The Agency. And then they would send me out to Keams Canyon. I didn't even know where it was except that someone of our relatives said that it was near Hopi. My uncles teased me about watching out for the Hopi men and boys don't let them get too close they said well you know how they are and they were pretty strict too about those things and then they were joking and then they were not too and so I said aw they won't get near to me I'm too ugly and I promised I would be careful anyway.

"So we all gathered for a while at my last auntie's house and then the old man my grandfather brought his wagon and horses to the door and we all got in and sat there for a while until my auntie told her father okay father let's go and shook his elbow because the poor old man was old by then and kind of going to sleep all the time you had to talk to him real loud. I had about ten dollars I think that was a lot of money more than it is now you know and when we got to the highway where the Indian road which is just a dirt road goes off the pave road my grandfather reached into his blue jeans and pulled out a silver dollar and put it into my hand. I was so shocked. We were all so shocked. We all looked around at each other we didn't know where the old man had gotten it because we were real poor two of my uncles had to borrow on their accounts at the trading store for the money I had in my purse but there it was a silver dollar so big and shining in my grandfather's hand and then in my hand.

"Well I was so shocked and everybody was so shocked that we all started crying right there at the junction of that Indian road and the pave highway I wanted to be a little girl again running after the old man when he hurried with his long legs to the cornfields or went for water down to the river. He was old then and his eye was turned gray and he didn't do much anymore except drive the wagon and chop a little bit of wood but I just held him and I just held him so tightly.

"Later on I don't know what happened to the silver dollar it had a date of 1907 on it but I kept it for a long time because I guess I wanted to have it to remember when I left my home country. What I did in between then and now is another story but that's the time I moved away," is what she said.[2]

There are a great many parallels between Pueblo experiences and those of African and Caribbean peoples—one is that we have all had the conqueror's language imposed on us. But our experience with English has been somewhat different in that the Bureau of Indian Affairs schools were not interested in teaching us the canon of Western classics. For instance, we never heard of Shakespeare. We were given Dick and Jane, and I can remember reading that the robins were heading south for the winter. It took me a long time to figure out what was going on. I worried for quite a while about our robins in Laguna because they didn't leave in the winter, until I finally realized that all the big textbook companies are up in Boston and *their* robins do go south in the winter. But in a way, this dreadful formal education freed us by encouraging us to maintain our narratives. Whatever literature we were exposed to at school (which was damn little), at home the storytelling, the special regard for telling and bringing together through the telling, was going on constantly.

And as the old people say, "If you can remember the stories, you will be all right. Just remember the stories." When I returned to Laguna Pueblo after attending college, I wondered how the storytelling was continuing (anthropologists say that Laguna Pueblo is one of the more acculturated pueblos), so I visited an English class at Laguna-Acoma High School. I knew the students had cassette tape recorders in their lockers and stereos at home, and that they listened to Kiss and Led Zeppelin and were well informed about popular culture in general. I had with me an anthology of short stories by Native American writers, *The Man to Send Rain Clouds*. One story in the book is about the killing of a state policeman in New Mexico by three Acoma Pueblo men in the early 1950s.[3] I asked the students how many had heard this story and steeled myself for the possibility that the anthropologists were right, that the old traditions were indeed dying out and the students would be ignorant of the story. But instead, all but one or two raised their hands—they had heard the story, just as I had heard it when I was young, some in English, some in Laguna.

One of the other advantages that we Pueblos have enjoyed is that we have always been able to stay with the land. Our stories cannot be separated from their geographical locations, from actual physical places on the land. We were not relocated like so many Native American groups who were torn away from their ancestral land. And our stories are so much a part of these places that it is almost impossible for future generations to lose them—there is a story connected with every place, every object in the landscape.

Dennis Brutus has talked about the "yet unborn" as well as "those from the past," and how we are still *all* in *this* place, and language—the storytelling—is our way of passing through or being with them, of being together again. When Aunt Susie told her stories, she would tell a younger child to go open the door so that our esteemed predecessors might bring in their gifts to us. "They are out there,"

Aunt Susie would say. "Let them come in. They're here, they're here with us *within* the stories."

A few years ago, when Aunt Susie was 106, I paid her a visit, and while I was there she said, "Well, I'll be leaving here soon. I think I'll be leaving here next week, and I will be going over to the Cliff House." She said, "It's going to be real good to get back over there." I was listening, and I was thinking that she must be talking about her house at Paguate Village, just north of Laguna. And she went on, "Well, my mother's sister (and she gave her Indian name) will be there. She has been living there. She will be there and we will be over there, and I will get a chance to write down these stories I've been telling you." Now you must understand, of course, that Aunt Susie's mother's sister, a great storyteller herself, has long since passed over into the land of the dead. But then I realized, too, that Aunt Susie wasn't talking about death the way most of us do. She was talking about "going over" as a journey, a journey that perhaps we can only begin to understand through an appreciation for the boundless capacity of language that, through storytelling, brings us together, despite great distances between cultures, despite great distances in time.

Salman Rushdie

Choice Between Light and Dark

Editor's note: This essay was written by Rushdie for The Observer *in London and published on 22 January 1989, after the demonstrations against* The Satanic Verses *at Bradford and London, but before the condemnation and death sentence imposed on Rushdie by Iran's Ayatollah Khomeini.*

Muhammad ibn Abdallah, one of the great geniuses of world history, a successful businessman, victorious general, and sophisticated statesman as well as a prophet, insisted throughout his life on his simple humanity. There are no contemporary portraits of him because he feared that, if any were made, people would worship the portraits. He was only the messenger; it was the message that should be revered.

As to the revelation itself, it caused Muhammad considerable anguish. Sometimes he heard voices; sometimes he saw visions; sometimes, he said, the words were found in his inmost heart, and at such times their production caused him acute physical pain. When the revelations began he feared for his sanity, and only after reassurances from his wife and friends did he accept that he was the recipient of the divine gift of the Word.

The religion which Muhammad established differs from Christianity in several important respects: the Prophet is not granted divine status, but the text is. It's worth pointing out, too, that Islam requires neither a collective act of worship nor an intercessionary caste of priests. The faithful communicate directly with their God.

Nowadays, however, a powerful tribe of clerics has taken over Islam. These are the contemporary Thought Police. They have turned Muhammad into a perfect being, his life into a perfect life, his revelation into the unambiguous, clear event it originally was not. Powerful taboos have been erected. One may not discuss Muhammad as if he were human, with human virtues and weaknesses. One may not discuss the growth of Islam as a historical phenomenon, as an ideology born out of its time. These are the taboos against which *The Satanic Verses* has transgressed (these and one other: I also tried to write about the place of women in Islamic society, and in the Koran). It is for this breach of taboo that the novel is being anathematized, fulminated against, and set alight.

Dr. Aadam Aziz, the patriarch in my novel *Midnight's Children*, loses his faith and is left with "a hole inside him, a vacancy in a vital inner chamber." I, too, possess the same God-shaped hole. Unable to accept the unarguable absolutes of religion, I have tried to fill up the hole with literature. The art of the novel is a thing I cherish as dearly as the book burners of Bradford value their brand of militant Islam. Literature is where I go to explore the highest and lowest places in human society and in the human spirit, where I hope to find not absolute truth but the truth of the tale, of the imagination, and of the heart. So the battle over *The Satanic Verses* is a clash of faiths, in a way. Or, more precisely, it's a clash of languages. As my fictional character "Salman" says of my fictional prophet "Mahound," "It's his Word against mine."

In this War of the Word, the guardians of religious truth have been telling their followers a number of lies. I am accused, for example, of calling Muhammad the devil. This is because I use the name Mahound, which, long ago, was indeed used as a derogatory term. But my novel tries in all sorts of ways to reoccupy negative images, to repossess the pejorative language, and on page 93 explains: "To turn insults into strengths, whigs, tories, Blacks all chose to wear with pride the names they were given in scorn; likewise, our mountain-climbing, prophet-motivated solitary is to be...Mahound."

Even the novel's title has been termed blasphemous; but the phrase is not mine. It comes from al-Tabari, one of the canonical Islamic sources. Tabari writes: "When the Messenger of God saw his people draw away from him...he would gladly have seen those things that bore too harshly on them softened a little."

Muhammad then received verses which accepted the three favorite Meccan goddesses as intercessionary agents. Meccans were delighted. Later, the Archangel Gabriel told Muhammad that these had been "Satanic verses," falsely inspired by the Devil in disguise, and they were removed from the Koran. Gabriel consoled Muhammad, however; earlier prophets had experienced similar difficulties for similar reasons, he said. To my mind, Muhammad's overcoming of temptation does him no dishonor; quite the reverse. The Archangel Gabriel felt the same way, but the novel's opponents are less tolerant than archangels.

The zealots also attack me by false analogy, comparing my book to pornography and demanding a ban on both. Many Islamic spokesmen have compared my work to anti-Semitism. But intellectual dissent is neither pornographic nor racist. I have tried to give a secular, humanist vision of the birth of a great world religion. For this, apparently, I should be tried under the Race Relations Act, or if not that, perhaps the Public Order Act. Any old Act will do. The justification is that I have "given offense." But the giving of offense cannot be a basis for censorship, or freedom of expression would perish instantly. And many of us who were revolted by the Bradford flames will feel that the offense done to our principles is at least as great as any offense caused to those who burned my book.

The Muslim world is full of censors these days, and many of its greatest writers have been forced into silence, exile, or submission. (The Joycean option of cunning seems unavailable at present.) To find Labour councillors in Bradford and Labour MPs in Westminster joining forces with the mullahs is hugely depressing. When Brian Sedgemore, Max Madden, Bernie Grant, and Councillor Mohammed Ajeeb start asking for censorship to be *extended* and for the blasphemy laws to be expanded rather than abolished, then it's time for the Labour leadership to respond by disowning such initiatives in the clearest possible terms.

The Satanic Verses is not, in my view, an antireligious novel. It is, however, an attempt to write about migration, its stresses and transformations, from the point of view of migrants from the Indian subcontinent to Britain. This is, for me, the saddest irony of all; that after working for five years to give voice and fictional flesh to the immigrant culture of which I am myself a member, I should see my book burned, largely unread, by the people it's about, people who might find some pleasure and much recognition in its pages. I tried to write against stereotypes; the zealot protests serve to confirm, in the Western mind, all the worst stereotypes of the Muslim world.

How fragile civilization is; how easily, how merrily a book burns! Inside my novel, its characters seek to become fully human by facing up to the great facts of love, death, and (with or without God) the life of the soul. Outside it, the forces of inhumanity are on the march. "Battle lines are being drawn up in India today," one of my characters remarks. "Secular versus religious, the light versus the dark. Better you choose which side you are on." Now that the battle has spread to Britain, I can only hope it will not be lost by default. It is time for us to choose.

Lynne Tillman

Critical Fiction / Critical Self

> Perhaps it is in this project of learning how to represent
> *ourselves* – how to speak *to*, rather than for or about,
> others – that the possibility of a "global" culture resides.
> – Craig Owens, *Art in America* (July 1989)

What I keep telling myself is that I want to make this simple, to make things simple; I want to be direct. I want to say why I write and what I write for, and out of, in as clear a way as possible – to cut to the chase or to the quick, to get to the heart of it. But nothing seems simple and I'm not certain why I write or in whose name other than my own, which is not really my name, but my father's, which is a made-up Ellis Island name, anyway.

To be able to make things simple I'd have to think that I was in control of myself, my language, my situation, my world. I'm not; I'm also not completely out of control. I write out of language, out of my world, out of myself, but I am not on top of the world and on top of the language that makes up the world and which makes me up, as I try desperately to make up other worlds. This essay is, in a way, for me, another world, one that I am now asking you to enter, which already seems a certain kind of demand. It has been hard for me, psychologically, and as a woman, to make demands, to negotiate a space from which I can demand – writing is a demand to be read and heard – and consequently it has been hard for me to become a writer.

I choose to write – fiction primarily, though I write nonfiction, too – because, especially lately, it gives me pleasure, though why that came about I'm not sure. I do know I decided to become a writer when I was eight and that I stuck to the idea; I held the notion deep inside me, for me alone and for a long time. I think it sustained me or gave me a me to sustain. What kind of decision could it have been then and even now? I need to write, I think, but need is an odd thing. I need to in the sense that writing gives me an identity, a thing to be in the world, gives me something to do, and so on. I never want to forget or diminish my own pleasure and narcissism, for while I may insist that I write fiction critically and not just for myself, it is also critical for me – whoever I am (I wish all my I's could be in quotes) – to write.

I hope this beginning doesn't put you off. Beginnings are difficult; in the beginning one must immediately impose a direction from which a character, a statement, a mood, or a frame of reference will be established or determined. And, most important, a voice, the ineffable voice. My unease – dis-ease – at discussing my writing of "critical fiction" is central to how I write, in any case. And one of the reasons I choose to write fiction is that just this kind of ambiguity and ambivalence can find its way into a story or into that complex cultural unit called a novel, where, as Bakhtin put it, a "struggle between one's own and another's word is being waged,"[1] and which represents the world as a multiplicity of voices, as heteroglossia.

It reassures me that Bakhtin thinks this, by the way; it is one of the theories I look to for sustenance and support when I feel that what I am engaged in is futile, that the forces I am or imagine myself fighting are so much bigger, so much more powerful that it's all hopeless. I know this is not a good attitude. I also take solace in sayings like Pessimism of the Intellect, Optimism of the Will. I look to many theories – psychoanalytic, literary, feminist, art, Marxist, sociological, film, cultural theories of all kinds – for help, for succor, for explanations and amplifications; they are heuristic tools with which to dig up, and into, the world.

If I assert I write fiction critically, I must set out what it is I oppose and am critical of, but I am dubious about asserting this, and so simultaneously – in a superimposition or as a split-screen image – wish to impose the question whether or not I can actually achieve this: a position of difference, writing differently, thinking differently, reading differently. All of these activities are related, requiring that others be captured by – and captive to – the same project and spirit. Whatever independent thinking is, if it is, it happens dependently; it depends on others, on the life of minds which, like one's own, are socially – nationally and internationally, if you will – and psychologically constructed. One is not entirely alone in being alone with one's thoughts. So the writing of critical fiction takes place within communities, some of which may not recognize themselves as such but in the act of writing and reading differently become known to themselves.

I am wary or shy of proposing my fiction as written in opposition to, or to pronounce that I write differently, as if I – or it – could transcend conditions of birth and development – its and mine – and was somehow able to escape them. Or even that I knew, and the writing could locate, the right problems. It's certainly on my agenda – to challenge the complacent, to question national, familial, racial, and sexual arrangements, to resist structures and institutions that serve the powerful and perpetuate powerlessness. But as I wrote of the narrator in my novel *Motion Sickness* – an American moving from place to place in foreign lands – "I must contribute daily, involuntarily, but in small and big ways toward keeping the world the way it is." (The question of agency haunts the novel.)

I'm struggling to find a way to think about all this, to be articulate and write something meaningful, which is supposed to be a writer's job. In this collection, Anton Shammas speaks of himself as a "Third World" person, a Palestinian citizen of Israel writing in Hebrew, who is "un-Jewing the Hebrew language," "undoing the culture of the majority from within." He quotes Gilles Deleuze and Félix Guattari's work on Kafka and minor literature – "that which a minority constructs within a major language."[2] Deleuze and Guattari work to empty the minor – the marginal – of unimportance: "There is nothing that is major or revolutionary except the minor."[3] And I take heart from "it is literature that produces an active solidarity in spite of skepticism."[4]

> If one is a woman one is often surprised by a sudden splitting off of consciousness, say in walking down Whitehall, when from being the natural inheritor of that civilisation, she becomes, on the contrary, outside of it, alien and critical.
> – Virginia Woolf, *A Room of One's Own*

I'm not claiming to be a Kafka, to write a dialect, or to be inventing a new language; I work within the American English language as a white, middle-class, second-generation American woman, at a particular moment in history, with my own particular biography. (Sometimes, like now, looking at the categories into which I fit, writing myself like this, I am, frankly, stultified.) So I must wrest this language and its forms away from or out of "the majority" (of which I am a part, in some ways and at some times, to others), to un-man it, to un-American it, even to un-white it, to inconvenience the majority language, to unconventionalize it, even to shame it, in an odd sort of way, to question privilege, my own, too, of course. (While I don't have to un-man myself – maybe de-man myself and my writing –

perhaps in the process of writing I may be able to approach un-Americaning and un-whiting myself.)

It seems odd – haughty (bad girl) – to write of un-manning language or un-Americaning it, especially un-whiting it, as if I could. Still when I sat down to write *Haunted Houses* (I remember being taught that Hemingway stood, as if that made him heroic and construed writing itself as virile activity), the challenge was to make unfamiliar the lives of girls in a language that is often hostile to "girls," that has a history of being hostile to girls and women. To construct "girls" in fiction, to represent them in writing, seemed to require a kind of wrestling match with an unwilling opponent. It was the case of writing against what I took to be the way women and girls were usually written. In fact the project was to take seriously female narratives, which often aren't, from masturbation fantasies to female friendship to girls' studying philosophy to women writing, and to make the writing of those narratives, the writing itself, the subject of the book as well. All the time, I was engaged with and writing to and against an invisible, implacable but indifferent enemy – I was no threat – and sometimes what it was I was against – up against – was beyond my comprehension, or so far inside me that I could never find it. In a way, too, I was just writing, and writing itself was sufficient for me.

> One goes into the room – but the resources of the English language would be much put to the stretch, and whole flights of words would need to wing their way illegitimately into existence before a woman could say what happens when she goes into a room.
> – Virginia Woolf, *A Room of One's Own*

"Whole flights of words would need to wing their way illegitimately" astonishes me – how accurate Woolf is about the unspeakable, the inadmissible, what cannot be said or has not been written. My emphasis, for this essay, would be on "illegitimately." It seems an existential fact of minority life that one feels illegitimate, is made to feel illegitimate. Mexican writer Elena Poniatowska remarks in her essay here that in a society hostile to women – and necessarily women writers – women are made to feel like freaks: "Isn't that a very refined, a very sophisticated form of repression?" Perhaps I was writing *Haunted Houses* "against" being a freak, at the same time I knew – and know – myself to be one, sitting there (here) writing.

Still, while I may want to un-man a language that reflects and produces conditions hostile to women, I don't imagine that I write a feminine language. I might have believed it possible, had I been a Frenchwoman who had learned to speak with *la* and *le* before masculine and feminine nouns, had this been part of my mother – my – tongue. But it wasn't. I haven't found another language to use; the language I was born into – and my inevitable blindnesses – is a limit I acknowledge. I've entered into one language (which from one point of view un-manned me) that has to be twisted around in order for me to make it work differently.

As I write this I remember the Rorschach test I was given by a psychologist friend years ago. I didn't want her to find out anything about me, so I went through the cards quickly, insouciantly. When we were done, she said: "You didn't take this seriously, but one thing I can tell you – whichever way I gave you the cards, you took them and you read them. You never once turned the cards around or upside down. The way I handed them to you, that's the way you looked at them." It hadn't occurred to me to do it differently. Now it does. But perhaps this is the limit I accept – I'm handed this grammar, this alphabet, this language embedded with cultural nuances, and I try to turn it upside down, to shuffle it, a deck of cards to build houses of cards – stories, essays, novels.

As part of a reshuffling, I reread a white Western male writer, D. H. Lawrence, and found that his literary "discoverer," Ford Madox Ford, marked Lawrence's entrance into "literature" with a certain *parti pris*. Of Lawrence's story, "Odour of Chrysanthemums," Ford wrote: "You are, then, for as long as the story lasts, to be in one of those untidy, unfinished landscapes where locomotives wander innocuously amongst women with baskets ... You are going to learn how what we used to call 'the other half' – though we might as well have said other ninety-nine hundredths – lives ... Because this man knows ... He knows the life he is writing about ... "⁵ Ford, himself a white Western man, positions Lawrence in "the other half," where women, as one minority among many, might place themselves or be placed. But to Ford, from the upper classes, the working class was other, as was ninety-nine hundredths of humanity, "other" to his "we." I suppose it's that use of "we" that produces "others" like me, makes "us" illegitimate – a "we" Lawrence was subject to as well.

This excursion to Lawrence is meant to take another step, a critical step, backward and forward, I hope, for I am just as anxious about totalizing "man" (and "American," and "white") as I am eager to decenter and defamiliarize him (them), by turning his (their) centrality into a question. If I totalize "man," I allow "woman" to be totalized and essentialized – or American, black, white, gay, straight, Gambian, Indian, Japanese, and so on.

From this point of view, and others, too, it was extremely useful (and moving) to read Edward Said's essay on the Gulf War, written in the midst of it, in which he stated: "The time has come where we cannot simply accuse the West of Orientalism and racism – I realize I am particularly vulnerable on this point… There are many Wests, some antagonistic, some not, with which to do business… The converse is equally true, that there are many Arabs for Westerners and others to talk to."[6] Reading his seminal work *Orientalism* some years ago, learning how "the Orient" had been invented, in a sense, by the West, I also recognized the problem he's referring to – the point of his "vulnerability" – presenting the West as monolithic. This recognition forced me to examine, and made me uncomfortably aware of, another of my vulnerabilities – how I, in the name of my version of feminism, had relied too heavily on "patriarchy," for one thing, for too many explanations.

So it's probably not surprising, given my concern with essentialisms of all kinds (and the construction of identity generally), that questioning national identity – how the nation state is inscribed in our different psyches, how each of us may be a repository of a national history and culture, how identity is inflected by nationality – that this was the impetus, even the mission (maybe impossible), for *Motion Sickness*, a novel whose narrator is a young, disquieted American woman traveling in Europe. But I have to admit, trying to be honest – although I question my ability to be honest – that I was also writing conscious of writing itself as a project, and that the desire to write *Motion Sickness* – the pleasure I derived from it, being its first reader – came from writing, and that the writing was of the utmost importance to me. I would never want to let go of that importance; it must coexist with the importance – to me – of what I think the book, the story, is about.

One writes in the cracks rather than by stepping over them, like a child playing a game as she walks on the sidewalk. My version: if I stepped on the crack, the line, I would die. Sometimes the rules of the game changed – I changed them, but rather paranoically: if I didn't step on the crack, I would die. Whatever the rule, the consequences were dire. Perhaps I didn't know how to play. I don't think I did. Maybe a portent, that child's game, of things to come. For while I can say I play with language, the game is dire, urgent, necessary. And the rules must change.

It's funny. Though skeptical and prone to depression, I write in the hope and spirit that each of us can think beyond our limits, while acknowledging limits.

I picture us all, like Bakhtin's idea of the novel, with many possible voices, as dialogical as words. There are identities, there are shifting subjectivities, and you and I are shifty subjects who may from time to time be many things, not essentially any one thing, except by desire perhaps and in certain moments, for certain reasons and for certain periods of time. I really am looking for new narratives to replace the old ones. I distrust words and stories and yet probably they are what I value most. Paradox rules.

Claribel Alegría

Latinidad and the Artist

In the broadest sense, as I understand the term, a *Latino* is simply an individual of Spanish-speaking, Latin American background, who finds himself or herself living in the United States, whether by intent or by force of circumstance. Many thousands of Latin American political refugees in the United States intend to return to their homelands when they no longer face the danger of being hunted down by death squads or security police – the two terms are interchangeable – in countries such as Guatemala and El Salvador. In addition, there are millions of economic refugees from Latin American countries, where the rate of unemployment and underemployment often runs as high as 40 to 50 percent of the active population. They have come to "the land of promise" to seek jobs that will enable them to send a monthly pittance to their families at home, and they intend to return to their familial roots when they have made their stake.

But members of either of the above categories may find a survival niche in the U.S. economy, may bring their families to join them, and may gradually abandon the idea of returning home. Perhaps the most "authentic" Latinos, then, are second-generation Latin Americans who have been educated in the United States and are competing on equal – or perhaps unequal – terms with "native born" Americans who are integrated into the society.

The past quarter-century has been a period of tremendous upheaval in Latin American societies, resulting in an unprecedented influx of Latinos into the United States and a consequent cultural shock on both sides. The first wave of political refugees washed ashore in Miami after the Cuban revolution in 1959, but there already existed sizeable Salvadoran ghettos in San Francisco, *pachuco* or Chicano ghettos in Los Angeles, and a huge Puerto Rican ghetto in New York.

The National Security State evolved out of U.S. panic over the Cuban revolution. National Security States developed throughout Latin America, wherever increasing misery and popular discontent had reached the boiling point. This system had actually been inaugurated in Central America during the depression years of the 1930s with the dictatorships of Anastasio Somoza in Nicaragua, Tiburcio Carías in Honduras, Jorge Ubico in Guatemala, and General Maximiliano Hernández Martínez in El Salvador. But the system was refined in Brazil in 1964 and in Guatemala in 1966, reaching its peak in the 1970s with counterinsurgency dictatorships installed in Chile, Paraguay, Uruguay, Argentina, Brazil, Guatemala, El Salvador, and Nicaragua.

The national army's task in each case was to defend the status quo, and the enemy was no longer defined as a hypothetical external foe. Instead, the enemy was found within the population of the country itself: any individuals or groups who sought structural reforms or social change, whether by democratic or revolutionary means. Consequently, a fifth of the population of both Uruguay and El Salvador, to take two examples, went into exile. Moreover, during the "lost decade" of the eighties, the ranks of the displaced throughout the continent have swelled as a result of the Third World economic crisis.

Despite the myth of the "melting pot," the WASP majority in the United States has always disparaged new ethnic arrivals, be they *niggers, micks, wops, hunkies, yids,* or *dagos.* Although virulent racist rhetoric has been muted in public discourse over the past decade or so, racist attitudes still form a strong and treacherous undercurrent in U.S. society. Let's face it – Latinos and blacks were the prime cannon fodder in the Persian Gulf war. Under the Reagan and Bush administrations, militant chauvinism has reached a fevered pitch. "America is back" has a fine, Yankee Doodle ring to it, but the obverse side of the coin is President Reagan himself evoking the nightmarish vision of hordes of brown-skinned illiterates streaming across the southern border of the United States to escape the "spreading cancer of communism" in America's backyard. Its legislative manifestation was the racist Simpson-Rodino Act, a fumbling attempt to send those undesirables back where they came from.

The truth, of course, is something else. The brown-skinned hordes, evicted from their homelands by genocidal counterinsurgency regimes in Guatemala and El Salvador, or driven by economic desperation out of Mexico and other countries, had already arrived and infiltrated U.S. society at all levels and in all geographical regions of the nation.

What should be the role of the Latino artist or scholar in this uneasy confrontation between two languages, diverse cultures, between the Third World and the First, and with the additional disadvantage of finding ourselves in the latter's ball court?

Like our brothers and sisters who have sought "refuge" for political or economic reasons, Latino writers, artists, and others working in the cultural arena in the United States face the problem of ignorance and indifference on the part of our hosts: the North American nation is as insular and provincial, as devoted to blind conformity and uniformity, as any traditional culture in the Third World. The average American speaks no other language than English. His life is centered on his job, his home, and the state of the national economy. To get ahead in the First World, he must specialize, and that specialization inevitably narrows his range of interests to occupational and professional matters. He believes what he reads in his newspapers and what he sees on his television, seldom suspecting that the manipulation of consent is the most sophisticated art form produced in his country.

Our first problem, then, is one of communication, of getting other Latinos and other Americans to listen to us. In today's world, we have lots to tell them.

We have things to tell them about how U.S. policies have been chewing up the peoples of our homelands, things that are of vital importance in shaping the historic role the United States can choose to play in the Third World during the remainder of the twentieth century. We Latinos must assume the roles of historians, politicians, journalists, sociologists, and teachers. We must take on the role of educators with respect to *latinidad*, because no one else is doing the job. To do that job effectively, we must celebrate cultural diversity, take pride in *la raza*, in our Spanish language, in our cultural heritage stemming from *la hispanidad*, which has given the world as rich a tapestry of prose, poetry, painting, drama, and music as any other major world culture. And we must be proud of our autochthonous roots: of the Aztecs who invented the calendar, of the Mayans who, before the age of telescopes, traced the orbit of Mercury about the sun, of the Incas who developed the art of irrigation and built the majestic terraces and edifices of Machu Picchu in polished stone.

The more we assert our culture and history, the more we insist on representing ourselves, the more difficult it will be for North Americans to ignore the extermination of our peoples.

Many of us will integrate into the larger U.S. society, or if we are unable to do so fully because of our undeniable otherness, our children will. There is nothing in that to be ashamed of. But it is one thing to desire to be accepted into a foreign society with a sense of shame and apology, with an inferiority complex imposed on one by the complacent majority, and it is a far different thing to integrate with the consciousness that one brings a cultural heritage that will enrich the host society.

Some will make the argument that I am prescribing an orthodoxy for the Latino artist or writer. Of course, the responsibility of the artist is to produce "good" art, just as the shoemaker's is to produce good shoes. No cobbler should limit herself to a certain kind of output or style of shoes, just as no artist should permit herself to be limited by outside pressures or constraints. Great art springs from deep sources of inspiration and from the artist's compulsion to reproduce her inner vision or the inner voice she hears. In my own poetry, I am incapable of producing anything on demand. I can write only out of what deeply moves me.

I am an El Salvadoran who has made her home Nicaragua. I realized years ago that I am too individualistic, too undisciplined, too lacking in self-abnegation to be a militant revolutionary. I am, however, in complete sympathy with the political and social objectives of the unified revolutionary movement in El Salvador, and if I sometimes appear to be speaking for my people, it is simply because I empathize with them in their long, bitter struggle for liberation from a bloody yoke of terror and five hundred years of repression. When I write poetry, however, I write poetry, and when I feel compelled to make another kind of statement I may write a novel, a book of contemporary history and testimony, or a newspaper or magazine article. For me the categories are clear and separate, and I am careful to keep them that way.

Every Latino writer, every artist, however, will make her own definitions and set her own goals. But we can all work toward the goal of increasing the quantity and quality of cross-cultural communication in the United States. Our resident artists and scholars have much to offer both the Latino community and the larger society as well. It is our responsibility to continue the search for ways to break into mainstream U.S. publishing, television, art: to open communications and public-interest channels to the larger society and not permit ourselves and our ethnic community as a whole to lock itself into a ghetto mentality. We must keep on producing, confident that we are not isolated, alone, but that our efforts are being supported and encouraged by our Latino sisters and brothers, confident that *latinidad* is a cooperative and not a cutthroat, competitive enterprise.

Abdelrahman Munif

Exile and the Writer

Translated by Peter Theroux

The exiled or emigré writer, by the mere act of setting foot in a new land, finds himself socially defined by a dubious assortment of ideas, dreams, and illusions on the part of people in his new home. Suddenly, the exile is transformed into the ambassador – unappointed by anyone! – of a cause or a people. He is beset by questions from his new hosts and equally overwhelmed by the questions he must ask himself. Far from home, he finds himself pondering things he had never given a thought to before, though they confronted him every day. An exiled writer finds himself constantly demanding of his friends, How are things at home? Why? When did this or that happen, and how? – and dozens of other questions. Summer and winter temperatures, which had never concerned him before, become issues. Rainfall, birds' migratory seasons, fruit-picking harvests become issues. His homeland's land and sea frontiers become issues. When it comes to geography, history, sites of ruins or events, even his country's "natural beauties," he finds he is more ignorant than he ever imagined. If he can, he will find an expert to educate him, for he must have the answers to these questions, and they must be the right answers.

For the writer in exile cannot help but take his responsibilities seriously. When he talks to others about his country, those responsibilities increase tenfold, and tenfold again. But it is not only that the writer in exile is trying to win over foreigners to an understanding of his country, but he is also trying to prove to the people in his own country that he still stands with them, that he still drinks from the same well they drink from; that though he is far away, he is still among them. At times, he will overdo it, invoking names once topical but now forgotten, or situating contemporary characters in places that no longer exist. But more on that later.

For a moment or two, I would like to talk about a particular problem faced by the writer in exile, and this of course is the problem of language. What language can and should the exiled writer use? How does one effectively resist becoming a prisoner to the demands of the past or to the exigencies of the present? The demands of the market for the Arab writer frequently require that the exile write in the tongue of his new, adopted country. There are obvious challenges to be faced here, for he must master not only the daily language of his host country, but also what we might call that language's "aura": he must learn its secrets and shadows, penetrate its logical peculiarities, get inside the language so that he can express the complexities and texture of his vision.

But it is far more complicated than this. For, in most cases, the language that the exiled writer must deploy is the language of the colonizer. Although learning that language offers deliverance for the writer – or the illusion of deliverance – as a bridge between two cultures for the transmission of a message, the exiled writer knows that the new language he is using has also served, historically, as the intellectual edifice on which the colonizing culture hangs its claims and assumptions of superiority.

Having "submitted" to the colonizer's language, some Arab writers in exile fiercely cling to the subject matter that will validate their country's distinctive heritage, tradition, and values. But often, rather than being able to follow his own heart in this project, the market requires that the writer deliver something new and different than other writers it has already heard from. And so he finds himself milking his memory for what is most strange and compelling in his past. Perhaps this goes some way toward explaining the large number of fantastic plots and bizarre characters in fiction written by Arab exiles. Consider the possibility that it is not because these subjects or characters are more important or have higher priority in Arab culture, but because they have the power to impress "the Other" with their titillating exoticism.

Although the individual writer of such tales may receive acclaim and recognition in his host country, he finds his true purpose undermined. For he is recognized, not as an organic part of that host culture – his work not a manifestation of its valued diversity – but as an exception, a token of the host country's vitality and supremacy in producing what it needs and wants. This dynamic turns the homeland and its culture into a mere one-dimensional text within a prescribed framework, however varied the societies are that are being written about, or however varied in talent, vision, and message their writers are.

It is not surprising, then, that we find a growing number of exiled writers abandoning subjects that relate to their own peoples and societies. The danger here is that of slipping into the production of those peculiarly competent "literary" efforts, assimilationist yet marginalized, what U.S. publishers would refer to as, and U.S. novelists know as the doom of, "the mid-list novel."

And so, there sits, very uncomfortably, the writer in exile, torn between regaining his homeland through writing – to the point of obsession! – or losing it – to the point of amnesia! These two conditions are prevalent in writing by exiles. Often, the reality of the native country, a reality that the writer seeks to reclaim, becomes submerged in a dream of the past. Geographical distance becomes psychological distance, for writer and country develop and change along different paths. The homeland of which he has a particular image, from a particular time, is no longer the same. Attempting to reinforce *his* reality, the exile can spend too much time trying to reconstruct the details of his country as he remembers it, as he lived it. For instance, the Iraqi writer Gha'ib Tu'mah Farman, who was exiled from his homeland for thirty years and who died in exile, was able to describe Baghdad only as he had known it, as he had left it. He spent all his years in exile evoking that Baghdad, even though the Baghdad he knew no longer existed.

And yet, there is no writer living in Iraq who has been able to summon and capture the image of Baghdad in the fifties as Gha'ib did. This is a fact worth exploring. The truth is that most people never *discover* their country in the true sense of the word until they lose it or are forced out of it. From the perspective of exile, one's homeland takes on an extra and deeper dimension. The exiled writer is, by necessity, endowed with the need to shape a homeland with roots in the past and with a view to the future, a view of that homeland as he would like it to be. It is the writer in exile whose work demonstrates to us most truthfully, most powerfully, that there can never be a fixed definition of country. Country is not an objective fact, but an ephemeral idea – an ever-shifting memory of the past and dream of the future.

I am a Saudi Arabian writer, exiled in Damascus, Syria. Now, while it may be that the overwhelming majority of Arab exiles set out for Arab destinations for reasons that require no explanation or analysis, Arab migrations in recent decades have been so numerous and varied as to merit serious study. We must take note, first, of the crucial role of oil in these migrations. Contemporary East-West relations have produced what one might call an "oil culture" in the Arab countries. Its powerful ally, the media (the press, publishing firms, television), has packaged and codified this culture – with a number of identifiable traits and tendencies: covertness, superficiality, consumerism, promotion of fantasy, pretensions to reclaiming our Arab heritage – through terrorist wars against reason, democracy, modernity, and scientific rationality. This oil culture has produced a degraded intellectual climate in which equivocation prevails.

As Arabs, we have already been inscribed in the memory of the West by way of Orientalism, its biases and its whims, and its abundant dose of hostility to incompatible interests. Oil culture has given a new "clarity" to this picture – Arabs are, in short, a collection of rich, lazy, lustful, cruel sheikhs, who, by chance, found fabulous wealth under their feet. But this substance, oil, which the whole world needs, cannot be left in the hands of these corrupt and immoral swindlers; it must be liberated, especially since its owners don't know what to do with it or how to benefit by it. Such an image – synthetic, politically and economically expedient – dogs Arab intellectuals, wherever they are. Wedged between the anvil of Arab regimes and the hammer of the West – which sees nothing in our region and its peoples but ancient history and some remnants of folklore – we are deprived of our actual rich and complex culture, our legitimate concerns and ambitions.

This is the West's doing. The West created our regimes, protects them, now colludes with its creations. The still-faint voices of exile are greeted by still-deaf ears. But they will be heard. For while truth may be silenced for a day, it will be heard the day after; conscience may slumber for a day, but it will awaken the day after – and a great many people will discover how they have been deceived.

Bessie Head

An African Story

It was a winter morning. Just before dawn the stars shone like bright, polished blue jewels in the sky and a half-eclipsed moon suddenly rose with a hauntingly beautiful light. And it was a summer afternoon. The summer rain had filled my yard with wild flowers. I seemed to be living, too, all the time, with animals' eyes –goats staring at me, cows staring at me, chickens staring at me. I slowly came alive with the background scenery. What have I said about the people of a free land, I who borrowed their clothes, their goats, their sunrises and sunsets for my books? Not anything very polite, it seems.

The wandering travelers of ancient times came unexpectedly upon people sitting around their outdoor fires.

"Who are you?" the people asked.

"I am the dreamer and storyteller," they replied. "I have seen life. I am drunk with the magical enchantment of human relationships. I laughed often. The big, wide free world is full of innocence..."

One imagines that those people always welcomed the storytellers. Each human society is a narrow world, trapped to death in paltry evils and jealousies, and for people to know that there are thoughts and generosities wider and freer than their own can only be an enrichment to their lives. But what happens to the dreamer and storyteller when he or she is born into a dead world of such extreme cruelties that no comment or statement of love can alter them? In the first place, in South Africa, who is one talking to? People there are not people but complexions and hair textures–whites, Coloureds, Indians, and Africans. Who can write about that? Where is that wedge of innocence and laughter that resolves so many human ills?

It has surprised me, the extent to which creative writing is often regarded, unconsciously, as a nationalistic activity, and perhaps this expression of national feeling is rather the subdued communication a writer holds with his or her own society. I have so often been referred to as "the Botswana writer," while in reality the Botswana personality isn't as violent as me. I wasn't born with the gentle, inquiring eyes of a cow but amongst black people who always said, when anything went wrong: "Why don't we all die?" And the subdued undertone was: "since the white man hates us so much."

Thought patterns change rapidly from one generation to another. We reformed the language of our parents because once the white man in South Africa started putting up notices "For whites only," he also dispensed with normal human decencies – like "please" and "thank you" and "I'm sorry" – while black people retained theirs as they have no benches to defend. It is impossible to translate a scene like this into human language. I once sat down on a bench at Cape Town railway station where the notice "Whites Only" was obscured. A few moments later a white man approached and shouted: "Get off!" It never occurred to him that he was achieving the opposite of his dreams of superiority and had become a living object of contempt, that human beings, when they are human, dare not conduct themselves in such ways.

It is preferable to have the kind of insecurity about life and death that is universal to humankind: *I am sure of so little*. It is despicable to have this same sense of insecurity – especially about a white skin – defended by power and guns. It seems to remove from them all fear of retribution for their deeds, and it creates in the recipient of their wild, fierce, savage cruelty a deep sense of shock.

Day after day one hears of unbelievable slaughter in Ireland. A traveler from England passed my way. "Why are people being killed like that in Ireland?" I asked. "The Catholics are fighting for their rights," he said. "They have always been discriminated against, never allowed to purchase their own homes and things like that. It's just like South Africa. There they call it racialism. In Ireland they call it religion."

Every oppressed man and woman has this suppressed violence, as though silently awaiting the time to set right the wrongs that afflict him or her. I have never forgotten it, even though, for the purposes of my trade, I borrowed the clothes of a country like Botswana.

South Africa made white people rich and comfortable, but their ownership of the country is ugly and repellent. They talk about South Africa in tourist language all the time: "This grand and sunny land," they say. The cheap, glaring, paltry trash who are living it up for themselves alone dominate everything, infiltrate everywhere. If one is a part of it, through being born there, how does one communicate with the horrible? That is why South Africa has no great writer: no one can create harmony out of cheap discord.

It is impossible to guess how the revolution will come one day in South Africa. But in a world where all ordinary people are insisting on their rights, it is inevitable. It is to be hoped that great leaders will arise there who remember the suffering of racial hatred and out of it formulate a common language of human love for all people.

Possibly, too, southern Africa might one day become the home of the storyteller and dreamer, who did not hurt others but only introduced new dreams that filled the heart with wonder.

Alicia Dujovne Ortiz

Buenos Aires

Translated by Caren Kaplan and Aurora Wolfgang

To Be *Porteño*

> Buenos Aires has no beginning to me, it feels as eternal
> as water or air...
> – Jorge Luis Borges

A Buenos Aires street, where vertical skyscrapers cannot break the curse of a boundless horizon. A street in one of those neighborhoods that sprawl endlessly, as if the city had been forced to repeat the earth's gesture. *Horizontal vertigo* . . . A woman passes. A man, leaning against a wall, watches her approach.

They both *know* that they have seen each other. They both prepare to replay a scene they have always known, the age-old ritual of virility to which they both must submit blindly. In a few seconds this man and woman will become Man and Woman, as essential as two numbers, as essential as the pampas – that distant line running horizontal to the sky.

Sensing that she is being watched, Woman fixes her eyes on that invisible line: the horizon is out there, behind the houses, vaguely entering our consciousness. But it is the shock of being seen that makes her exist. When she passes in front of him, Man moves away from the wall, chooses the best angle, and drops a word or two into her ear. Words: aggressive, lyrical, erotic, romantic, crude, comical, inspired, dull . . . it doesn't matter. He has said his *piropo*, replaying that Spanish tradition of spirited flattery. (Here is an example overheard in Madrid: "You are built better than the Ten Commandments!") His honor is safe. In playing his *piropo*, he is Man. He has declared that she is Woman. Hallelujah! All's right with the world.

But another man has seen and heard. There is no question of his turning a deaf ear. The planet would crumble to dust if he didn't rekindle the flame of the *piropo*. He has to move, in his turn, toward the woman: not out of sentiment but for the ritual. To say his *piropo* or not to be. He says it. The world stays on an even keel. And here comes a third man who has seen, has heard . . . You know what happens next.

We could ask plenty of troubling questions about this chain of desire. Aren't the men of Buenos Aires really linked . . . to each other? What's the point of this soccer game, where the men pass the *piropo* like a ball between them? Is it really the woman? These questions lead us in a direction I'd rather not follow . . . at least for the moment. I'd rather not uncover the reason for this anxious virility, nor delve into the anguish of this insecure machismo. I'm just trying to describe a city where you exist solely through your reflection in the eyes of others: shimmering sex, a burning mirage of passion in *trompe l'oeil* which keeps us alert, alive, our gaze on the prowl.

From the age of twelve, the Buenos Aires woman learns to be seen, and thus, to exist. The gaze of the Other constructs her. Her skeleton is forged in the intensity of this gaze. This is where her strength comes from, the way her joints are put together without a hint of creaking. The pride of her bearing: chin up, clicking heels, the "two-by-four" rhythm of her hips which repeats the tango's beat. The gaze is an inexhaustible language. It costs nothing, requires nothing, runs, floats, undulates, free and easy as air. The woman blossoms like a flower in a hothouse. Used to such glances, she cannot live without them. Without this mirror which structures her identity, she would live – of course – but her life would be clouded, dulled, without brilliance.

This is exactly what happens when she leaves her city to come to Europe. Outside the Mediterranean countries, she finds herself not before eyes but before eyelids. No one sees her. Or rather, she is seen in an extremely modest manner that makes her feel invisible. Then, her skeleton cracks and droops. Her spinal column sags; a marionette suddenly dangling. In Buenos Aires, the gaze was like a life-line stretched over the abyss. She always walked on this line. Now, if it disappears, she falls. To the bottom of the abyss? No, because this Europe that is so very blond, so atrociously Nordic, indifferent, and polite is not an abyss. She falls into a very soft, reassuring, and comfortable net. But on this fluffy mattress at the bottom, where no one sees her, bothers, or hassles her, she sometimes dreams of the days when she proudly walked in the streets of the razor-sharp gaze.

If Buenos Aires has such sharp eyesight, it's for a good reason: it is distant.

Distant from whom? From what?...Distant from everything. Distance is always
relative. For Buenos Aires it becomes absolute. First, because Buenos Aires is
situated at the bottom, to the left of the heart of the planet. Second, because this
distance is part of its very essence. It's true, it feels far away from other cities
in the world. Yet, it was founded on this relationship; facing others, existing only
through others. A geographic fate doubled by a self-distancing destiny. Eccentric
city, off-center – Buenos Aires has an oblique identity. That is why, in the strange
house of cards that the tangoing couple creates, the position of the leg is crosswise
and perverse.

I always thought I hated the tango for its nostalgia for the past just as I always
thought I detested Buenos Aires, the city of my birth, for its propensity to destroy
all traces of this past. Strange parallel: the tango laments the old neighborhoods of
childhood, and my city, in its aggressive modernity, condemns these neighborhoods to oblivion. As for me, I always wanted to construct an identity counter to
the tango and my city, by loving the present – ah! naive!!...As if it were possible!
As if detesting this music of the past and this city of the future were not so clearly
inscribed in their double centrifugal movement! In despising them, I gave in to
their secret rule. Can you become attached to this monster of ten million inhabitants, spewing smoke on the edge of emptiness, to this dance of absence? Detesting
Buenos Aires is an inverted, therefore totally normal, way of loving it.

Buenos Aires always brings the ego into question. She pretends to turn her
back on South America in order to face Europe. What could be more natural?
That's where she comes from. For doesn't the child try – worried, hopeful – to
catch the same look in his father's eye? Isn't the child disappointed if this look is
not reciprocated? So, we have Buenos Aires' conditional identity – it exists only if
Europe is looking. The city was born in this play of mirrors, in this complicity of
reflection. A certain way of life was born as well. An anxiety about being stared at
doesn't come just from the colonial condition, from infantilization. One explanation lies in the land of Argentina itself.

"*Horizontal vertigo*," wrote Drieu La Rochelle. And Roger Caillois wrote: "I trust
the soul that takes its law from so pure a land. I give thanks to this land which so
exaggerates the role of the sky." An ideal metaphysical space, a baroque space as
well (the baroque of too much emptiness, not too much fullness; of the concave,
not the convex: like the imaginary stories by Borges where the storyteller creates
through omission, writing through the very act of nonwriting), where through absence the pampas raise the oldest and most fundamental questions: "Who are we?

Where are we going?" Everywhere else the earth is round. Here on the pampas it is more round than anywhere else. More round; that is to say, more infinite. This is where the terror comes from. Back to Borges – I cannot read him without picking up his own fear. But what is he afraid of? Or who? He never admits it, yet, he describes the shape of his fear: round, circular, spherical. Like the pampas. Borges uses the word "circular" to describe time, to connote the eternal return. His visions of eternity are spherical (the Aleph, the Zahir) or circular (the Wheel, the Disk). Borges cites Pascal, who saw the universe as a horrifying sphere: "Nature is an infinite sphere, whose center is everywhere and whose circumference is nowhere." This definition applies perfectly to the land that this city and this fear are rooted in.

Could you build a circular city on the pampas, a kernel-city, a city curled up like a tightened fist? Apparently not, since Buenos Aires is the epitome of expansiveness: the city pours itself out like liquid. A city without boundaries. Or rather, a port city; a gateway that never closes. I have always been astonished by those great cities of the world that have such precise boundaries that you can say exactly where they end. Buenos Aires has no end. It needs a beltway around it so you could point an index finger, trembling with uncertainty, and say: "You end there. Up to this point, you are you. Beyond that, God only knows!" Buenos Aires couldn't care less, just as the gaucho, drunk on space, scoffed at the barbed wire that tried to divide his pampas. Buenos Aires laughs and continues her endless development – a city that stretches farther than the eye can see or the mind imagine. So, what does it mean to say that you are a native of Buenos Aires? To belong to Buenos Aires, to be *Porteño*, to come from this port? What does it mean? What or who can we hang onto? There are no mountains, no memories of times gone by. Usually you cling to history or geography. In this case, what are we supposed to do? Here, geography is merely a vague line that marks the separation of earth and sky. Two lines, rather: the line that marks the pampas is green; the Río de la Plata is a mass of brown mud whose other bank is indistinct. Above, a blue, blue sky; a sky of "naive candor," with an enormous sun shooting out rays like a spider web, as if drawn by a child. So beautiful. Outrageously big. Incredibly exaggerated. As for our history, it's brief. First, the Indians disappeared, leaving us without roots. Then, numerous immigrants appeared to infinitely multiply this rootlessness – like the spherical "Aleph" where all the objects and beings of the universe swirl together. For Borges, the "Aleph" is a catalogue, a swarming universe, one of those lists that he laments – just as he laments a certain cluttered Buenos Aires that is oblivious to this essential emptiness; the Italian, pizza-eating Buenos Aires.

It's as if the only way to keep anxiety at bay is to fill ourselves up as quickly as possible. Everywhere else the Indians left traces behind them; here there is nothing left. No other South American Indian people have disappeared as completely as ours. All that remains can be held in the palm of one hand: an arrowhead, a black and white drawing to scale of a poncho – turned to ashes. Hunters and nomads, these Indians must have been, before Borges, metaphysical questioners. "Where are we going," they must have asked, "on this round earth?" The void was their answer. And we who call ourselves Argentinians, we *Porteños* from Buenos Aires, where are we going – with the heavy legacy of these ashes, this Indian dust, this ghostly flock which howls in the cold south winds?

The varied origins of the immigrants are abundantly evident, first of all, in our faces: our eyes are often blue. Then, there are our unpronounceable names, which tag us as Argentinians when we're in Peru or Venezuela. Finally, there are the photographs taken back when the pampas penetrated every street in Buenos Aires, even in the middle of the city. In those days, toward the end of the last century, the tango had barely been born. It still had a naive, shrill tone and a marvelous aroma of wild grass. This early tango spoke of the present. Since then, all the tangos speak in the past tense; celebrating the past, lamenting its passing. What exactly were the good old days like? It was a time of new arrivals: Spaniards, Italians, Russian or Polish Jews, Armenians, Arabs, Yugoslavians, Bulgarians, Irish! ...Rough, dark men from Wales!...Men from Provence! One day, in ecstasy, I saw a photography exhibit of these new-arrivals. They were standing stiffly on the dock, their patched canvas bags at their feet. In spite of their different origins, they all had the same expression on their faces, the same crazy look, their eyes too fixed, sunken-in, bright and feverish...

Let's take a closer look at the yellowed aura with which time has surrounded these images. It reminds me a little of religious painting, where gold backgrounds isolate certain exceptional beings in a sacred space. In these photographs the golden space isolates a shivering, rumpled group: sullen, fat women – sometimes with the shadow of a mustache above their pale upper lips, always with a dark scarf encircling their sad, madonna faces; frail men in wrinkled jackets, with Chaplinesque bowler hats and skinny mustaches, who press against each other as if for protection from the golden future which surrounds them. Actually, it is the excess of air and land around them which makes them huddle together like that. "What are we going to do with all this and in all that?" they seem to ask, shrinking together more and more. Ultimately, the only possible response to such excess would have been to open their arms rather than gluing them close to their sides, as if they were crucified by the recognition that their destiny would be this vast expanse.

And so, a herd of the humiliated and oppressed came to replace the proud, defeated ones. Once the Indians were wiped out, the place was wide open for all the conquered people of the earth to congregate. They came to bequeath the memory of their own fears to us who have a fear without memory. But they had hardly arrived before they lost a fragment of themselves, a piece of their identity, a bit of their proper names. "What is your name?" asked the port commissioner with his tanned face, ironic smile, and eyes slightly slanted from some aboriginal ancestor. "Waschziszchicz." "Fine! I'll put: Bachich. Where do you come from?" "From Turkey, but I am Armenian." "Your passport is Turkish, so you're Turkish, damn it!" In this way, the Armenians who had fled the Turks and the Jews who had fled the Russians found themselves turned into Turks and Russians in Argentina. History plays some good jokes! In Buenos Aires, the word *Turk* means Arab or Armenian and the word *Russian* means Jewish. Some good jokes, indeed! Buenos Aires was born and grew to be a big, industrial city thanks to the massacre of a people and, then, thanks to the arrival of those who had run away from more or less the same fate. Almost immediately, the tango began to sound sad.

After I had been away from my country for five years, I went to an absurd and touching performance of a tango orchestra. I suddenly understood everything. Buenos Aires was there in front of me, complete, in the form of an orchestra. A paunchy accordionist of Italian origin pumped his instrument of German origin in and out as if he widened and narrowed the smile of some wrinkled lips. A guitarist of Spanish origin with scowling eyebrows had a somber air about him. An unbelievably blond pianist appeared to have the same ancestry as the accordion. A violinist with red hair seemed to have escaped from one of Chagall's paintings. I had the feeling that he had never left the Moldavia of his ancestors (and of mine). He made his notes undulate like an oriental serpent. His violin sobbed in ingratiating and shifty half-tones, zigzagging like the trail of a gypsy car through a field of sunflowers. You didn't just hear his music, you felt it along the nape of your neck and down the twin serpent of your spinal cord. And I said to myself: "There is my city. There it is, such as it is: bastard, mulatto, impure, mixed-up, and drenched in nostalgia. And that is its music: music from everywhere and nowhere." Music of lost memories, of times past, an immense territory of sound where all the victims of the depopulation and population of the Argentine republic meet: the moan of the Indian and the moan of the Jew, the Spanish and the Moorish arabesque, with the trills of the Neapolitan *canzonetta*, punctuated by African drums, soaked in *morriña*, the sadness of Galicia. Always the ancient question: "Who are we? Where are we going?" All these musicians were struggling together in "two/four" rhythm to reach a tragic climax as if they played with a woman's body; violent, sentimental, enraged, continually pulling my heart toward their emptiness, my heart which threatened to unwind like a skein of wool . . .

Then I danced. First, you must understand that an Argentinian woman never dances a tango perfunctorily, like people do these days. She dances only with certain partners, just as she makes love only with certain men. What happens between two people who tango is unique each time. The tango is constructed each time they dance. It is invented anew. Just as there are no two identical fingerprints, there are never two identical tangos. I danced, therefore, with the man who seemed better able than all the others to join his legs to mine to create that fabulous animal, that two-headed monster we call: tango. It's a beast with four legs, languorous or lively, that lives just for the length of a song and dies, murdered by the final note.

Dancing like this I felt the oblique sensation of being a *Porteña* in my entire body. Can you imagine fully facing your partner in a tango? A square tango? In a straight line like a Tyrolian dance? The tango is fundamentally crosswise and baroque. The essence of classical style is to advance directly. Baroque style offers mischievous, delicious detours. It is beside the point to arrive as quickly as possible. In fact, it doesn't matter if you arrive at all. The point is to enjoy the journey. Where were we going, my cavalier and I, crosswise (not like the right angles of the Christian cross, but like the bones beneath the skull on the pirate's black flag)? Where were we going? Or, more exactly, where was he going, my private dictator who commanded my every move by tracing a secret sign on my back? A woman who tangos must have a gift for intuition. She has to make herself transparent, crystal clear, to divine the intentions of her partner several seconds in advance, even before he, himself, knows which lopsided, depraved, perverse position in which he is going to put his foot. It reminds me of a horse I used to love to ride. I remember the delicate way he paid attention. He could sense my slightest hesitation over which path to take. My hand would not have to move, not a tremor would shake the reins, but he already understood the new idea budding within me. When a woman dances the tango she becomes this sensitive, intuitive horse. She obeys the subtlest and most silent commands of the cavalier with legs of steel . . .

So, Buenos Aires, a city far from the center of the world, a city founded on the disappearance of the Indians and then on the arrival of immigrants from various countries, invented music that is sideways, weepy, and crossbred, a music which gives *Porteña* identity its foundation of emptiness and absence. Other South American countries, and even the northern provinces of Argentina, have a wounded identity. Their inhabitants have dual identities, half-Spanish/half-Indian or half-Spanish/half-Black. Or, sometimes, they even have three identities – but they are always tangible. They can recognize each other through their wounds. In Buenos Aires we cannot. Mourning the massacre of the Indians is an abstract idea. We've never seen these Indians who fought so proudly against the Spanish conquistadors in the sixteenth century: the ones who, toward 1516, ate Don Juan de Solís, the first explorer of the Río de la Plata. Their blood no longer courses through our veins, only in the people of the provinces. But Buenos Aires condescendingly calls provincials "the little Black ones." They do everything they can to reject this unwelcome reminder of the past. The major obsession of the city is summed up in one phrase: "Do the Europeans think we wear feather headdresses?" As for the immigrants, they adapted themselves to the country, here they're the establishment, the nouveau riche, the reproducers. If the tango mourns its wounds, they are the soul's, not the body's. Identity is not wounded in Buenos Aires. It's almost worse: it is unreal.

What is the product of this gigantic unreality – the *Porteño* – really like? For the truest ... and the most malicious insights, you always have to turn to Borges. According to him, the Aleph, that "copious universe," is subjected to the Italian influence of those perfectly ridiculous, loud Zunnis, Zunninos, and Zungris. After the wave of immigrants in 1900, Buenos Aires-the-copious became even more expansive, in effect, more exuberant, and less distingiushed, according to the social class Borges belonged to, for whom "Italian" meant "tomato vendor." This deeply Argentinian, very South American prejudice, constructed the following image of the *Porteño*: he is big, not too thin; he has very pale skin, exaggerated gestures, a superiority complex, a terror of ridicule, a studied elegance, bright laughter, brash jokes; he is lazy, has a taste for comfort and an excessive appetite; he is sentimental, crude, and above all, he is unshakably certain of himself. He is the shrewdest, most calculating, and (of course) the most "macho" man in the entire world. Any similarity to the popular, neorealist image of the Italian male is purely accidental ... This expansive *Porteño* sings in Spanish with an Italian accent even if he has a Polish father and a French Basque mother. Our music's Italian origin, mixed with Spanish phrases, also gives us a unique oral product that is as impure as the tango:

the speech of Buenos Aires. Aside from this, the Italians have brightened our existence thanks to an element of revolutionary ingeniousness: the salad. And thanks as well, to the pizza.

Since my mother came from a traditional family, whose Spanish heritage stretched way back, she never tasted a tomato until after she married my father, the son of immigrants. "Fresh vegetables? *Gringo* stuff!" my mother declared with disgust. She was referring not only to North Americans (whom we rarely saw) but to all the "blond strangers." To us, a *gringo* can be an Italian from Milan or someone from Poland or Germany. The real *gaucho*, the horseman who embodies the worst faults of both Indians and Spanish, this proud man, independent, slow-moving, thin-skinned, violent, mocking, the Cossack of the pampas, ate meat only. Back when the pampas were wide open, this solitary *gaucho* (always without women, of course) proudly pranced through an infinite space scattered here and there with herds. Hungry? He lassoed a steer, slit its throat, cut out the tongue, savored this choice morsel, and abandoned the rest to the crows. For holidays, on the other hand, he cooked the whole cow in its skin and threw the leftovers to the dogs. Country of waste: in spite of the persistent efforts of the immigrants who brought their love of economies with them, Argentina inherited from the wasteful *gaucho* an aristocratic extravagance.

Not counting *maté*, nothing green is part of the Argentine diet. Buenos Aires is the capital of meat. It's the capital of barbecue and crispy fat; a city of giant steaks, of chops the same shape as Argentina on the map. It's a city of slaughterhouses, whose odor of terror I can never get rid of – a smell that evokes one image and one feeling: the image of panic-stricken cows driven in green-stained trucks to the slaughterhouse in Mataderos, leaving a trail of terrified mooing behind them. It's impossible to erase this terror and this smell from my memory. Something responds in me, in my own stomach, a kind of pity, horrified sympathy, and a strange agitation. It would be going too far to blame our political violence on our carnivorous habits. I'm convinced, however, that the Italians came to Argentina to gently soothe the cry that we inherited from the Spanish, "Long Live Death!" Given a choice between powerful alternatives, so typically Argentinian – "Rosas or death!" "Perón or death!" – given a choice, each time, between the name of an incredibly macho *caudillo* whose speeches strike fear in the hearts of the people, and … death – in the face of these alternatives, Buenos Aires-the-jovial, the progeny of Zunnis, Zunninos, and Zungris, have invented another slogan, one that is certainly more tender: "Pizza … or death!"

I began with metaphysical questions and followed them with a meditation on mixtures: mozzarella, oregano, and tomatoes must seem paradoxical. However, I don't mean to get off the track. My subject is really the anxiety of existence. The *Porteño*, not a big drinker, is a big eater. To explain where this comes from (and I know it as well as anyone), I have to tell you about my grandmother.

She was born in Moldavia, survived the pogroms, and followed her husband, a young, delicate intellectual, to the Jewish colonies of Argentina that were founded by Baron Hirsch. She had known hunger, and she never forgot it. In the face of the pampas' immensity out in the province of Santa Fe, the young, delicate intellectual went crazy with terror and found no other response to this excess of sky than suicide. My grandmother busied herself in front of her kitchen stove, multiplied her Jewish specialties (gefilte fish, *varenikes*), and above all, above all, gave my father (who was born in Argentina) the following advice: "Eat some bread. Eat everything with bread. If not, you'll never be full." *Eat some bread.* Sacred watchword, watchword of my ancestors. We are frightened because we lost our land in Russia; we are frightened because the earth here is too vast; we have known hunger; we are frightened of experiencing it again, so, my little one, eat everything with bread, eat as much as you can, as long as there is something left. My father obeyed. All his life he ate like a true Argentinian immigrant. He ate, stifling the sobbing questions that had tormented his father. He became one of the founders of the Argentinian Communist Party, making sure that the poor could eat as well... Argentina's emptiness, the metaphysical space of the pampas, the birthplace of the literature of the fantastic, which is the very symbol of the Río de la Plata (for Roger Caillois, the *fantastic* is the abrupt eruption of the supernatural terror, while the *marvelous*, which you never find in Argentina, is the simple acceptance of the supernatural in daily life)... through reversal this emptiness becomes fullness: pizza or death, gefilte fish or the terrifying feeling of ignoring the why and wherefore, the true meaning of one's destiny.

Anxiety of existence. Identity conflict. Uncertainty of the personal self, the national self, the sexual self: lament, endless lament! So, we come to the tango and, at last, we can tackle the prickly problem of Argentinian *machismo*.

You always hear that the tango was "men's music." This was true back when the dance first appeared in the slums of Buenos Aires. What happened between the appearance of the masculine couple of 1900 – two mysterious *machos*, dressed completely in black, hats pulled low over their brows, tight-fitting jackets, inky black mustaches, dancing somberly together – and the free and flamboyant *chanteuses* we know today? Woman arrived on the scene. And the couple formed by these two naively ambiguous men who proudly displayed their masculinity, leaning against each other, complaining bitterly of woman's evil, all the while claiming that, from their point of view, there is no saint like mother (suffering soul!) – this couple is as dead today as the grass between the cobblestones.

At the turn of the century Buenos Aires was a city of men: immigrants, *gauchos* – there were only men. It makes sense, therefore, that men were the first to do this new, shady, suspect dance. One dances with whoever is available. So no one found it strange that, in the service of the tango, the first *chanteuses* dressed like men while they risked their fragile and clumsy little voices on the streaming trills of the *zarzuela*. Masculinity being valued most highly, it was necessary to resort, with a complicitous wink, to *trompe l'oeil*, and long live the look! It was so funny! The transvestism of the plump, pouting, overly shrill *chanteuses*, disguised as *gauchos* with boots and sombreros or wearing a tight jacket that they unbuttoned to place a hand, in a "virile" gesture, on an ample thigh ... The bizarreness of this somewhat ambiguous gender did not stop there. In those days the men themselves were all tenors, singing with hand over heart, stringing trill after trill, eyes cast heavenward like the Virgin. It's perfectly possible for a man to have a delicate voice. But, with Carlos Gardel, voices became lower; and then, when the orchestras became Italianized and expanded in the forties, adding deeper and fuller-sounding instruments, much lower. Yet, high or low, these macho voices have always had one single complaint: "*Mama mia*! How evil women are!" A highly coded complaint and the perfect counterpart to the courtly love poem. Idealization or denigration: two ways to invoke the same strikingly rigid system of signs with the same effect: ignoring the personality, the whole person, considering only the gender to which the other belongs. And there you have it: whether a tango, or a courtly love poem, it's always a code.

But children grow up and the anxious *machos*, in love with mother, become men. In the seventies Astor Piazzolla changed the tango's weepy style. He invented a grating music, even more darkly sinister, but – how can I describe it? – a vital darkness. He brought the tango up to date. These are not happy times. The hellish aspects of the big city are a given; but he accepts these aspects, perhaps in order to change them. It was Piazzolla who chose a woman to become the priestess of this kind of tango that is so completely modern à la Rimbaud. History's strange morality ... The tango's renaissance is due to a positive, antinostalgic, optimistic spirit inspired by women like Susan Rinaldi. Oh yes! It is as difficult for a people to mature as for an individual. Will we ever be able to sing about pain instead of about this incredible fear of women? Is Buenos Aires on the verge of discovering the center of its being, even if it turns out to be empty?

Why do we have such an absurd need for a solid, deep-rooted, robust, and pink-cheeked identity, a peasant identity anchored for centuries to the same land? Why not embrace an empty self? What is so awful about emptiness once you get used to it? I have no roots. It's a fact. A tragic mixture of blood runs in my veins: Jews, Genovese, Castilians, Irish, Indians, maybe Blacks, find in me a bizarre and motley meeting place. I am a crowd, a one-woman march, procession, parade, masquerade. For a long time I used to see a strange sight: just before I fell asleep each night, right before dreams begin, before my closed eyes, I saw battalions of vanquished soldiers advancing across a plain. Whole armies. They never came toward me. They moved slowly on horseback into the distance: humiliated, wounded, slumped over. I could see each precise detail of their uniforms. There were Tartars, soldiers from Napoleon's army, others I couldn't identify. Who were they? Why did they cross this region of myself, zigzagging toward the darkness, just before I fell asleep? Were they trying to tell me that I was not alone, that a legion of the defeated kept me company? Were they trying to tell me, in their own sad way, that I was descended from an endless violation, from a long line of defeated, violated people?

Let me start again, then, by saying: to be a crowd, what a marvelous gift! For a long time, those who are not a crowd will not know the falsehood of the self. They will take their masks seriously, staying attached to them. What would be simpler for us *Porteños* than to break these links? Internal exile. The feeling of belonging only to Paradise Lost. The sensation of strangeness, everywhere and always. To know you are a carnival of characters, nations, genders, epochs... Aren't all these elements of complete uncertainty part of the human condition? To be a *Porteño* is like being a Jew. Yet, for Jews, uncertainty comes from a lack of land and an excess of roots. With us, it's just the opposite.

Actually, Buenos Aires is a Jewish town! It differs, however, from New York; for example, you never see ecstatic Hasidics (with their corkscrew sidecurls) dancing. The Jews of Buenos Aires have lost their colorfulness. Yet, in fading, they have colored others, lending a profoundly Jewish nuance to the city. The proof is in our sense of humor. Could you laugh in Paris, in a non-Jewish milieu, at psychoanalytic jokes about "Jewish mothers"? Paris is a city much too full of itself. Jewish nostalgia has no place there. Buenos Aires, empty herself, ceaselessly opens her lungs to let in the same sighs as her people. Psychoanalysis is another case in point. In Buenos Aires, when you get up from the couch you continue to probe your psyche at length around the café table – subtly, almost to the point of exasperation, plunging into labyrinths of interlocking questions. And interlocking questions, you know, are the structure of Jewish dialogue. "Why are you *Porteño?*" Judeo-Argentinian response: "Why wouldn't I be?"

The North and Good-bye

> Sadness of things past
> Sands that life has carried away,
> Sorrow of neighborhoods changing
> Bitterness of dying dreams
>   – lyrics from a popular tango

When did I realize it was time to say good-bye? Did it sneak into the neighborhoods I've lived in? Childhood in the west. Adulthood in the east. This was very typical, very traditional, very "tango." For *Porteños*, growing up means leaving the old neighborhood for the city's center, then – if possible – leaving the city and going elsewhere. So, my good-bye to Buenos Aires began very early – when I lived in Ramos Mejia. It surfaced when I lived in a neighborhood in the north. A whole life lived between those two points in the labyrinth of the city. When I was on the verge of leaving Buenos Aires the city seemed to be marked by crossroads that resembled my own doubts, full of poorly made decisions, zigzagging with interrupted beginnings just like ant tracks. So, as I was deciding what to put in my suitcase (a letter with drawings of bears and lions from my father? old poems? a toy? the skirt I wore the day when . . . ? a packet of *maté?* a jar of that brown, preserved milk, muddy and nourishing like the river?), at that very moment I found myself able to see my own city both tenderly and cruelly. Mercilessly. The piercing vision of one's final hours on earth.

    The northern section of the city is very chic, very snobby, and very predisposed to these kinds of insights. It has been nicknamed "Freud City" because an overwhelming majority of psychoanalysts live there. And when these psychoanalysts were persecuted by the *junta* and accused of keeping the secrets of the guerrillas who confessed on their couches, they moved to Spain and recreated "Freud City" in Barcelona. The poor Spaniards, who, until that point, still firmly believed in their mothers!.... As for me, I was drawn to the atmosphere of the northern part of the city, where my family once had a home in the old neighborhood of Palermo, with its patios where magnolias bloomed in a blaze of white blossoms, evoking the moonlike faces of long-ago *Porteñas*, round and pale beneath jet-black hair. These patios no longer exist, but their legend remains. Their aura haunts the present. The calle Billinghourst is just an alley between two rows of modern buildings, where you have to crane your neck to see the sky. But, thanks to my mother's reminiscences, I can always summon the past and remember what it looked like once upon a time.

The principal artery of the Palermo quarter is the very elegant Avenida Santa Fe. High above it, even further north, flows the wide, majestic, impetuous, opulent river of Avenida Libertador, bordered by luxurious houses and crisscrossed by gigantic American shiny cars, honking furiously. Avenida Libertador loves contrasts. It travels, breathtakingly high, toward the Presidential Residence of Olivos, which is closely guarded by brick walls, and toward the beautiful neighborhoods of Martinez and Vicente López, where stately homes spring up, like the one Victoria Ocampo gave to Rabindranath Tagore while she was alive and bequeathed to UNESCO after her death. Then, it heads back toward the aristocratic cemetery, La Recoleta, curving toward café "La Biela," and runs right into a small group of young people, very blond, very suave, very hip, who talk about yachting while getting out of their sporty convertibles. Finally, showing no prejudice, Avenida Libertador runs past "Misery City," a vast shantytown that can't be hidden. It's right there, within reach; practical, because you can show it to tourists without having to leave town. You can see the miserable, cardboard huts that surround it, where children wallow in stagnant pools of water – green with rot and decay. This Misery City, in fact, is well located. Its inhabitants come to us from the north, from Bolivia and Paraguay. So, it holds that more or less swarthy population that all capitals worthy of the name keep around for their obvious usefulness: Algerians in Paris, Puerto Ricans in New York, *Salteños* in Buenos Aires.

Above all, Palermo is associated with the huge park of the same name that is full of marvelous lakes, lanes, and rose gardens. Around 1830, this park was the ranch of the first in a long line of dictators, Don Juan Manuel de Rosas. Palermo is also synonymous with its botanical garden, full of luxuriant plants that wave their leaves at us, visited by cats and old ladies with sacks full of meat and liver. But above all, Palermo means the zoo. Oh, that zoo! I deliberately left it for last. The animals always seem musty, covered with a greenish moss, but they live in splendid, crazy buildings, designed by a feverishly insane architect. That Hindu palace where the dusty elephant lives, those temples erected for who knows what primitive and bloodthirsty divinity where the hyenas live, and then those walls that imitate trees, and finally, the fine, steel-mesh nets enclosing a heap of artificial rocks painted white to look like snow, themselves topped by a proud and solitary condor, a Zarathustra with black feathers! And you buy those lion and giraffe-shaped cookies covered in pink sugar for the children to give to the bears who wait behind the bars, holding out their paws. All those balloons shaped like ducks and mice!... Everything here imitates something else, every gesture mimes another. Planted in front of a Japanese bridge, a tree pretends to be a bear asking for a cookie; stretching out a branch, obviously trying to be first, the favorite, the most petted. It pleads. It insists. It's Sunday. The men are watching the animals in a distracted way. They are listening to their transistor radios because it's the sacred day for soccer. From each radio a passionate murmur escapes; the voices of the commentators who talk and scream at an incredible pace, whose passion suddenly peaks in endless, shrill howls, just like the ones that must have frozen the blood in the pale veins of Don Pedro de Mendoza: Goooooooooooooooooooooal! Goooooooooooooooooooal!

How can I leave? How can I leave, I ask, with the cry of joy or rage frozen in my ears! And yet, I must. I must, because this is a land that casts you far away. Each inhabitant of Buenos Aires is thrown like a pebble into water. The outer ring that the falling pebble makes on the surface is the city, lost city, distant city, whose deepest essence is to be somewhere else in time. Yes, leave-taking is an Argentinian way of life. Argentina's most beautiful novel, *Don Segundo Sombra*, by Ricardo Güiraldes, ends with the legendary words: "I left, like someone who is losing his blood." Because leaving by way of the pampas is horrible. You watch the traveler becoming smaller and smaller, crushed by the sky and the enormous horizon. Leaving by mountain trail is not as sad. You disappear immediately behind the rocks. Across the pampas, the departure is drawn out, infinitely stretched out, like certain very long tango moans, or like that eternal Goooooooooooooooooooooal, love's climax that never, never ends.

So, my friends got together one summer evening for a farewell dinner. We did it the right way, everything exactly as it was supposed to be. Where else could this farewell dinner take place if not on the banks of the river? What could we eat for this farewell dinner if not a giant *asado*? And toward what city could I go, if not toward Paris? Some *Porteños* go to other cities but they know, deep inside, that it isn't truly right. Going to Paris is the natural, unique *Porteño* accomplishment. Seated on the terrace of a *carrito* on Avenida Costanera, we watched the lights' reflections on the river and our ancestors came from everywhere to join us. For us, going to Paris is a kind of homecoming. In Buenos Aires, we say that storks bring us babies . . . from Paris. So, all grown up, we return to Paris as if it were our birthplace. This was so obvious during the farewell dinner that the usual Judeo-Argentinian dialogue was pointless. No one asked me: "Where are you going?" I didn't give the sly, expected response: "Where should I go?"

After dinner, we went down the Costanera to the edge of the river. The summer air was as wet as a tongue. The humidity in Buenos Aires is a presence, a living being. You can touch it, caress it. The river, too, was alive, waiting to be petted. It had an animal-like smell and came creeping to lick our toes. The street lamps were encircled by a moist, glimmering halo. A cloud of shiny insects fatally swirled around them. The river was softly breathing. It had become invisible, but it looked out for us in the dark, winking conspiratorially in the swirling reflections. Come closer, Río de la Plata! Come! Come on! Lie down! Lie down! Lie down! Come along, my beautiful river dog – dear old river, we are destined to leave each other even if we stay in Buenos Aires, because *Porteños* are intrinsically absent and the Río de la Plata is the path of their oblivion.

But if I don't have roots, why have my roots made me suffer so?

Walter Mosley

The Black Dick

Poverty causes people to pay attention to detail. You know to the penny how much a can of beans will cost; how long a pair of trousers you bought will last. You know precisely how many weeks you can slide on your rent before the marshall comes to evict you. And you know the streets.

You can tell when the men standing on the corner are up to no good, or when it's just too quiet in the apartment next door. You notice automatically when someone is flashing large bills, when a door is left ajar.

Poverty makes you a plumber, an electrician, a painter, and a carpenter. Poverty teaches you how to sew and how to cook.

There are also lessons in philosophy for the poor. You know how hungry you have to be before you will steal and just how much abuse you will take before digging that .38 out of the bottom drawer next to the bed.

You know that the set of carving knives you bought in the street for five dollars was stolen. You might even know the name of the man you bought it from. He's moved on from elementary ethics to the weightier realm of law and chaos.

The man down the hall is dying of alcohol poisoning, but he may kill one of his children before he goes.

You can see, smell, and hear poverty. I suspect that this has always been true. You learn to identify the shoes and shirt of poverty in yourself and in others. And if you want a good job you have to wear a different shirt, a shirt without its collar frayed, and good shoes, so that your potential employer won't see the desperation in you. You have to use an uncle's address so you won't be identified by neighborhood.

And if you bathe and dress right and speak without an accent (without the truth about you coming out of your mouth) – then maybe you'll get a toehold in another world. Maybe your children won't know as much as you did.

Hiding poverty and working hard is how most Americans have migrated from ghetto to suburb.

It works

for people with white skin.

But poverty is tattooed on black and brown skins. Ignorance and violence, sex and criminality are deeply etched in Hispanic and African hues. If you're not white it is hard to get out of the slums. Clothes won't do it; midwestern articulation won't either. You have to work harder and you have to work longer to prove that you've "overcome" your poverty, your skin. And you have to prove yourself over and over again.

I wrote a novel. It was what you might call a "literary" work of fiction. It was a story of two young men. One man had been abandoned by his father when he was eight years old. The other hates his stepfather and wants to either humiliate or kill him. At the insistence of Raymond (the man who hates his stepfather), these young men embark on a journey. The other young man, Ezekiel, drives. And while he drives he begins to have memories, and a deeper understanding, of his own father.

Different journeys on the same road; not a new idea. But the setting and the characters were unusual: the drama unfolds in a mythical bayou town in Texas, called Pariah, and almost all of the characters are black.

I sent this novel to fifteen literary agents. They all liked the book and the writing, and they all rejected it for the same reason – not commercial enough. The look and the sound of poor rural blacks wouldn't, in these agents' opinions, sell books. Raymond and Ezekiel couldn't get a foot in the door; they went unemployed.

I put the book away and went on writing.

This time I wrote about two men in forties L.A. Still young, but a little older, Raymond and Ezekiel find themselves in postwar America. Ezekiel has lost his job and is about to lose his house to the bank. So when a white gangster offers to make his mortgage payment, Easy (Ezekiel's nickname) jumps at the chance. All he has to do is search the ghetto jazz clubs of Watts for a white woman who likes the company down there.

Once he starts his search people start to die. Easy finds himself in so much trouble that he has to call on his patricidal "friend" Raymond (a.k.a. Mouse) to fight his way out.

In short, I cast my characters into the mystery genre.

I had created a reluctant detective who is poor and black with middle-class aspirations.

Easy knows how to pay attention to details. He can read the streets as well as a woodsman can read skat. He is educated in the ways of desperation and crime by a lifetime of poverty. Now when Easy gets around white people they may be afraid of him, but they never suspect that he has the smarts of some kind of agent trying to glean their secrets. Turn the coin over: when Easy comes into a bar or church in the Watts community everybody thinks they know by his color that no white man would trust him with a mission.

Easy has become invisible by virtue of his skin.

The characters and their language are the same in this book as in the earlier novel. They are poor and black and hungry to get those things that racism denies them.

I had no problem selling this book. Poverty is the driving force of this novel, but it's poverty with a new pair of shoes.

Easy has become a detective, a title that you better not dress for, you'll become too obvious. Like Joe Louis stripping down and climbing into the ring, Easy and Mouse just have to jump in and go after the answers until they are the only ones left standing.

In a sense, the genre has made Easy stronger. Even though he speaks in a strange dialect, I think people want to listen to him because they know that he is asking questions and looking for answers that are important to them. And if people respect Easy, I think it's not because of his hard past, but because he has taken on a tough job in the real world: he's trying to define himself in spite of the world, to live by his own system of values. He's trying to do what is right in an imperfect world. The genre may be mystery, but the underlying questions are moral and ethical, even existential.

I have tried to stay true to my characters while getting them a toehold in the world of publishing. I gave Easy a new suit, but his skin is still black. He still talks like the street that spawned him. He has a little money now, and some respect. But he still puts his hand down to his crotch after he's had dealings with the white population, and they still count their fingers after shaking his hand.

III.

"THAT CAPACIOUS TOPIC":

GENDER POLITICS

CONFERENCE PRESENTATIONS

MAY 12, 1990

Michele Wallace

Angela Carter

Jessica Hagedorn

Ama Ata Aidoo

Nawal El Saadawi

Michele Wallace

I would like to use Toni Morrison's *Beloved* as a springboard for a proposal that I hope you will find both provocative and useful.

Beloved seems to me our preeminent example, in an African-American feminist context, of what I think of as a critical fiction, because it remakes, demystifies, and transforms the character of history as the master narrative. It problematizes and pluralizes how we think of what the West calls "myth." *Beloved* fundamentally restructures and challenges the prefabrication of the West, or at least that small portion of Western history known to us as slavery in the antebellum South. Most importantly, it focuses on the lost, irretrievable portion of that history – the voice and the imagination of the black female slave who could neither read nor write nor even bear to remember.

Myth, *Beloved* seems to propose, is not only a viable alternative to the narrative of mastery called history, it is an essential corrective to the way in which the vision of mastery in the past continues to hamstring the applications of history in the present. It is true that the category of "myth" has served as a convenient vessel for trivializing non- and anti-Western discourse. But it would be a great mistake, I would argue, to throw out the term, for it describes as well a crucial historical reality.

To recall our history, it is not enough that we recall our loss; we must recall the *process* of loss. For African Americans, who can turn to no unviolated homeland in culture or history, it is too late to correct the discarding and discounting of Afro-centric myth, magic, or spirituality that attended our brutalization and domination by simply reincluding it. What has been discarded and discounted has been lost forever. Instead, as *Beloved* tells us, and as African-American literature by women has been helping us to understand, we must choose to recount and recollect the negativity, the discount, the loss. In the process, we may ultimately make a new kind of history, a kind of history that first recalls how its own disciplinary discourse was made in brutality and exclusion, and second, a history that selects as its starting point the heterogeneity of the present.

For the time being, we are forced to turn to such critical fictions. Black women in the United States are already making a new kind of literature. What we need desperately as well is a new kind of black feminist literary and cultural criticism, the boundaries of which will reach beyond strictly academic audiences. It is essential that this cultural criticism engage with the dominant discourse. By dominant discourse, I'm talking not only about the rhetoric of ultra-right think-tanks like the Heritage Foundation, but, equally important, about the various knowledge productions of the art world and other cultural avant-gardes of the left. I am talking about becoming visible and audible in institutions like the Dia Center for the Arts and the New Museum and publications like *The Nation* and *The Village Voice*. We must do this, quite simply, because the racism and sexism of this and other cities are threatening to kill us if we do not speak against them. We cannot settle for any ghettoization, however attractive that ghetto may be, of black women's writing.

The purpose of this critical activity will be, in addition to direct political engagement: (1) to diagnose and describe our exclusion from past and contemporary creative, intellectual, and academic life in the United States; and (2) to precipitate our inclusion in critical discourse, not only in the humanities and the arts, but also ultimately in the sciences, medicine, technology, politics, law. I don't fool myself, on the basis of any essentialist naiveté, that the mere inclusion of phenotypically black, biologically female persons will serve to correct all our woes. Rather, the guiding principle here is that the project and process of seeking inclusion will raise consciousness and provide alternative strategies in revising intellectual, artistic, political, and economic agendas in the United States.

So the necessity for black feminist critical engagement has become my primary concern and has led me to be very interested in developments in African-American literary criticism, for that is the academic and disciplinary home in which much black feminist critical engagement finds itself. This is so precisely because, since the emancipation of blacks from slavery in the 1860s – which made it no longer illegal for most blacks to read and write – the bulk of a black female intellectual or discursive contribution has been made in literature – fiction, poetry, plays, autobiography, essays, and, to a lesser extent, journalism.

Of course, the shortcomings of such a disciplinary home are of precisely the same character, as Cornel West points out, as those that plague African-American political leadership when it focuses its energies entirely on electoral politics. Just as there are specific limits on the degree to which problems that beset the black community can be addressed or corrected at the electoral level, there are specific limits on the degree to which the problems that plague black women can be addressed at the level of academic African-American literary criticism, African-American studies, or women's studies. Nevertheless, the tenor of recent press coverage of issues related to this problem (especially in *The New York Times*, as usual) suggests that it would be entirely incautious to dismiss at this stage the continued necessity for the most basic kind of equality discourse, affirmative action, and clarification of goals in regard to women of color in academia.

Therefore, rather than suggesting that feminist or even identity politics have become a bad project in the neoimperialist, neocolonialist, appropriating West, I would agree with art critic Griselda Pollock that not only feminist but also identity or minority politics mark out three fluid horizons in the West, each of which, when critically engaged, can create what Pollock calls new knowledges. These three horizons I will tentatively call equality, difference, and the deconstruction and de-mystification of the dichotomizing of equality and difference. I know the unwieldiness of the name offends, but part of the solution lies, in fact, in the accurate naming of it. The importance of mobilizing on these three basic horizons simultaneously is best indicated by recognizing the fact that the basic assumptions of equality and difference are constantly being challenged and eroded in the dominant discourse and on the left. When this happens, one is forced to drop back to square one and to reassess the most basic kinds of claims to equality and difference.

The first level of struggle, for equality, asserts the notion that black women and black men are just as good as white men and white women in producing literary texts, fiction, poetry, plays, and literary criticism. This is the simplest and most uninteresting strategy of feminist minority identity politics and yet, as I have said, must necessarily be the foundation for all further theoretical, speculative, and interventionist cultural operations and processes. Since it is constantly being challenged, equality continues to be something that we need to argue about and for. But it becomes a hegemonic barrier to all other discourses if it is seen as an end in itself. On the other hand, to exclude equality claims from a black feminist critical practice would be playing political and economic Russian roulette.

On the second horizon of struggle is difference. Blacks, women, gays, lesbians are different, special, unique, and not to be collapsed into other categories; not to be subsumed, invisibilized, appropriated, or otherwise discarded in favor of other priorities. Every category has its own priorities that must be taken into account in any discussion and forging of coalitions. Difference should be celebrated for its own sake and on its own terms. This level of critical discourse is not to be taken for granted as self-evident or already safely achieved. It is essential that we keep acknowledging difference as a process rather than as a *fait accompli*. We must, at the same time, diligently stand guard against any institutionalized definitions of difference. An example: a black studies department such as the one at City College in New York City, in which the chair of the department maintains, against the notion of white philosopher Michael Levin that blacks are different and therefore inferior, the notion that blacks are different and therefore superior. The reason that arguments of superiority have to be fought against as diligently as arguments of inferiority is that the two positions cannot be extricated from one another. Each argument makes the other inevitable, so much so that they can even be taken to be precisely the same argument. It's worth noting that I'm willing to make this argument from the politics of my position as a black feminist madwoman in the attic who is struggling to come down from the attic. It seems to me that only those who have never been required to question their "membership" in a group feel entitled to make claims of superiority for that group.

Of course, the level of struggle that interests me the most is ultimately the deconstruction of the binary opposition of equality versus difference, for this is the level on which language wreaks the havoc of indeterminacy versus premature closure. Anti-essentialism is one of the philosophical responses to this problem. But in the absence of a profound critique of dichotomizing practices in general, it is, at many junctures, structurally and institutionally impossible to wage struggle at that level. In other words, it is not always possible to insist that as we speak about the problems that plague us, we call the language we speak into question. Of course, this is where critical fictions come in to save the day. The question for me, and I suppose this has always been the question for cultural critics, is how this energy can be tapped for all critical and political enterprises.

Angela Carter

I know that whenever a group of women are gathered together, the grandmother always makes a phantom appearance, hovering above them. I should like to invoke my grandmother, who used to say whenever a birth occurred in the immediate vicinity, "It is a wise child that knows its own father." This is my lead-in to a joke that was part of the repertoire of a British comedian named Max Miller, who had a number of wonderful attributes, one of which was a floral suit. Miller was a sort of Boy George prototype. He would appear on stage wearing this floral suit and accept in an ambivalent way the jeers of the audience. The joke goes like this:

There is this boy, you see, and he wants to marry the girl across the road. So he says to his father, "Dad, I fancy marrying that girl across the road." And his father looks very mournful and regretful and says, "Son, I have a confession to make. When I was a young lad I used to get around, and I am sorry to have to tell you this, but you can't marry her because she is really your sister." So, the boy becomes somewhat downcast, but happily he is able to recover. Now we used to have a good public transport system in those days, so according to the joke, the boy gets on a bus. And he comes back and says to his father, "Father, I want to get married. I want to get married to that girl who lives three streets away." And his father looks glum and says, "Son, I've got something to tell you. When I was a lad we didn't have buses, but I had a bike, and to make a long story short, that girl's your sister." Now the boy, increasingly downcast, buys a railway ticket. He comes back from his excursion and says to his father, "I bet you've never been to Birmingham." And his father replies, "Oh yes I have." So, extremely disconsolate, the boy goes to his mother and says, "Looks like I'm never going to be able to get married, Mum." "Why is that?" she asks. "Well, it seems every girl I fancy turns out to be my sister." And his mother says, "You go ahead and marry whoever you want, lad. *He's* not your father."

He's not your father. It's a phrase that knocks down all the sacred cows – or, in this instance, bulls – of cultural history. Imagine, you could throw out everything with this phrase: Hamlet, Oedipus, the Brothers Karamazov, King Lear, Superman. It is the ultimate Freudian joke. And it illustrates wonderfully not only some of the manners of the British working class that may be unfamiliar to you, but also that *father* is a social and legal fiction, that the term is only important as a social construction designed to facilitate the transmission of property. Since the people of this story probably lived in what we call a Council house – that is, a state-subsidized accommodation – the transmission of property is perhaps less important than the transmission of a whole set of ideas. Property could just as well be transmitted through a maternal vein (which is much less amenable to a sleight of hand, if that be the appropriate organ), and in some cultures, obviously, property *is* transmitted through the maternal line. But even in cultures in which the biological father is perfectly well known, some male relative, usually a mother's brother, fills in the space that we fill with father to teach a boy what a mother cannot – how to kill things, how to clean his foreskin, and so forth.

In *The Rebel*, Camus, thinking of Oedipal theory, says it is a foolish thing for a dictator to call himself the father of his people. It always puts the wrong idea in the minds of young men. I think I am correct in saying of the head of state of Malawi that he rules over a predominantly matrifocal people and therefore calls himself the maternal uncle of his people. But this doesn't make his regime any less repressive, nor apparently has it prevented people from trying to kill him. There is obviously more to the idea of the male authoritarian figure than simply the word *father*. The name of an Italian film, *Padre Padrone*, about feudal relationships in Sardinia, translates as "father/master." It is very difficult to find an equivalent in female terms: mother/mistress has a completely different set of connotations.

We often speak about something referred to as "legitimate power," power that has a right to exist, like the right a legal father exercises over his children. The correlative to legitimate power, I suppose, is illegitimate power, power that has no basis in legality. Whereas a mother's rights over a child are considered natural, they are the *woman*'s birthright, not the child's. And it now turns out, given the advances in reproductive technology, that a woman has a *right* to have a child, even if her body is not naturally equipped to do so. Which is to say that the term *mother* can also be a fiction, a social construction.

I am British by nationality, citizen of a nation that between the mid-nineteenth and mid-twentieth century exercised power over a larger empire than that administered by ancient Rome. (Although the Roman, Chinese, and Ottoman empires lasted longer. We outlasted the Soviet empire, but the U.S. empire is still in the running, and I think may make the century.) We acquired this empire by the most ancient right of all, the right of conquest. But we exercised power over it both by authoritarian structures of legality – patriarchal structure – and by coercion. Britain thought of her empire, and indeed she still thinks of it, in female terms, as a *natural* acquisition, like a pregnancy. Sometimes the British even like to think of the various parts of the empire as unwanted acquisitions, acquired inadvertently, like an unwanted or accidental pregnancy. (When I was in school, it was still possible for our history textbooks to claim that Britain acquired her possessions in Africa in a fit of absentmindedness.) But once impregnated, Britain was forced to carry through to term. The phrase *white man's burden* can very easily be turned into the *white woman's burden,* once you imagine poor old Britannia forcibly impregnated.

The idea of the mother country is still quite strong in both Britain and the former imperial colonies. I remember being very taken aback once when I met a writer in London who said she had come to visit the mother country, her voice cold with irony. She comes from Trinidad. I should say that to some people from the predominantly white ex-colonies, Australia and New Zealand, the idea of the mother country seems equally odd. In the case of Australia, especially, we find an instance of bad mother: severe rejection drove the first fathers to Australia.

We also speak of a mother tongue. Ever since Britain's inception, our women have been used as imperial symbols. In the sixteenth century, before Britain as such existed, before the annexation of Scotland, Elizabeth the Virgin Queen was the iconographic figure of colonizing adventures in America – Virginia was named for her. There was a conscious desire to make the Virgin Queen the equivalent of the Virgin Mother: the Protestant Virgin Queen, the Catholic Virgin Mother. She advanced through the Americas not only with a quasi-halo around her head, but also with many of the connotations of the Holy Mother. Queen Victoria finally did it in the nineteenth century. And Margaret Thatcher used her femininity in the most extraordinary ways – bad mother power.

These are all pieces of a fragmented discourse, if you like, around the idea that patriarchy is one form of repressive power among many; pieces of a fragmented discourse to suggest that there are different forms of repressive power, and that maybe power itself is the problem.

Jessica Hagedorn

Now I will discuss Virgin Mary Power.

The writer Ntozake Shange said in a 1989 newspaper article:

I refuse to live and to create from a defensive position. I write to fight...And I would hope that my choice of words and my choice of characters and situations reflect my experience as a woman on the planet. I don't have anything that I can add to the masculine perception of the world. What I can add has to be from what I have experienced. And my perceptions and my syntax, my colloquialisms, my preoccupations, are founded in race and gender.[1]

Last night, as I sat in the audience, I kept wishing I had brought a dictionary. Certain words kept cropping up: *transgressiveness, hegemony;* certain names, like Walter Benjamin; certain phrases, like *territoriality of language.* Pretty interesting for me, a nonacademic Filipino who thrives on confusion and chaos. The culture in which I was born and raised is indeed chaotic, hybrid, and exhilarating. For us, there is no either/or, for us there is both/and, with many levels happening at the same time. My head ached with words and with connections made to Anton Shammas's language dilemmas and Arturo Islas's Border ease and unease. It was with great relief that I ran off to a bar with my friends Luis and Angel for a brief but necessary dose of what I call Filipino therapy: a few hard drinks, one or two cigarettes, *tsismis* ("gossip") about Imelda's trial. We lamented the need for tribal gatherings and wondered if what is passing for a kind of intellectual tribal gathering this weekend at Dia is now commonly referred to as "panel" or "symposium" – words that I am uncomfortable with.

All this, by the way, is my attempt to respond to the young woman from Canada who was questioning the framework of this meeting. As a performance artist, I thought, well, this is a very interesting question. Here we are: *we* are looking at *you.* We are sitting on this platform, we are sitting on these hard chairs. Hope we don't have to pee. It's very stiff, and the lighting is especially harsh. Bless me, mother, for I have sinned.

I want to quote from Trinh Minh-ha's astonishing book, *Woman, Native, Other*:

Learned women have often been described in terms one might use in describing a thief. Being able to read and write, a learned woman robs man of his creativity, his activity, his culture, his language. Learning "unfeminizes". . . . Women writers are both prompted to hide in writing and feel prompted to do so. As language-stealers, they must yet learn to steal without being seen, and with no pretense of being a stealer, for fear of "exposing the father."[2]

It is my nature to be cynical, suspicious, and ungrateful. Blame it on the mambo, and the cha-cha, on hunting amulets worn on the same chain as tiny crucifixes, and scapulars blessed by the Pope. Blame it on the Spaniards who colonized us, baptized us, and imposed a patriarchal system in the name of the Father, the Son, and the Holy Ghost. Blame it on the barbed-wire crowns we wear with pride, on our fatalistic humor that keeps our sanity intact, but also trivializes our own expression. Blame it on a legacy of brutal tropical generals stuffed in khaki uniforms, their eyes shielded by impenetrable sunglasses worn Douglas MacArthur-style. Blame it on the simplest of explanations: the Philippines spent four hundred years in a convent and fifty years in Hollywood.

I was born in Manila, the Philippines, forty years ago. My upbringing was privileged, typically colonial, and Catholic. It is a familiar story. My heritage is mixed Filipino, Spanish, Scotch-American, and Chinese. In this mestiza mixture I was considered fortunate, although I was often told I wasn't light enough and my nose was *too* Filipino–whatever that means. Ironically, my family was somewhat progressive.

Marrying well meant upgrading your class and your race by finding a rich man or a white man who could take you to that fabulous consumer wonderland known as the U.S.A. Like most Filipinos, I was brainwashed from infancy to look outside the indigenous culture for guidance and inspiration. Taught that the label "Made in the U.S.A." meant automatic superiority, taught that Filipinos are inherently lazy, shiftless, and undependable. Our only talent, it seems, is for mimicry. Weren't the best bands in Asia Filipino? We are proud of our Filipino versions of Stevie Wonder, Barbra Streisand, Johnny Mathis, and so on. The colonizers did their job only too well, for if you ask me what is indigenous, I'm not so sure I could give you an honest answer except to say animism, paganism, matriarchy: what was long ago, before the Spaniards with their imperialist Christianity, and before the Americans with their pseudo-rescue missions and insidious media. We learned our native language, Tagalog, as if it were a foreign language. It was also the language used to address servants. English was the preferred language–expert, mock-English, which everyone spoke mixed with Spanish slang. No one in my day thought to question why a so-called independent nation so close to China and Vietnam chose to conduct most of its schools, white-collar businesses, and even media in English. Perhaps one way we have conquered this trilingual nightmare is to claim it as our own. As Filipino critic Luis Francia said to me last night, "To go forward, Filipinos and Filipino Americans may have to transcend the corruption of our culture by turning what is now perceived as negative to our advantage."

In this same way, women of my culture seek to claim what was once theirs. I don't relate to Western feminism comfortably – although my upbringing was incredibly Westernized, it was also (in spite of itself) Filipino through and through. It's a bundle of contradictions that never ceases to amaze me. Corazon Aquino is a prime example of this. When she first took over, she was practically a saint in most people's eyes, a profoundly religious Catholic woman who was also a member of the ruling, ruling, ruling class. She came to represent the hope of salvation for repressed Filipinos, the leftist Filipinos, and the so-called progressive types from the middle and upper classes. She has lasted this long only because she has learned to compromise with her husband's assassins and has retreated to the shelter of her almighty church. In most circles nowadays she is referred to as the Tarnished Madonna.

My novel, *Dogeaters*, is a love letter to my motherland. It is a fact and a fiction born of rage, shame, pride, and my ongoing struggle and resistance to what I will simply refer to as white supremacy. Call it what you will: male domination, phallocentrism, Eurocentrism, colonialism, postcolonialism, postcoitalism, or postmodernism – it is on the margins of the empire of white supremacy that I have lived all my life. I know it well, and the anguish of that is more keenly felt every time I go back to Manila, which has become more Western consumer-crazy, more cynical and corrupt than I ever thought possible.

I wrote *Dogeaters* on my own terms, in the English I reclaim as a Filipino: the English mixed with Spanish and Tagalog. I did not want to use a glossary. I sought to subvert, exorcise, celebrate. Taking on the voices of characters from all levels of society, using fragments of overheard dialogue, newspaper clippings, found historical documents, soap opera plots, the script for a radio melodrama as foreground for the torture and rape of a young woman. The litany of prayer is both sacred and profane final chapter. The antihero of the book, the quintessential, mongrelized Filipino voice I chose to inhabit, is not female but feminine and belongs to the ambivalent homosexual character, Joey Sands, a male prostitute and drug addict, a G.I. baby who is half-black, an illegitimate, illiterate whore and son of a whore. Because he never knew his father or mother, Joey borrows his last name from the Sands casino in Las Vegas. He reconstructs himself, he improvises himself, and he is a noble survivor.

I want to close by reading a few brief excerpts from the book.

I've had my share of women since, but they don't really interest me. Don't ask me why. To tell you the truth, not much interests me at all. I learned early that men go for me; I like that about them. I don't have to work at being sexy. Ha-ha. Maybe it's my Negro blood.

Uncle says I prefer men because I know them best. I take advantage of the situation, run men around, make them give me money. For me, men are easy. I am open to anything, though. If I met a rich woman, for example . . . If I met a rich woman, if I met a rich woman, if I met a rich woman who was willing to support me to love me no matter what. You'd better believe I'd get it up for her too. Be her pretty baby. I know how to do that. Make them love me even when I break their hearts, steal, or spend all their money. Sometimes, you'd be amazed.

Maybe I'm lying. Uncle says I was born a liar, that I can't help myself. Lies pour out of my mouth even when I am sleeping. The truth is, maybe I really like men and just won't ad-mit it. Shit. What's the difference? At least Uncle is proud of me. I know it, though he'd never say so.

Hell. Sometimes I feel the days go by too fast. I get worried. I won't be young forever, and then what? . . . I know I deserve something better. Right now I'm biding my time. I take good care of myself. I'm in control, my life is simple. I do okay spinning my records and turning a few tricks. I'm dressed, fed, and high. I can take it or leave it, break hearts wherever I go. Life can be so sweet, sometimes.

And the final:

Our Mother, who art in heaven. Hallowed be thy name. Thy kingdom come, thy will be done. Thy will not be done. Hallowed be thy name, thy kingdom never came. You who have been defiled, belittled, and diminished. Our Blessed Virgin Mary of Most Precious Blood, menstrual, ephemeral, carnal, eternal. Rosa Mystica, Black Virgin of Rhinestone and Velvet Mystery, Madonna of Volcanoes and Violence, your eye burns through the palm of my out-stretched hand. Eye glowing with heavenly flames, one single Eye watching over me, on earth as it is in heaven . . .

Our mother who art, what have those bastards gone and done now? Your eyes are veiled and clouded by tears, veiled but never blinded. Dazzle us with your pity, let the scars tattooed on your face be a reminder of your perennial sorrow. Kyrie eleison. Kyrie eleison. Lamb of goddammit who taketh away the sins of the world!...

Ave Maria, mother of revenge. The Lord was never with you. Blessed art thou among women, and blessed are the fruits of thy womb: guavas, mangos, santol, mangosteen, durian. Now and forever, world without end. Now and forever.

Ama Ata Aidoo

I would like to claim your indulgence as I recall two concepts that have gained international currency and have cropped up on this platform, concepts that some of us consider negative in their implications. I would like to discuss them in order to dissociate myself from them.

Number one: *Third World*. (And thanks for making my job a little easier this afternoon, Angela . . .) I feel that one of the weapons that Western patriarchal systems have used to magnificent effect in their quest to dominate the rest of the world has been the strategy of *mis*naming. For what exactly are "First World" and "Third World," but formulations connoting superiority and inferiority? The notion of *third* eliminates choice. A third option is not much, is it? In terms of quality? Third-rate is not even mediocre. In sports? Third is neither gold nor silver, but bronze. To be more blunt, third is always one step from failure. And the question is: why should the majority of the people of this world agree to be so desecrated? The answer is: we did not agree. The fact that so many of our spokespersons acquiesce in its use does not make it legitimate.

What everyone nicely forgets is that these areas now referred to as the Third World were once the cradles of humankind, site of the earliest and most vibrant civilizations. Egypt was very African and very black, despite the caucasianization of Classical Egypt that was initiated at the beginning of this century and is still going on. (I am referring to the whitening of visual images from pre-Pharaonic and Pharaonic times, the thinning and raising of noses, the thinning of lips, and so on.)[1] Indeed, there is virtually a panic in some African artistic and intellectual circles that by the time the ongoing renovation of the Sphinx is finished and it looks "as good as old,"[2] there will hardly be anything left to remind future African and world generations that, in fact, the face of the Sphinx was originally modeled on the very "negroid" features of the Pharaoh who built it, Khafre, the IVth King of the IVth Dynasty. Nor can we easily forget the pre-Columbian Mayan, Aztec, and other empires of the Americas, or India and China. Clearly the great biblical prophecy has been fulfilled in modern economic and political parlance: the first has been made last!

We cannot overlook the many grotesqueries and absurdities the term *Third World* connotes. For instance, if a writer wrote a story beginning with, "Once

upon a time, a Third World boy and a Third World girl met and fell in love...,"
it would sound like pretty weird science fiction, wouldn't it? In the meantime, the
flawed nature of the paradigm becomes even more evident when we remind ourselves that in a supposedly three-tiered formation, no one has so far clearly and
unequivocally identified which sections of our contemporary world make up the
"Second World."

But what term(s) can we substitute for Third World? Perhaps *Africans, Asians,
Latin Americans, Caribbeans?* People often protest any attempts to get rid of misno-
mers like "Third World" and "First World" because, they claim, the alternatives
are too much of a mouthful. This view clearly adds insult to injury. Because it insists that in order for some people to easily identify some other people the latter
should agree to have their identities truncated. What is certain is that behind the
euphemisms is the hard reality of power relations: the conqueror versus the conquered; the rich versus the poor; the technologically advanced versus the technologically backward. Therefore, since there seems to be a need sometimes to bunch
us – the disadvantaged of the world – together, in terms of how we relate to the
so-called First World (the advantaged), we should be absolutely honest in our
characterization. For instance, we could go back to two of the most meaningful
descriptions of power relations that have ever been suggested: *bourgeois nations*
and *proletarian nations.*[3]

Postcolonial. This is the other term that some of us balk at. Perhaps the concept
was relevant to the United States after its war of independence, and to a certain extent, to the erstwhile imperial dominions of Canada, Australia, and New Zealand.
Applied to Africa, India, and some other parts of the world, "postcolonial" is not
only a fiction, but a most pernicious fiction, a cover-up of a dangerous period in
our people's lives. For unlike "neocolonial," for instance, "postcolonial" posits a
notion of *something finished.* (And "post" definitely is not "ante.")

But, let us look at the average African in the rural areas of the continent or
urban shantytowns, with no shelter, no education for her children, malnourished,
and aged beyond her years. She has not experienced an end but a continuation
of colonial oppression. Furthermore, the plunder of Africa's mineral and other
natural resources by multinational corporations and multilateral agencies continues unabated. And need we go into the devastation caused by foreign debt servic-
ing? Again, in terms of bilateral and multilateral grants and loans, the whole "aid"
system has been analyzed to show that colonialism has not been "post"-ed anywhere. At the end of the day, the poor countries pay lots more than they borrowed

to the rich (and former colonial) powers. So-called.

It could be argued that the term *postcolonial* offers a rational and neat construct in terms of literary critique. But as we know all too well, literature and other forms of artistic expression have an unruly way of not only reflecting but also actively spilling into reality. Therefore, those of us involved in the trade – whether as writers or critics – have to exercise the most extreme caution when we are bandying around terminologies.

At this point, I would like to speak briefly on the subject I originally planned to discuss, the situation of the African woman and African women writers. It is, I have written elsewhere, rather unfortunate but true that the African woman is the most invisible of all invisibles and (we might as well face it) the most despised. This has nothing to do with anything that African women themselves did or failed to do. It has to do with the sexual politics and the politics of the wealth of this earth: who grabbed it and who held it. Meanwhile, since women everywhere at all times have been mercilessly used and abused, you can then imagine what it has been like being an African woman.

Without wanting to apportion too much blame, from all the evidence at our disposal we can safely conclude that, outside the power appropriated by Western men as colonial masters, our own men have monopolized leadership positions over the last five hundred years. Now many African women are convinced that the oppression of women that modern African men indulge in and claim as "genuine" African culture is, in fact, a legacy of the European colonizers. Because, apart from their muddled views, first, of the European woman, then about other women, European colonizing men brought a few Victorian notions along with them on their "civilizing" missions. They ended up with some very twisted and disturbing fantasies of the sexual prowess of Africans, and of course their own (imagined) lack of it. This bundle of confusing notions of African and European sexuality is part of the psychological violence that accompanied the physical and spiritual violence of colonization.

However, when one views the situation of the African woman from inside her own society, we get another story altogether. For when we discuss gender politics in the African context, we quickly find that we must lay the blame for our present predicament squarely on the doorsteps of African men. They took the family house, denied access to the womenfolk, sold parts of our birthright off to strangers and the highest bidders; then sat and stared as the walls caved in on us.

Last October [1989], I was in Berlin, and one of my more persistent nightmares became reality in an incredible scenario. I was one of a group of writers who had been invited to a workshop on African literature. One panel was dedicated to issues facing African women and African women writers. But it became apparent soon after the panelists made their presentations and the discussion was opened to the floor that, on the issue of the status of African women in their own societies, the audience was split into two clear factions. On one side were the white (in this case, European) feminists who were almost bullying us, the African women on the panel, to declare for their brand of feminism. Because as far as they are concerned, they know much more about the oppression of African women than those of us African women who had allowed ourselves to be flown to this conference all the way from wherever we had been to tell them about ourselves and our environment.

On the other side were the male Africans who formed part of the audience, a mixed group of students, workers, and professionals. It became apparent that the sole reason some of them had come to the conference was to remind us that we should say we did not want feminism at all in Africa. They, too, knew more than we African women on the panel, what the African woman in Africa needs. Which definitely does not include feminism!

In the end, and out of sheer exasperation, we told both the European feminists and the African men resident in Europe that, strange as it may seem, we African women are perfectly capable of making up our own minds and speaking for ourselves. This in response to a comment by one European feminist to the effect that we "bourgeois African women are in no position to speak for the ordinary African women in the village." And, of course, it had not struck her as odd that, by the same token, it was even more ridiculous that she – a European bourgeois woman – was trying to speak for "the ordinary African woman in the village."

As this story indicates, colonialism survives in many forms.

Nawal El Saadawi

The first time I visited the United States, an American woman asked me my nationality. I told her that I am from Egypt. She said, "You are Arab?" I said, "Yes, I'm an Arab woman." And she said, "You're sure you are an Arab woman?" I said, "Yes, I'm sure I am an Arab woman." Then I realized that the image of Arab women here in the United States is limited to either the veiled woman or the belly dancer. There is nothing in between. Now, several years later, I am still astonished by Americans who question my nationality. "Are you sure you're an Arab woman?" Today, they are likely to follow up with the question, "Then why aren't you veiled?"

There are many misconceptions about the identity, character, and diversity of Arab women, most certainly about the diversity of the culture of Arab women. Feminism is a part of our culture, our history. In the Arab Women Solidarity Association, we call ourselves historical socialist feminists. We insist on these three words. Historical, because we have a long history of struggle and because we must know our past before we can conceive a nonpatriarchal future. Socialist, because we cannot separate patriarchy and class; we are oppressed because we are women *and* because we are poor. Finally, feminist, because we have formulated a powerful critique of patriarchy.

As a writer, I am often invited to international conferences, and I must say that I hate this division between Eastern and Western feminists. Because, in fact, many women in the West are quite backward and many women in the East are very progressive, and vice versa, so the division between East and West is ambiguous and misleading. And when I attend such international meetings I am frequently asked a question by Western women that I know is well intentioned but, even so, is grounded in assumptions that are quite racist: "You have come from an impoverished, backward country. How can we help you?" It is always assumed that we women of color need assistance and that so-called First World women must help us. And so we often hear, "How can we help you?" We usually respond by saying, "Well, you can help us by fighting here in your country against the same system that is oppressing us all."

Here's another example of this misapprehension of our common problems. Many Western women know very little about African/Arab cultures (although this is changing, particularly over the past decade). Consequently, upon meeting a woman from Sudan or Egypt, many Western women respond with the cursory "Oh, you are the women who are circumcised. This is very barbaric." Now, this circumcision is a terrifying and horrible business, but it also has its sensationalist side, and to know nothing but this about another woman's culture borders on racism. After all, there are other kinds of circumcision under patriarchy – psychological, for instance. My point is that we must recognize the similarities in our oppression and fight oppression together.

Patriarchy exists everywhere, it differs only by degree. In the Middle East and North Africa, we are experiencing a revival of Islamic fundamentalism – oppressive to women, of course. But here, in the United States, under Reagan and now Bush, you are experiencing a revival of Christian fundamentalism, equally oppressive to women. Westerners refuse to see or acknowledge these similarities. But the point is that women are oppressed under Christianity, Islam, Judaism, Hinduism – under all religions – because all religions are class-patriarchal structures.

Arab women live in a formerly colonized area of the world. The colonial repression continues, but it is more subtle now – not a colonization through military means, but through economic means and through systems of representation. Representation is quite important, because, as in your country, the media is very powerful in Egypt. The problem of representations of our culture in the media are a problem that women writers must contend with. What are the best means of struggle against this misinformation? The problem is acute in my country, because printed material is censored in Egypt. In fact, two days before I left for the United States, while I was still in Cairo, the government censored the only feminist magazine (of which I am an editor) in Egypt, which deals with class, patriarchy, and sexuality.

In 1972, all of my books – novels and nonfiction – were censored. I went to jail under President Sadat because of the content of my work, because I am a writer – not because I am a member of any particular political party or group, but simply because I expressed myself in written form on a variety of subjects having to do with Arab women. My arrest proved for me the tremendous power of the pen. It was actually exhilarating to know that Sadat was afraid of one woman with a pen! And the state's fear was demonstrated to me every morning when the jailer would search my cell and say to me, "If I find a pen or paper in your cell, it is much more dangerous to you than if I find a gun." I understood then the power of the word.

Margaret Atwood

The Female Body

> ...entirely devoted to the subject of "The Female Body."
> Knowing how well you have written on this topic...this
> capacious topic...
> — letter from the *Michigan Quarterly Review*

1.

I agree, it's a hot topic. But only one? Look around, there's a wide range. Take my own, for instance.

I get up in the morning. My topic feels like hell. I sprinkle it with water, brush parts of it, rub it with towels, powder it, add lubricant. I dump in the fuel and away goes my topic, my topical topic, my controversial topic, my capacious topic, my limping topic, my nearsighted topic, my topic with back problems, my badly-behaved topic, my vulgar topic, my outrageous topic, my aging topic, my topic that is out of the question and anyway still can't spell, in its oversized coat and worn winter boots, scuttling along the sidewalks as if it were flesh and blood, hunting for what's out there, an avocado, an alderman, an adjective, hungry as ever.

2.

The basic Female Body comes with the following accessories: garter belt, panty-girdle, crinoline, camisole, bustle, brassiere, stomacher, chemise, virgin zone, spike heels, nose ring, veil, kid gloves, fishnet stockings, fichu, bandeau, Merry Widow, weepers, chokers, barrettes, bangles, beads, lorgnette, feather boa, basic black, compact, Lycra stretch one-piece with modesty panel, designer peignoir, flannel nightie, lace teddy, bed, head.

3.

The Female Body is made of transparent plastic and lights up when you plug it in. You press a button to illuminate the different systems. The Circulatory System is red for the heart and arteries, purple for the veins; the Respiratory System is blue, the Lymphatic System is yellow, the Digestive System is green, with liver and kidneys in aqua. The nerves are done in orange, and the brain is pink. The skeleton, as you might expect, is white.

The Reproductive System is optional, and can be removed. It comes with or without a miniature embryo. Parental judgment can thereby be exercised. We do not wish to frighten or offend.

4.

He said, I won't have one of those things in the house. It gives a young girl a false notion of beauty, not to mention anatomy. If a real woman was built like that she'd fall on her face.

She said, If we don't let her have one like all the other girls she'll feel singled out. It'll become an issue. She'll long for one and she'll long to turn into one. Repression breeds sublimation. You know that.

He said, It's not just the pointy plastic tits, it's the wardrobe. The wardrobe and that stupid male doll, what's-his-name, the one with the underwear glued on.

She said, Better to get it over with when she's young. He said, All right but don't let me see it.

She came whizzing down the stairs, thrown like a dart. She was stark naked. Her hair had been chopped off, her head was turned back to front, she was missing some toes, and she'd been tattooed all over her body with purple ink, in a scroll-work design. She hit the potted azalea, trembled there for a moment like a botched angel, and fell.

He said, I guess we're safe.

5.

The Female Body has many uses. It's been used as a door-knocker, a bottle opener, as a clock with a ticking belly, as something to hold up lampshades, as a nutcracker, just squeeze the brass legs together and out comes your nut. It bears torches, lifts victorious wreaths, grows copper wings and raises aloft a ring of neon stars; whole buildings rest on its marble heads.

It sells cars, beer, shaving lotion, cigarettes, hard liquor; it sells diet plans and diamonds, and desire in tiny crystal bottles. Is this the face that launched a thousand products? You bet it is, but don't get any funny big ideas, honey, that smile is a dime a dozen. It does not merely sell, it is sold. Money flows into this country or that country, flies in, practically crawls in, suitful after suitful, lured by all those hairless preteen legs. Listen, you want to reduce the national debt, don't you? Aren't you patriotic? That's the spirit. That's my girl.

She's a natural resource, a renewable one luckily, because those things wear out so quickly. They don't make 'em like they used to. Shoddy goods.

6.

One and one equals another one. Pleasure in the female is not a requirement. Pair-bonding is stronger in geese. We're not talking about love, we're talking about biology. That's how we all got here, daughter.

Snails do it differently. They're hermaphrodites and work in threes.

7.

Each female body contains a female brain. Handy. Makes things work. Stick pins in it and you get amazing results. Old popular songs. Short circuits. Bad dreams.

Anyway: each of these brains has two halves. They're joined together by a thick cord; neural pathways flow from one to the other, sparkles of electric information washing to and fro. Like light on waves. Like a conversation. How does a woman know? She listens. She listens in.

The male brain, now, that's a different matter. Only a thin connection. Space over here, time over there, music and arithmetic in their own sealed compartments. The right brain doesn't know what the left brain is doing. Good for aiming though, for hitting the target when you pull the trigger. What's the target? Who's the target? Who cares? What matters is hitting it. That's the male brain for you. Objective.

This is why men are so sad, why they feel so cut off, why they think of themselves as orphans cast adrift, footloose and stringless in the deep void. What void? she says. What are you talking about? The void of the Universe, he says, and she says Oh and looks out the window and tries to get a handle on it, but it's no use, there's too much going on, too many rustlings in the leaves, too many voices, so she says, Would you like a cheese sandwich, a piece of cake, a cup of tea? And he grinds his teeth because she doesn't understand, and wanders off, not just alone but Alone, lost in the dark, lost in the skull, searching for the other half, the twin who could complete him.

Then it comes to him: he's lost the Female Body! Look, it shines in the gloom, far ahead, a vision of wholeness, a ripeness, like a giant melon, like an apple, like a metaphor for *breast* in a bad sex novel; it shines like a balloon, like a foggy noon, a watery moon, shimmering in its egg of light.

Catch it. Put it in a pumpkin, in a high tower, in a compound, in a chamber, in a house, in a room. Quick, stick a leash on it, a lock, a chain, some pain, settle it down, so it can never get away from you again.

Ana Castillo

Massacre of the Dreamers

REFLECTIONS ON MEXICAN-INDIAN WOMEN IN THE U.S.:
500 YEARS AFTER THE CONQUEST

Anyone dreaming anything about the end of the Empire
was ordered to the palace to tell of it. Night and day emis-
saries combed the city, and Tenochtitlán paid tribute in
dreams...
   But finding no good in the thousands offered, Mocte-
zuma killed all the offenders. It was the massacre of the
dreamers, the most pathetic of all...
   From that day there were no more forecasts, no more
dreams. Terror weighed upon the spirit world...
   — Laurette Séjourné, *Burning Water: Thought and
   Religion in Ancient Mexico*

Queen Xochitl... legendary queen of the Toltecs. During
her reign women were called to war service. She headed
the battalions and was killed in battle; legend has it that
as she died, blood streamed from her wounds, foretelling
the scattering of the Toltec nation.
   — Martha Cotera, *Profile of the Mexican
   American Woman*

Perhaps the greatest harm patriarchy has done to us is to
stifle, coopt, and deform our powers of imagination.
Moralisms, dualistic dogmas, repressive prohibitions
block our imagination at its sources, which is the fusion
of sexual and spiritual energies.
   — Monica Sjöö and Barbara Mor, *The Great Cosmic
   Mother: Rediscovering the Religion of the Earth*

Un Tapiz: The Poetics of *Concientización*

I

"Now i think i know how you saw me that first summer... i was part of the culture that wouldn't allow me to separate."

"I left the church in tears, knowing how for many years I had closed my heart to the passionate pull of such faith that promised no end to the pain. I grew white. Fought to free myself from my culture's claim on me."

"Culture forms our beliefs. Culture is made by those in power—men."

*"dark women come to me
sitting in circles
I pass thru their hands
the head of my mother
painted in clay colors..."*

"We were drawn to each other by the Indian spirit of mutual ancestors."

"I am visible—see this Indian face—yet I am invisible. I both blind them with my beak nose and am their blind spot. But I exist, we exist."[1]

II

"... once being born it would no longer be innocent, for being was to survive, and to survive, one must hurt weaker beings. No, the end of harming another living being was not the destruction but the saving of oneself, which becomes the true objective."

"In the shed behind the corral, where they'd hidden the fawn, Prieta found the hammer. She had to grasp it with both hands. She swung it up. The weight folded her body backwards. A thud reverberated on Venadita's skull."

*"Women do not coagulate into one
hero's death; we bleed*

*out of many pores, so constant
that it has come to be seen
as the way things are."*

*"Love? In the classic sense, it describes in one syllable all the humiliation that one is born to
and pressed upon to surrender to a man."*

*"It is our custom
to consume the person we love
. . . I'll wear your jawbone
round my neck
. . . Nights I'll sleep cradling
your skull sharpening
my teeth on your toothless grin
. . . Sundays there's Mass and communion
and I'll put your relics to rest."*

*"Still, I feel
the mutilated body
swimming in side stroke
pumping twice as hard
for the lack
of body, pushing
through your words
which hold no water
for me."*

III

*"Only fear could harm one. i told you to close your eyes, what you might see your logical
mind could not rationalize and it would cause you to weaken. It would gain power from your
very fear."*

*"That power is my inner self, the entity that is the sum total of all my incarnations, the
godwoman in me I call Antigua, mi Diosa, the divine within, Coatlicue-Cihuacoatl-
Tlazolteotl-Tonantzin-Coatlaopeuh-Guadalupe they are one."*

"With this knowledge so deeply emblazoned upon my heart, how then was I supposed to turn away from La Madre, La Chicana? If I were to build my womanhood on this self-evident truth, it is the lover of the Chicana, the lover of myself as a Chicana I had to embrace, no white man."

IV

"Once I looked into her blue eyes,
asked, Have you ever had an orgasm?
Finally she looked into my brown eyes,
told me how Papagrande would flip the skirt
of her nightgown over her head
and in the dark take out his palo, his stick,
and do lo que hacen todos los hombres
while she laid back and prayed
he would finish quickly."

"i was pliable clay to be molded and defined, to envelop him, suit his proportions until a pillow was placed over the mouth to stifle a cry of insatiable hunger."

"You reach for me in bed
Look at me, you say, turning
my chin into your hand what do you see?

It is
my face, wanting
and refusing everything.

. . . I want to feel
your touch outside
my body on the surface
of my skin.

I want to know, for sure,
where you leave off
and I begin."

V

"We are afraid to look at how we have failed each other. We are afraid to see how we have taken the values of our oppressor into our hearts and turned them against ourselves and one another."

"We needled, stabbed, manipulated, cut, and through it all we loved, driven to see the other improved in her own reflection."

"I will not be ashamed again. Nor will I shame myself."

Ours is a poetics no different
than any other literary movement throughout the ages. We are looking at what has been handed down to us by previous generations of poets and, in effect, rejecting, reshaping, or restructuring that legacy, reconstructing and making language and structure ours – suitable to our moment in history.

What makes the Mexican-Indian woman's literary expression questionable (and indeed, ours is under suspicion as legitimate literature by all) is essentially the same mechanism that has always kept us invisible as human beings and suppressed our contributions to the changing process of society. The "mainstream" doubts the value of our cultural endeavors because it measures them against self-serving standards. If we learn to use language that conforms to these standards, then, of course, our work proves itself worthy (though often deemed imitative). The *individual* who adopts the prevailing standards will be rewarded; the one who refuses is ostracized. This punishment and reward system for individual assimilation is not simply "the American way," it is the last resort when blatant rejection on the basis of class, race, and gender is no longer considered acceptable by society.

"Privilege grants language which escapes me."
I have also written elsewhere of the "vulgar limitations of language." As a utilizer of symbols – the written word – my dilemma is not only that of social marginalization and disenfranchisement from the language of dominant society, but also the diminishment of my potential and responsibility as a poet, as one who attempts to give some *tangible* interpretation of life's meaning. For if there is one aim of poetry, that is its relentless attempt to free human desire: to inspire the will to

live, to rejoice, to let the imagination flourish. Part and parcel of this endeavor is the poet's willingness to accept death, death with dignity, as part of life. All poets are as intimate with death as they are with breathing. That is why the "political" poet is outraged at death *without* dignity, death caused by the insanity and greed of war instigated by special interest groups who have it in their power to catalyze and manage such destruction.

The arena of the written word was, historically, the exclusive realm of a particular class of people: white, upper-class, well-educated men. Over time, a handful of "exceptional" women were admitted to this exclusive circle. Women who had access to only mediocre and often inferior public or parochial schooling, institutions bent on the repression of the human will, were not meant to take up the pen as a way of life. Being of the generation that globally rebelled against authority, we have managed, remarkably, I think, to change that.

Choosing to be conscious transmitters of literary expressions, Mexican-Indian women writers have become excavators of our culture, mining for our *own* metaphors, legends, folklore, and myths. Our foremothers and fathers are not Homer but Netzahualcoyotl, not Sappho but Sor Juana, not Athena but Coatlicue. Our cultural heritages were "discovered" in the era of our generation's rebellion. They were not directly passed on to us from the previous generation, which, because of social ostracism, lack of education, migration, dispersion, and poverty, was not in a position to uncover and share such a rich and illustrious legacy.

Yet what is most provocative and significant in our literature is that, while we claim and explore these cultural metaphors as an act of rebellion against the dominant culture, we must also take on the *revisioning* of these metaphors. As an example, we need only look at the figure of Malintzin/doña Marina/La Malinche. Masculinist ideology has cast Malintzin in the role of betrayer of the Indian race. But in recent years, women writers have taken on the responsibility of re-imagining Malintzin's life; she has emerged, in our writing, as everything from slave victim to heroine, to mother to the mestizo race, to genius linguist, to brilliant military strategist. No "facts" have been added or altered to make this possible. The difference is not in the telling, but in who does the telling. We have attempted to clarify how the patriarchal conquest ultimately left this young Indian woman little choice but to obey in the name of God the Father.

In the early years of the Chicano movement, as we sought legitimate acknowledgment by dominant society, the granting of greater educational and economic opportunities, and the affirmation of our unique cultural identity in Anglocentric society, our poetry, using the language of everyday life, played an important part in stirring the hearts of the pueblo. We have, however, reached a new phase in our poetics of self-definition. As mestizas, we must now take a critical look at language, *all* our languages and patois combinations, with the understanding that, explicitly or implicitly, language is the vehicle by which we not only represent ourselves but perceive ourselves in the world. If we as writers no longer feel bound to a collective Chicano movement, we are each individually accountable now for our vast use of language and the ideas communicated through it.

The vast majority of Mexican Indians or mestizos were taught to be afraid of a certain type of English: the language of the Anglos who initiated and sustained our social and economic disenfranchisement, who consciously or unconsciously instigated our traumatic experiences in monolingual Anglo-based schools, and who subscribed to and exacerbated the racism under which we have always lived in the United States. At the same time, we were equally intimidated by the Spanish of middle- or higher-strata people who come from Latin America. For how could a language of those so different from us speak for those of us here who have so long been denied a sense of belonging, a sense of historical ties to this nation?[2]

Our choices have been difficult. On the one hand, we may choose to adapt standard English and white writing standards, yet use our cultural heritage as a "motif." But this, in my opinion, reduces our poetry to Oaxacan paper cuts strung from beam to beam: white standards the firm structure, with Hispanic "flourishes" lending the local color that sanctions the celebrated fallacy of the melting pot. By white writing, I refer to the current Anglophone trend being processed through workshops and M.F.A. programs across the United States. Ivan Argüelles puts it succinctly: "Evocative, finely crafted, witty, urbane, sophisticated, occasionally troubling, but always safe, white writing is easily the most pervasive literary fashion today... White writing can sometimes be politically correct, but sanitized and with only faint air-brushed innuendos of anger."[3]

On the other hand, if we categorically reject the influence of English and "refined" Spanish, we may equally limit our perceptions by refusing to explore the fertile convergences and congruences of our tongue with others. Word-play (thus, idea-play) is in the very blood of the Mexican people. In the process of our word-play, of actively transforming one word into another and then another based on the similarity of sounds, we not only express our sense of irony and humor. We also create *new* meaning, or give the original thought a fusion of multiple meanings.[4] In attempting to do this with English-dominant speakers – especially but not

exclusively white people – I am always disappointed to find how their unimagina-
tive way in which they have been taught to hear language makes a complete disaster of my attempt at word-play.

Of course, not all of our writers have suffered from the "language trauma"
I have described. Some have, in fact, been encouraged – to read, to explore language, and to pursue higher education. But so many of us, *too* many of us, do
suffer the anxiety induced by the pressure to speak "correctly," and therefore we
come to doubt our writing skills. And, whatever our relationship to language, all
mestizas are products of the hegemony that has instilled in us contempt for our
cultural identity. We have been immersed in a North American value system that
honors the competitive spirit and the desire for individual recognition as the sine
qua non of success. This frenzy for individual immortality is not my concern here.
What *is* my concern is when the appetite for society's "carrots" inhibits the poet's
initial instinct: her primary desire to reconcile with her *impermanence*. Existential
angst, mortality, the sense of one's humble transcience through life – whatever
term one prefers for one's impermanence, it has always been a vital motivation behind artistic creation.

Doubtless this has been a core concern since the early times of literary history.
Woman, herself, has always known that she is connected to the cycle of birth and
death of all living things. She experiences it organically. It was man who, feeling
himself alienated from that cycle, marked out a spiritual split in humankind's collective psyche and forced its irreconcilable dualisms, dichotomies, and polarized
opposites upon women. A profound anxiety about man's capability of creating and
sustaining life generated an even deeper anxiety about man's death. If women now
share this masculinist anxiety about death, it is because they have been psychically
and physically beaten not only into amnesia, but also into actual denial of their
primordial connection to the cycle of life and death.

This dominance of man over woman's psyche, the alienation from his own connection to living matter, the subsequent objectification of her existence, is the basis
of man's view of woman as Other. And the dark-skinned woman, because it is in
her form that archaeologists have found the first traces of goddess worship, has
become the paradigmatic Other for men.

It is, therefore, a misunderstanding of the psycho-historic dynamic that gives
rise to the concept of the Other that can strip this term of its meaning. Woman is,
most assuredly, the Other of man. But a man cannot be the Other of woman, and
most certainly the white male image of power in the United States today is no-

body's Other. Other is that which man has denied himself to be. As he shaped his phallic, Sun-Father-God world, he defined the Other: as enigma, as his mysteries. But Other, when she comes to know herself, is truly not Other to herself, and man is never an enigma or mystery to her. His thoughts, his fears, his deepest secrets, are plainly reflected in the civilization he has built around her.

As the post-World War II generation, or the generation of the "Baby Boom,"
we were incarnated when the United States was truly *on top* and *projecting* into the great, endless, fantastic future – where nothing was going to stop it. We were literally *rocketed* to the moon with a mission to penetrate its virgin soil for the betterment of all. Yet we are now living to hear quite the opposite message reluctantly being delivered to us by every kind of "expert" and authority (with the exception, of course, of politicians, who are not "experts" so much as keepers of the gate): that is, environmentalists and economists alike are affirming that the United States, along with the rest of the world, is in deep trouble. Nations are not immortal after all, and neither is our planet.

We must realize then that not only are our physical beings vulnerable, but so is everything else – from nationhood (as we were taught as children to conceive of it) to the earth's resources. This to me is the work of the conscienticized writer: whether we choose to use cultural metaphors familiar to our elected audience (for instance, Chicanas) or to introduce images borrowed from other cultural legacies, we must remind ourselves and others that nothing is separate from anything else, matter and energy are one, in a constant state of flux: this fusion can only be expressed in our work if we allow ourselves to be open to the endless possibilities of associations.

If we continue, for example, to view the Virgin of Guadalupe as the metaphor for mother, the chain of associations traditionally follows thus: Virgin of Guadalupe = Mother = Nurturer = Fertility = Nature = Earth = Female = female. Woman is locked exclusively into the historically traditional role of procreator and nurturer, and given our Western orientation of dualism, we are automatically programmed to juxtapose the male as penetrator/protector. But what would happen if we began to imagine earth, nature, in an un-gendered way? What would happen if we refused these learned associations, dualisms, metaphors? We might begin to introduce previously unimagined images and concepts into our poetics, into our lives.

"The author is the poem's first reader." [5]

Language and ideas are our points of departure because they are, perhaps, the only elements that a poet is conscious of at the time she picks up the pen. At a subconscious level (and pardon the term *subconscious,* which I am first to concede is only marginally descriptive), the poem is materialized from thought to hand to pen. Consciously, the poet gropes for the image or metaphor that "feels" right, but she does not know what she is creating until it is done. At times, she doesn't know if it *is* done, or how to finish it, or even what to make of it.

That is why, to use a popular analogy, when we finally send a poem out into the world, like a child who has come of age, one whom we have schooled to the best of our abilities, we are sometimes amazed at the stories we hear told about it. Critics and university professors go about their business evaluating, interpreting, measuring, comparing, and placing into social and historical context our "child." If we as poets like what we hear, we beam with pride at what we most surely *deliberately* instilled in our prodigy. If we don't like what we hear, we are quick to question the authority (the critic) or to doubt the author (ourselves), wondering if we have failed at our endeavors. But the construction of poetics and prose, the development of ideas, is not the achievement of any one individual writer of her generation. Together, we create a tapestry. At times it is vibrant with color and movement, and during other periods it is dull and redundant, and still at others – just poorly done. No one of us is infallible, no one of us alone achieves the perfect confluence of elements in her individual creation.

Conscienticized poetics,

then, takes on everything and everyone at once – or at least, that is its mission. If we view the hierarchy of literary history as a pyramid, the mestiza writer is indeed situated at the bottom – with a Mexican scribe, European monk, a nineteenth-century British gentleman, and U.S. mogul publisher/editor today clambering on one another's backs all the way to the top. It is even difficult to persuade those in our lives who respect and trust us, one's male lover or sister (or even female lover, for that matter), that we are creating not only a new poetics with our own language but a new *concientización.*

I want to discuss three books that I believe are part of this new tapestry of *concientización:* Gloria Anzaldúa's *Borderlands/La Frontera: The New Mestiza,* Cherríe Moraga's *Loving in the War Years: Lo que nunca pasó por sus labios,* and my own first novel, *The Mixquiahuala Letters.*

"Her body had betrayed her."[6]

Borderlands requires close reading in order to appreciate its schema of ciphering and deciphering, its interweaving of a journey of self-understanding and the challenge of the writing process itself. "This book, then, speaks of my existence," Anzaldúa declares in her preface, and for her readers, *Borderlands* is a blood-curdling scream in the night.

In the early days of Chicano literature much attention was focused on writers who explored social conditions. There was a tendency to exclude from academic or critical purview those writers whose work and life did not fit comfortably within the campesino archetype. Gloria Anzaldúa, a Tex-Mex with a background as a field worker, would seem, then, the likely successor to the late Tomás Rivera. His book, *Y no se lo trago la tierra/And the Earth Did Not Part,* dealt with (from the "universal male perspective") the coming of age of a campesino, the role that achieved recognition as the "true" Chicano experience.

Yet, Anzaldúa's exceptional physical eruditions lead us into remote psychic labyrinths. The inner self is the one that Anzaldúa feels to be her truer representation, although her interior life is deeply bound to her physical being. Anzaldúa, we learn, began to menstruate at three months of age and underwent a hysterectomy as a young woman. And this rare and painful condition informs every aspect of her story, even as she speaks of her development as a poet and political activist.

Now, one of the strongest taboos in Judeo-Christian theology has to do with woman's menses. While in some cultures, such as the Native American, woman's blood is still considered potent and magical, the authors of the mythical texts of the Bible tell us that we are despicable and wanton *because* we bleed. During puberty, at the time a girl usually begins to menstruate, she is immediately separated from the world of men, from the world itself.

Thus, as her title suggests, Anzaldúa's vision originates in marginalization; this marginalism shapes her vision of the future. The masses of people who are forced to live on the borderlands of not only the dominant culture but their own culture as well, her story demonstrates, develop a sixth sense as a strategy for survival. Anzaldúa's inherent sense of difference, of "otherworldness," permits her to see and know what others cannot. Her spiritual informants are Mexican, especially Indian. Her guide is Coatlicue, multiple deity and mother of the gods of the Aztec pantheon. In Aztec culture, Coatlicue is both creator and destroyer, both exalted and denigrated. Anzaldúa, like other feminist historians of religion, believes that the Aztecs disarmed Coatlicue of her greatest endowments as mother goddess and reshaped her role according to the needs of the imperialist patriarchy.

I would venture to add that Anzaldúa's spiritual affinity for Coatlicue serves as a resonant reflection of this particular writer's desire for a disembodiment that would free her of tremendous physical and emotional anguish. "She felt shame for being abnormal. The bleeding distanced her from others. Her body had betrayed her," writes Anzaldúa.[7] Though specifically Anzaldúa's experience, this desperate desire to distance oneself from one's body is a feeling shared by many women. So many of us have been taught by the church and our Mexican traditions that our bodies are sin-ridden, untrustworthy, and in any event, do not belong to us.

While Anzaldúa struggles with the acknowledgment of her physical self, Cherríe Moraga celebrates the connection between her interior life and her sexuality. Anzaldúa declares her sexual preference to be a conscious decision: "*I made the choice to be queer.*"[8] Moraga, on the other hand, says of herself in her preface: "My mother's daughter who at ten years old knew she was queer. Queer to believe that God cared so much about me, he intended to see me burn in hell... Todavía soy bien catolica – filled with guilt, passion, and incense, and the inherent Mexican faith that there is meaning to nuestro sufrimiento en el mundo."[9]

For the political activist, sexuality has been the last frontier to liberate. Anzaldúa and Moraga pave the way for an open dialogue about lesbianism crucial to the understanding, affirmation, and recognition of our personal and public selves. Using autobiography, essays, journal entries, and poems, *Loving in the War Years,* like *Borderlands,* represents one woman's attempt to unravel the conflicts facing and within a conscienticized writer. In an essay entitled "A Long Line of Vendidas,"[10] Moraga explores the various influences that control the lives of poor and working-class women of color in the United States in order that we may begin to understand how we might respond, rather than simply react, to women of different classes and colors.

Moraga and Anzaldúa also grapple with the identity issues shared by those of "mixed blood." (This "mixed blood" concept is troublesome for me since, as Mexicans, we are already mestizos – of mixed blood – and perceived as such by both Mexican Indians and Native Americans, as well as the rest of society.) Moraga's Mexican-American mother is married to an "Anglo"; Moraga is neither "fully" Mexican nor "fully" Anglo. Did her mother betray her culture? Moraga is forced to ask. And yet, Moraga also wonders, has she betrayed her mother's culture by rejecting the mandated roles of wife and mother? Anzaldúa takes another tack. She feels she has no reason to question her *mestizaje,* and indeed, she reaffirms the long-denigrated blood of her Indian heritage, yet claims: "So *mamá, Raza,* how wonderful, *no tener que rendir cuentas a nadie.* I feel perfectly free to rebel and rail against my culture. I feel no betrayal on my part because, unlike Chicanas and other women of color who grew up white or who have only recently returned to their native cultural roots, I was totally immersed in mine."[11] In fact, none of us "tenemos que rendirle cuentas a nadie," but the unfortunate truth for us is that we are all, in one way or another, provoked to that end the instant we set pen to paper and declare an "I" or even the implied collective "i."

But of course, an Anglocized brown woman always walks a tightrope. Denial of her *mestizaje* does not change what she is. The point for *us,* in our identity analyses – through prose, poetry, and essays – is a self-evaluation that brings us closer to the truth about ourselves in an affirming way. Carmen Tafolla, in her publication on and for "la Chicana," *To Split a Human,* tells us as much:

Don't play "Will the Real Chicana Please Stand Up?" Much as we have heard different groups compete for "charter membership" in the Most Oppressed Club, Deep in the Barrio Bar, Pachuca of the Year Award, Mujer Sufrida ranks, and Double Minority Bingo, we must admit that membership dues must be continuously paid and advertised. It is irrelevant to try to justify how "Chicana" we are or to criticize others for being "Anglicized."[12]

If Moraga did not affirm her Chicana affiliations until she was an adult, she had long given consideration to the agonizing conflicts generated by the sexual proscriptions of "proper" Catholic society and her own desires. Her heightened awareness of the complexities of identity have helped Moraga (and Anzaldúa) to formulate a blend of feminism suitable to Chicanas, in which self-reflection (sharply attuned to the spiritual dimensions of Mexican-Indian culture), material analysis, and the revisioning of gender roles all carry equal weight.

"Releasing her readers from what could be referred to as her personal biases or subjective interpretations"

is how critic Alvina Quintana, in an unpublished paper, characterized my project in *The Mixquiahuala Letters.* Quintana's subtitle, "Working Toward the Construction of the Chicana Cultural and Feminist Identity," is a succinct description of the goal of my first novel. Quintana is referring to two deliberate ploys used to dissuade readers from interpreting the novel as autobiography. The first was a disclaimer at the beginning of the novel. The second was the construction of the novel as a series of letters, accompanied by my suggestion that the reader read them in a variety of orders, thus producing diverse interpretations beyond my narrative control.

Subversion of all implied truths

is necessary in order to understand the milieu of sexist politics that shape the lives of women. Moraga and Anzaldúa suggest this in their texts. Teresa, the main character of *Letters,* although she does not always see it, is also an insurgent.

Chicanalove

Teresa is a Chicana of working-class background. During a summer of study in Mexico she befriends Alicia, to whom the letters are addressed. Alicia is of mixed Latina/white middle-class background and a burgeoning feminist. Thus begins Teresa's confrontation with herself as a conventional married woman from a conservative Mexican background.

Whereas male writers may express criticism of institutions such as the church and state that have controlled our lives, they do so with the benefit of male privilege. That is, they write on the premise that even as brown men of little economic means, the world has been defined by other men for the benefit of men: as a discussion among men. On the other hand, women *know* they have little, if anything, to do with society's signs. That is why, I believe, it is equally painful and important to read of Anzaldúa's search to claim the "wound" that is the symbol of her existence, as it is to hear Teresa's self-admonishment as she writes to Alicia in Letter 32: "You had been angry that i never had problems attracting men. You pointed out the obvious, the big breasts, full hips and thighs, the kewpie doll mouth. Underlying the superficial attraction men felt toward me is what you did not recognize. i was docile."[13] We Mexican women so often go for the jugular in ourselves. Yet in Letter 24, we listen to her draw on the resources of folklore, Catholic mythology, and woman-identified beliefs to combat a negative energy force that threatens her and her friend. The gesture of wrapping a rosary around the fingers of her nonbeliever friend (which in this passage seems to infer that the source of danger may be male as much as it is supernatural) is a demonstration of her loyalty to woman. Throughout the book, Teresa is both protector and nurturer.

As Teresa evolves as a feminist, she is placed in the dangerous position of being viewed as a traitor to the male-dominated Chicano movement. (As Cherríe Moraga explains in her essay, "A Long Line of Vendidas," "The woman who defies her role as subservient to her husband, father, brother, or son by taking control of her own sexual destiny is purported to be a 'traitor to her race' by contributing to the 'genocide' of her people – whether or not she has children. In short, even if the defiant woman is *not* a lesbian."[14]) Ultimately, however, Teresa, like many other women characters in contemporary Chicana poetry and prose, is emphatic in her refusal to be viewed as Malinche, a betrayer of her race. In a section of *Loving in the War Years* entitled "La Malinchista," Moraga asserts that "Chicanos' refusal to look at our weaknesses as a people and a movement is, in the most profound sense, an act of self-betrayal. The Chicana lesbian bears the brunt of this betrayal, for it is she, the most visible manifestation of a woman taking control of her own sexual identity and destiny, who so severely challenges the anti-feminist Chicano/a."[15] "Not me sold out my people but they me," Anzaldúa declares.[16] In Letter 22, Teresa plays a verbal chess game with a Mexicano who hopes to have her in bed that night:

He began, "I think you are a 'liberal woman.' Am I correct?" [She replies]... "What you perceive as 'liberal' is my independence to choose what i do, with whom, and when. Moreover, it also means that i may choose not to do it, with anyone, ever."[17]

It may be said (and indeed, it has) that neither the character of Teresa nor the works of Anzaldúa and Moraga are representative of the thoughts or lives of the majority of women. Yet in the history of civilization, when can it be claimed that a poet is the typical citizen marching in step with the times? Poets and artists are visionaries. They are dreamers who weave stories out of their dreams, which *are* reflective of their times, but which most people do not, cannot, or refuse to see.

I see *Borderlands* and *Loving in the War Years,* and I would like to see my own novel, as meaningful examples of public risk-taking. The woman writer cannot fail to be aware of the possible consequences of her cultural interpretations and her claims as feminist, both within her own culture and within the dominant one in which her works are received. The ideological problem that the personal is political does not include a formal, theoretical solution. As Sigrid Weigel states in her essay, "Double Focus," "Love, pain and happiness, the desire to overcome personal boundaries and self-assertion cannot be distributed according to rules; that would result in the collapse of human relationships."[18]

Thus, in all three texts discussed here, the principal thematic concern is that of relationships or connections – with all their complexities: woman with man, woman with woman, woman as daughter, woman as mother, woman with religion, woman with Chicano/Mexicano culture, mestiza with Anglo society, among many others. As writers, as Chicanas, as conscienticized women, we must live with the very problems presented in our narratives. Each of us, as Weigel states, "must learn to voice the contradictions, to see them, to comprehend them, to live in and with them, also learn to gain strength from the rebellion against yesterday and from the anticipation of tomorrow."[19]

Alix Kates Shulman

The Taint

"Yuck!" said my friend when I asked her to tell me her reaction to feminist fiction.

I stare at her. Is she being provocative or sincere? A feminist activist and journalist who has no problem with either feminism or fiction, who claims she eagerly gobbles up feminist nonfiction as it rolls from the presses and is in fact writing her own book of it, my friend now goes even further, admitting she would probably avoid a novel presented to her as feminist. When she chooses fiction, she declares, she tries to select novels known to be delicious, moving, wonderful – and forget the politics – although naturally she would consider it a bonus if a good novel turned out to be feminist, too.

I'm shocked. Some of the most delicious, moving, and, yes, wonderful fiction I know seems to me patently feminist, from *Jane Eyre* to *The Golden Notebook* to *The Woman Warrior* (thinking only of novels written in English). What can be going on if even a self-proclaimed feminist like this friend has a prejudice against feminist fiction? What of the rest of the world? Am I – a veteran of the women's movement who has been writing fiction for more than two decades, including one novel about the rise of the contemporary women's movement – am I so out of touch that my friends must go out of their way to tell me?

Like every writer, I hope to be read sympathetically. Maybe I need to slow down and rethink this label before brazenly parading around in it in print. I feel fairly comfortable as a feminist and as a novelist; but as a feminist novelist? What's in a name? What is feminist fiction anyway? And who sez?

My first two novels were knocked or praised as feminist novels, but my second two, which personally seem to me equally feminist from the point of view of themes, controlling vision, audience, aim, author's politics, or any other approach I can think of, were each praised or knocked for *not* being so. For example, the late Anatole Broyard – no friend to feminism, fictional or otherwise – began his *New York Times* review of my third novel with: "After two rather trendy [read: feminist] novels, Alix Kates Shulman has written a selfless, careful, and satisfying book [read: not-feminist]."[1] Maybe a step up from being judged by my gender, but possibly only a sidestep. I'm confused.

As someone practiced in examining intellectual and political issues in company with her women friends, I decided to ask a few more people what they think about feminist fiction. Those I consulted include not only fellow fiction writers but also a few critics, an editor, a scientist, journalists, several academic feminists – all writers and word-people who, I figured, would be savvy about the meanings and implications of at least the key terms. In their own work these women write perceptively about women. All are deeply engaged in reading, teaching, writing about, encouraging women writers, rescuing forgotten women writers of the past from oblivion, and generally countering the entrenched, exclusionary, white male literary elite guard. How surprised I was to find them as hesitant as I in the face of my questions – some enthusiastic, but some suspicious, confused, wary, defensive, or even hostile. The very idea of feminist fiction is surprisingly charged.

Eventually, everyone calmed down and turned thoughtful. What is feminist fiction? Spiraling downward from the broadest to the narrowest descriptions, my friends' tentative answers included fiction that: demonstrates the authenticity of women's experience, centers on what it is to be a woman in culture, dramatizes the constraints on women under patriarchy, examines patriarchal institutions, is self-conscious about gender and traditional gender arrangements, challenges patriarchal modes of writing, portrays strong, independent women, embodies feminist attitudes, explores feminist themes, centers on feminist characters, aims to advance feminist causes, or is written by a feminist.

Whew! It seems that feminist fiction can be an oceanic category, large enough to encompass a good part of the totality of women's fiction, or a deep puddle, including only a handful of works by a select group of self-proclaimed feminist writers whose works are saturated with feminist consciousness or portray feminist life – as, say, gay fiction reflects gay consciousness and portrays gay life.

Is this because the winds of deconstruction have left all general categories and identities notoriously shaken? When such formerly seaworthy terms as *woman*, *feminist*, and *fiction* are wobbling like rowboats in a hurricane, the term *feminist fiction* must be at least as unstable. But I suspect there's another reason. For even if we could provisionally agree that the vessels *feminist* and *fiction* are sound enough for this short trip, some fiction writers who confess to being feminists would still balk at climbing into the vessel *feminist fiction* with their treasured, vulnerable manuscripts. I sympathize. Who wants to capsize in shark-infested waters?

The first novelist I consult asks warily, "Feminist fiction – what exactly do you mean?" – as if I were setting a trap. With one breath she wants to be invited along on the trip, even resents a critic who once complained in print that her fiction was insufficiently political. But with her next breath she confides, "Frankly, I think people are turned off by the whole category. If they [or did she say *I*?] read a feminist novel it's *despite* not *because* it's feminist."

Again! Only this time it's a fiction writer saying it. "Really?" I ask, registering my surprise as I think of such feminist favorites as *The Color Purple* and *To the Lighthouse*. "People are turned off?"

And yet, I can't be all that surprised since I must admit that when strangers ask me what kind of novels I write, I don't always volunteer straight out, "feminist novels" – not unless I know who's asking, and why. Sometimes when it's Open Season on Ladies' Lit and the critics are out there pillorying feminists as polemicists ("that busy battalion of American women novelists who have been flooding the market with their crudely polemical morality tales of liberation," runs a typical tirade), I wouldn't mind slipping quietly away like some of my writing friends who leave town when their books are coming out to avoid seeing reviews – though in fact, as an activist, I feel duty bound to stand and fight. On the other hand, when I am credited with changing someone's life, whether blamed (as by the Ohio man who wrote that it was my fault his wife took off with the baby and left him after reading one of my novels) or thanked (as in the frequent letters from women telling the stories of their lives), then I'll wear the label in the same spirit with which I wear one of my hundred political buttons to a demonstration – slightly uncomfortable about condensing my impossibly complicated views down to a phrase, but proud to lend my body to the cause. Since my own voice talks on in my books, I'm willing to submerge it temporarily in the unified roar of the crowd for the sake of something I believe in.

"Why do you suppose it turns people off?" I ask. But this question too is slightly disingenuous. In the unending game of Naming-the-Despised no one wants to be tagged It at the moment the music stops. Everyone scrambles for a safe seat. So, in another area, the acceptable name has passed from Person of Color to Black to Negro and back to Black and Person of Color again. I know perfectly well that whereas not so long ago many women writers bristled at being considered "women writers," dreading the label as limiting, disparaging, even dismissive, now, when, thanks to feminism, gender is no longer a legitimate category of dismissal in the arts, the new bugaboo seems to be the label "feminist writer," even among women who may no longer mind being called women writers or, for that matter, feminists.

Why?

Too – well – *political.*

"Don't you read feminist fiction, then?" I continue.

"Not if I can help it," replies my friend unabashedly. "Unless I happen to know it's good art."

I look at her, a sometime feminist who has occasionally expressed regret that she missed out on the high times of the movement. Why this presumption that feminist fiction is bad art? Badass maybe, but bad art? Not that I haven't read my share of preachy, pompous, dull, sentimental, haranguing, or unconvincing fiction, but I can't say it's been especially feminist. Assuming that good art and bad occur in feminist novels in about the same proportion as in any other type, I want on the contrary to presume for this discussion that we're talking only about the good-art ones. Why bother with the other kind at all? A serious discussion of any genre will involve the best, not the worst, of the type. I consider proposing that maybe a feminist novel is a novel that moves or delights one's feminist bones, which would mean it must be "good art." But I doubt my friend would buy it.

And then I see it overhead clinging to the wall, that scaly green lizard, Politics versus Art, looking down on us with its beady eyes and flicking its lightning tongue. I'm astonished at my friends – political and engaged! – for still harboring that peculiarly American presumption that politics and art don't mix. Or that when they do mix, what comes out is poison propaganda. As if feminist fiction meant putting the needs of feminism over those of fiction; as if feminism were more narrowly ideological than visionary; as if there could be fiction without political implications; as if one invariably had to choose. Why is it that in other countries novelists (particularly celebrated male ones) are expected to explore political questions in their work and express opinions on every political subject without compromising their art, are even looked to as spokespeople, but not here in the United States? Here, it's widely presumed that you must choose either art or politics, not both. Given the suspicion surrounding the artist who dreams of political consequence, this very presumption may itself produce constricting pressure on artistic integrity equal to the presumed pressure produced by political commitment. Alas, most fiction writers I know meekly, if regretfully, accept the necessity of the choice and choose the safety of art – particularly if the politics in question are feminist.

Because, let's face it, feminism – initially perceived as daring, sexy, rebellious, gutsy, new – is now suspected in certain circles of being tainted, like food that's been around too long: even if it's still all right, better not take a chance on it, better be safe and toss it out. I recognize the distaste in my friend's response, her fear of having her work contaminated by association with two potent contaminants, women and politics, both implied by feminism, and to her mind inviting dismissal of her work as trivial, as ideological, as boring. If it's feminist, she intimates, it won't be considered art.

How did this dissociation happen? Sadly I recognize the trivializing taint as the very one that has long infected everything associated with women, from motherhood to makeup, that feminism was founded to eliminate. I believe this is why many women, particularly the young, even those with fairly feminist politics, shy away from the term *feminist*: it is too closely associated with – oh, you know – women. What irony! After its bold strike for wholeness and health, feminism, instead of cleansing women of the taint, as it set out to do, itself became tainted, until now, again, fiction writers like my friend, ambitious for as large an audience as possible, avoid an association of their work with that compromising parochial word.

(If this avoidance is much less true of critics and academics than of artists, it's probably because they are not only permitted but required to deal in ideas, while artists, amazingly, are not. The highest praise T. S. Eliot could give Henry James was that he had "a mind so fine no idea could violate it." There are quite a few excellent journals devoted to feminist theory, hardly any to feminist fiction. Besides, some feminist critics have tenure.)

The troublesome suspicion between feminist art and politics, writers and activists, has actually gone both ways. Back in the early days of the women's liberation movement, it was widely thought that anyone who wrote about the new feminist ideas, especially for a large audience, was probably "ripping off the movement" for personal gain. As part of the debate over individualism within feminism, some people held that since the ideas of the movement belong equally to everyone, not just to those who write them down, any writing feminist ought to leave her work unsigned. Others went further and thought that since no one has a right to speak for anyone else (yes, feminists were saying that way back then!), and writers are often treated by the world as spokespeople, writers should keep (contradiction in terms) quiet and not write at all. Kate Millett, Robin Morgan, and Ellen Willis themselves did not escape the ire (and envy?) of the movement. This peculiar historical anomaly seems almost incomprehensible today; who in the movement would dream of criticizing Mary Gordon, say, or Barbara Ehrenreich for publishing under their own names? Yet at a time when, because of the encouragement of the movement, many women were for the first time developing the confidence and analytic skills necessary to write, hardly any feminist writer I know escaped a certain uneasiness about publishing feminist work. This was true even of fiction, though fiction aroused less suspicion in the movement than did theory – perhaps because on the surface fiction seems more personal, idiosyncratic, and to ideologues even frivolous.

But this peculiar idea that if your writing embodies feminism you can't be a loyal feminist seems to me precisely as absurd as the complementary notion that if your writing embodies feminism you can't be a good fiction writer. Isn't it obvious that your best writing will embody what you know best and feel most passionate about? – that if you have feminist values, your fiction will have feminist values, too? Why would you ever have to choose?

Just as I was beginning to worry that I might be the only fiction writer I know who isn't nervous about being described as a feminist one, another writer, one whose large and devoted following is not particularly associated with feminism, outdid me in her confident embrace of the term. "Yes!" she responded to the question, Do you consider yourself a feminist writer? – almost before it was out of my mouth. Far from skulking about in fear of the *F*-word, she takes the largest view of feminist fiction, large enough to include not only her own work (which she twinklingly allows was feminist even before there was a movement) but the work of certain writers she most admires, including some who decline the label, like Christa Wolf and Doris Lessing. "But that doesn't mean their work isn't feminist," argues my friend. Revered by men and women alike, and heaped with literary honors, her access to readers is not endangered. "I'd argue with them. I'd say their work is definitely feminist, whether they say so or not."

("And I'd say *her* work, though wonderful, is *not* feminist, no matter what *she* says," appended another friend, a critic, *sotto voce*.)

So – some say they aren't who are, some say they are who aren't, and some aren't saying. Overhearing us, another writer enters the discussion to insist that the very question is counterproductive, that any representation of the writer's work is misrepresentation. Instead, she insists, people should just read the books, allowing each fiction to fall where it may, like Pick-Up-Sticks, and the hell with what *ist* it is. More anxious than the others I've been talking to, younger and less successful, her voice is unusually soft for this crowd. Not that she would deny her feminism, she says in an aside, no more than she would deny being Jewish; still, what's the point in being "ghettoized"? She's against all labels, which, she says, are always used against us.

An example of the power of names leaps from my memory, and I have to admit they do have their lasting effects. In 1969 I wrote an article called "A Marriage Agreement," which proposed, in a set of principles and a flexible schedule, that men and women share housework and child care equally. First published in the feminist journal *Up From Under*, the controversial piece soon stimulated wide debate as it was reprinted in *New York Magazine*, the premiere issue of *Ms.*, *Life*, *Redbook*, and various anthologies from sociology textbooks to a casebook on contract law. The call for domestic equality was so threatening to middle-class male privilege that the article was attacked by, among others, Russell Baker, S. I. Hayakawa, and Norman Mailer, who wrote in *The Prisoner of Sex* that "he could love a woman and she might even sprain her back before a hundred sinks of dishes in a month, but he would not be happy to help her if his work should suffer, no, not unless her work was as valuable as his own," concluding that "if he were obliged to have a roommate, he would pick a man."[2] But in the course of the debate a peculiar thing happened: with increasing frequency, reprints of and articles on my "Marriage Agreement" referred to it not as an "Agreement," as I had titled it, but as a "Contract." Even when, in exchange for my permission to reprint, I got it in writing that it would be called an agreement, not a contract, it was still called a contract, suggesting a legally enforceable and adversarial document rather than a voluntary and friendly one. The label "contract" undermined the spirit, and thus the effect, of the agreement. Even now, when the ideal of domestic equality, though seldom practiced, is widely embraced, the notion of a contract, as against an agreement, is usually greeted with distaste. The name matters.

Finally, I consult a feminist critic I much admire, a smart, avid reader and teacher of fiction. She dismisses the large questions and definitions as "no longer interesting" following upon fifteen years of sophisticated, often brilliant, feminist literary criticism. Instead, she proposes that the smallest and least mushy category, the most neglected and thereby the most interesting one, is Feminist Fiction with capital *F*'s – that is, fiction by political women for whom the contemporary women's movement was one of the major experiences of their lives, an experience leaving its traces in virtually all their thought and work. This, she contends, is probably what most people think of when they hear the term Feminist Fiction, anyway: politically engaged fiction. I wonder: is this the reason for the purported turnoff reported by my informants? For though feminism is everywhere alive, the movement is, at least in the United States, quiescent. Much more than feminist ideas, which turn up everywhere nowadays, it's the movement that currently suffers image trouble.

Together we review the fiction we know and come up with a short list of Feminist Works, including books by Margaret Atwood, Angela Carter, Marilyn French, Ursula K. Le Guin, Maxine Hong Kingston, Marge Piercy, Joanna Russ, Jane Rule, Alice Walker, Fay Weldon, Monique Wittig – but I won't go on. Some of these writers are acquaintances and might be distressed by my naming names. Better to risk their feeling slighted at being left off the list than exposed by being put on it; they may be grateful to me later. I suspect that even they (even I?) would prefer to be considered not by their gender or their politics but simply as writers, if that were only possible. One of the advantages of fiction over theory, after all, is its unarguable particularity, with all characters, events, ideas, and opinions drawn solely from the imagination, where any resemblance to others is purely coincidental. No forced outings in my article! I'll protect my sources and let you each compile your own list.

Still, the list my friend and I compiled seemed surprisingly short. Why? Perhaps because revolutions, social or political, may be just too noisy and intense to give rise to an extensive literature, which must be created in hours and years of reflective calm. From experience I know well that activists' energies are directed outward, writers' energies inward. It's probably as easy to record a revolution from the midst of it when everyone is working at fever pitch as it is to write a novel standing in a rush-hour subway train. Plus, as Lenin said on the eve of the October Revolution, laying aside the incomplete manuscript of his *State and Revolution*, "it is more pleasant and useful to go through 'the experience of the revolution' than to write about it."

But Lenin was not a novelist. And not every artist transformed by the great social movements of her time is confounded by the oppressive either/or of art and politics. In *Meridian*, her feminist novel about the civil rights movement, Alice Walker offers another possibility. Speaking in the voice of the artist, she writes:

Perhaps it will be my part to walk behind the real revolutionaries – those who know they must spill blood in order to help the poor and the black . . . And when they stop to wash off the blood . . . I will come forward and sing from memory songs they will need once more to hear. For it is

*the song of the people, transformed by the experiences of each generation, that holds them to-
gether, and if any part of it is lost the people suffer and are without soul.*[3]

In the end, it was not one of my literary friends but a well-read scientist, Naomi
Weisstein, who came up with the description of feminist fiction I plan to live with.
(A longtime feminist working in another field, she doesn't worry about the consequences of publicity in this one, so I dare to reveal her name.) Sensible, expansive,
and illuminating, her description allows me to include on my list a wide range of
writers I admire, from the past as well as the present, without unduly stretching
the term. Here it is:

*Feminist fiction is fiction that does not admire patriarchy or accept its ideology. Nor does it
portray its male characters as naturally more exciting, more important, or more valuable
than its female characters. In addition, the female characters are valued enough to be presented in their full humanity, whether they be villains or heroes, and the sympathetic female
characters are neither necessarily nice nor necessarily beautiful. In this way, feminist fiction
challenges the patriarchal belief in the fixed and eternal nature of men and women.*

You get the drift. While I would probably add the qualification that the work be
centrally concerned with the condition of being woman, Naomi's generous, if negative, description leaves the imagination free of restrictions and is clear enough to
counter the prejudice I keep bumping into. Who could object? True, it is one of the
looser ones; but, then, one of the most hopeful aspects of the women's movement
is its struggle to be widely inclusive. In each of its particulars, Naomi's description
closely resembles the vision that inspired me to become both a feminist and a novelist in the first place. Without that vision, instead of soberly declaring myself a
feminist novelist whatever the consequences (for I can't recant and refuse to
choose), I would probably still be playing the game of Name Tag and scrambling
like crazy when the music stops.

Alice Walker

The Right to Life

WHAT CAN THE WHITE MAN SAY TO THE BLACK WOMAN?

Pro-Choice/Keep Abortion Legal Rally
The Mayflower Hotel, Washington, D.C.
April 8, 1989

What is of use in these words I offer in memory and recognition of our common mother.
And to my daughter.

What can the white man say to the black woman?

For four hundred years he ruled over the black woman's womb.

Let us be clear. In the barracoons and along the slave shipping coasts of Africa, for more than twenty generations, it was he who dashed our babies' brains out against the rocks.

What can the white man say to the black woman?

For four hundred years he determined which black woman's children would live or die.

Let it be remembered. It was he who placed our children on the auction block in cities all across the eastern half of what is now the United States, and listened to and watched them beg for their mothers' arms, before being sold to the highest bidder and dragged away.

What can the white man say to the black woman?

We remember that Fannie Lou Hamer, a poor sharecropper on a Mississippi plantation, was one of twenty-one children; and that on plantations across the South black women often had twelve, fifteen, twenty children. Like their enslaved mothers and grandmothers before them, these black women were sacrificed to the profit the white man could make from harnessing their bodies and their children's bodies to the cotton gin.

What can the white man say to the black woman?

We see him lined up, on Saturday nights, century after century, to make the black mother, who must sell her body to feed her children, go down on her knees to him.

Let us take note:

He has not cared for a single one of the dark children in his midst, over hundreds of years.

Where are the children of the Cherokee, my great grandmother's people?

Gone.

Where are the children of the Blackfoot?
Gone.
Where are the children of the Lakota?
Gone.

Of the Cheyenne?
Of the Chippewa?
Of the Iroquois?
Of the Sioux?
Of the Akan?
Of the Ibo?
Of the Ashanti?
Of the Maori and the Aborigine?

Where are the children of "the slave coast" and Wounded Knee?

We do not forget the forced sterilizations and forced starvations on the reservations, here as in South Africa. Nor do we forget the smallpox-infested blankets Indian children were given by the Great White Fathers of the United States Government.

What has the white man to say to the black woman?

When we have children you do everything in your power to make them feel unwanted from the moment they are born. You send them to fight and kill other dark mothers' children around the world. You shove them onto public highways into the path of oncoming cars. You shove their heads through plate glass windows. You string them up and string them out.

What has the white man to say to the black woman?

From the beginning, you have treated all dark children with absolute hatred.

Thirty million African children died on the way to the Americas, where nothing awaited them but endless toil and the crack of a bullwhip. They died of a lack of food, of lack of movement in the holds of ships. Of lack of friends and relatives. They died of depression, bewilderment, and fear.

What has the white man to say to the black woman?

Let us look around us: Let us look at the world the white man has made for the black woman and her children.

It is a world in which the black woman is still forced to provide cheap labor in the form of children, for the factory farms and on the assembly lines of the white man.

It is a world into which the white man dumps every foul, person-annulling drug he smuggles into Creation.

It is a world where many of our babies die at birth, or later of malnutrition, and where many more grow up to live lives of such misery they are forced to choose death by their own hands.

What has the white man to say to the black woman, and to all women and children everywhere?

Let us consider the depletion of the ozone; let us consider homelessness and the nuclear peril; let us consider the destruction of the rain forests – in the name of the almighty hamburger. Let us consider the poisoned apples and the poisoned water and the poisoned air, and the poisoned earth.

And that all of our children, because of the white man's assault on the planet, have a possibility of death by cancer in their almost immediate future.

What has the white male lawgiver to say to any of us? Those of us who love life too much to willingly bring more children into a world saturated by death.

Abortion, for many women, is more than an experience of suffering beyond anything most men will ever know, it is an act of mercy, and an act of self-defense.

To make abortion illegal, again, is to sentence millions of women and children to miserable lives and even more miserable deaths.

Given his history, in relation to us, I think the white man should be ashamed to attempt to speak for the unborn children of the black woman. To force us to have children for him to ridicule, drug, turn into killers and homeless wanderers is a testament to his hypocrisy.

What can the white man say to the black woman?

Only one thing that the black woman might hear.

Yes, indeed, the white man can say, your children have the right to life. Therefore I will call back from the dead those thirty million who were tossed overboard during the centuries of the slave trade. And the other millions who died in my cotton fields and hanging from my trees.

I will recall all those who died of broken hearts and broken spirits, under the insult of segregation.

I will raise up all the mothers who died exhausted after birthing twenty-one children to work sunup to sundown on my plantation. I will restore to full health all those who perished for lack of food, shelter, sunlight, and love; and from my inability to recognize them as human beings.

But I will go even further:

I will tell you black woman, that I wish to be forgiven the sins I commit daily against you and your children. For I know that until I treat your children with love, I can never be trusted by my own. Nor can I respect myself.

And I will free your children from insultingly high infant mortality rates, short life spans, horrible housing, lack of food, rampant ill health. I will liberate them from the ghetto. I will open wide the doors of all the schools and the hospitals and businesses of society to your children. I will look at your children and see, not a threat, but a joy.

I will remove myself as an obstacle in the path that your children, against all odds, are making toward the light. I will not assassinate them for dreaming dreams and offering new visions of how to live. I will cease trying to lead your children, for I can see I have never understood where I was going. I will agree to sit quietly for a century or so, and meditate on this.

This is what the white man can say to the black woman.

We are listening.

Sarah Schulman

Why I Fear the Future

W. H. Auden wrote, "Not one of my poems ever saved one Jew."

When the AIDS activist organization ACT UP first began, we believed that hard work, education, diligent activism, and creativity would produce solutions to the AIDS crisis. We did not anticipate the extent to which the government would obstruct our every initiative. With 106,000 AIDS deaths as of June 1991, this nation still does not have a needle exchange or condom distribution program, explicit safe sex material, protection for people with AIDS, adequate health services, or an efficient and humane research procedure. The obvious conclusion I draw is that the government does not want to end the AIDS crisis. As poet Kenny Fries says, we know that Silence equals Death, but we have just recently realized that Voice does not equal Life.

As I was sitting in the New York University Medical Center, visiting my friend Phil Zwickler, I ran down a checklist in my mind of all the reasons why we massage the feet of dying people. Because they have been in bed for a long, long time and have poor circulation. Because they need to be touched, but chest catheters and IVs get in the way. Besides, they can't sit up. Because, by rubbing their feet, you can sit on the edge of their beds and they can see you. Because you can talk to them and touch them at the same time and they don't have to move. Because you can take one last look.

At Phil Zwickler's memorial service, I really had to smile because the guy was such a control queen that he had planned how we should memorialize him. In fact, there was even a moment when we had to sit and listen to Phil's favorite songs. He made us listen to Steely Dan. The food afterwards was coffee and Danish. When his mother stood up to speak, I was really worried because that is everybody's nightmare – to die and your mother has the last word. But actually it turned out that she really knew who he was. So often, at these services, the parents do not really know their child.

Phil Zwickler was a filmmaker, and one of his films, *Rights and Reactions*, was about the passage of the Gay Rights Bill in New York City in 1986. The bill finally passed after years of humiliating defeat. As I was watching the footage he chose for his own memorial, I suddenly realized, for the first time, that I had lived as an adult homosexual in a city without a gay rights bill. In fact, I was thrown out of two restaurants on two separate occasions in the early eighties for kissing women. They could do that then because there was no gay rights bill. Sitting there, at Phil's service, I suddenly started to cry, half for Phil and half for me, because they threw me out.

This brings us to Tompkins Square Park, from which three hundred homeless people have been thrown out. I live one block from the park, and my neighborhood is currently under police occupation. The city is spending $100,000 a day, in the middle of its worst fiscal crisis, to keep homeless people out of the park. So now there are police everywhere. They're in every coffee shop. They're in every store. They're talking on every pay phone. When you stand on the corner waiting for a light, you're standing in front of the police. When you run into a friend and have a chat on the street, it takes place right in front of the police. In the meantime they do let people into the park if they are going to play basketball, walk their dog, or take their kids to the playground. But if you are homeless, you can't go in. The definition of who constitutes The Public is rapidly changing. Now homeless people – that is, people with no private space, people who must live in public space – are being told that their homelessness is their *private* problem. That they are no longer part of the "general population." What is permissible in the public sphere is also shrinking. Women who want abortion information can't get it in federally funded clinics *even if they ask*. Women who are nude dancers now have to wear pasties (which are far more lascivious than nudity). The court has decided that it is really the nipple that is obscene. *The New York Times* reports that AIDS has not spread into the heterosexual, non-drug-using world and therefore is not a concern for the "general population."

But so many of my friends are dying.

I'm thirty-two years old. I read the obituary page first.

Recently ACT UP held a demonstration at the United Nations. We're asking the World Health Organization for disaster relief services. We're asking for food, shelter, and medical supplies. There's a small park across the street from the U.N. where people are allowed to demonstrate. But the police would not let us walk on the sidewalk to get to that spot. They began to arrest ACT UP members simply for standing on the sidewalk. Usually we *try* to get arrested, to attract media attention, since the deaths themselves are not newsworthy enough for them. But this time, people got arrested for no reason. We had joined the ranks of the nonpublic: the people who are not allowed to use the sidewalks, not allowed to go to the park, not allowed to discuss abortion, not allowed to show their nipples. We are on the losing side of the great divide.

My friend calls from San Francisco. He can't walk or swallow.

I don't know which issue is more significant for gay writing – how we are to represent AIDS in our literature or the fact that so many writers are dying. I cross my fingers hoping that George Bush will die of a heart attack soon. I can't imagine any other scenario that would actually get rid of him. I know it's humiliating to be reduced to crossing my fingers, but I have to try everything I can.

At the Lambda Literary Awards, Allen Barnett, author of *The Body and Its Dangers*, arrived in a wheelchair from Co-op Care to receive his award. He announced that he had picked out his tie to match his Kaposi's sarcoma. Then he took his Hickman catheter out of his chest and started talking into it as though it were a microphone.

At that point I realized that when I first began to comprehend the enormity of what was happening to my community, I anticipated only that we would lose many people. But I did not understand that those of us who remain, that is to say, those of us who will continue to lose and lose, would also lose our ability to mourn fully. I feel that I have been dehumanized by the sheer quantity of death, so that now I can no longer fully grieve each person – how much I love each one, and how much I miss each one.

However, knowing that no large social gains can be won in this period, I still remain politically active. I do this because small victories are meaningful in individual lives. I do this because I don't want to be complicit with a future in which people in need will die and everyone else will be condemned to a vicious banality. But also because I believe that in long, hard struggles there is a value to what Gary Indiana calls the "politics of repetition." Even if it takes all our energy, I still intend to do everything I can to at least keep these issues alive.

Lauretta Ngcobo

African Motherhood: Fact and Fiction

A girl born in Africa is born to fulfill a role. She is made aware of the destiny awaiting her and is prepared from the earliest age possible for motherhood. However well she may be loved, her rights within the family are limited compared to those of her brother. A daughter does not belong to her parents as a son does. She is constantly made aware (perhaps playfully) that she is "on her way out." (It is significant that in some of the Bantu languages the word *marriage* is synonymous with the word *journey*.) In short, the time spent with the family she has been born into is time spent being prepared for the central role in her life: the future role of wife to a man from another family; the role of obedient daughter-in-law to his parents; and most important, the role of mother to her husband's children. Many young girls eagerly anticipate their marriage and a place where they will finally belong. This is double jeopardy, for they will never really belong anywhere.

In African societies, children – particularly male children – are essential "human capital." Marriage among Africans therefore is essentially an institution enabling the control and management of procreation. (This is true in most other cultures as well, of course. The notion that a woman fully expresses her "womanhood" through marriage and motherhood is not restricted to my continent.) The basis of marriage is the transfer of woman's fertility to the husband's family group. To facilitate this transfer of fertility, a dowry must be paid. The dowry, or "bride price," does not, as some think, symbolize the buying of the wife; it represents, more accurately, the claim on any children she will bear. The dowry not only gives exclusive sexual rights to the man, but also provides a means of social control over the children.[1] Finally, the dowry cements the new relationship between the two families. It should be noted that there is little said about the young couple and their relationship to each other after marriage. The notion of love and the public expression of personal emotions is confined to the courtship period. Marriage is a relationship between two groups, not merely two people.

The all-important need for children has led to the institutionalization of motherhood through fertility rites, taboos, and religious beliefs. Central to many African belief systems is that there are three states of human existence, all equally important: the land of the living, the land of the unborn, and the land of the ancestors and the dead. The land of the unborn and the land of the ancestors and the dead make strong claims on the land of the living. It is a man's sacred obligation to "immortalize" his ancestors; failure to do so would be considered an unbearable shame. The "blame" for childlessness is, then, shifted to women. Belief has it that the children of any given family are always "out there," waiting for mothers to come and rescue them from oblivion, to bring them into the land of the living. In cases of childlessness, community members do not think of sharing or soothing the couple's or woman's disappointment; instead, they hear the cries of the unborn children indicting the woman who does not come to "rescue" them.

Motherhood is a powerful institution in African societies. But women as mothers must exercise their power from a peripheral position. In her husband's home, the woman soon discovers that she is another kind of "second-class citizen" —the title, by the way, of a powerful novel by Nigerian writer Buchi Emecheta. A woman in the community of her in-laws does not move in to assert her independence or find her place of centrality. Instead, she finds herself reduced to a permanent state of dependence and estrangement. She will always be an outsider among her husband's people, always the first suspected when things go wrong. She will work hard and long to help provide food for the family. She will remain marginalized until old age, at which time, as a senior wife, she will be empowered to exercise authority over the younger women and train them in the art of walking the tightrope.

From the earliest stages of a marriage, there is a conscious effort to distance the wife from her husband. Men and women live quite segregated lives. In most societies they will not eat together, and, as among the Bemba of Zambia, young girls are taught that a "good wife" does not talk to her husband much. This distancing of the young bride will affect all aspects of her life. In some societies, like the Nguni, she will never be called by her own name. She might be called by her father's name—"the daughter of so and so"—or she may simply be called "the bride" until she has her first child. Then she will be referred to as "the mother of so and so"—thus her identity is always determined through her father or her child. Her alienation is further intensified by many taboos. For instance, depending on the society, there are complicated patterns of behavior demanded toward each member of the new family. She will call none of them by name (except the very youngest), sometimes not even her husband. She might call him "the brother of so and so," referring to his youngest brother or sister, until she has his first child; then she will call him "the father of so and so." She cannot call her father-in-law by name and must avoid contact with him as much as possible. In extreme cases, she is expected to avoid using any words that sound like his name.

A young woman works hard to contribute to the economic well-being of her husband's family. In spite of her great economic input, however, she has neither property rights nor rights of inheritance; nor can she give legacies to anyone. She cannot own land or cattle, nor can she participate in debates or negotiations concerning property. As a "minor," she cannot be party to a legal action, but must be represented by her father or brother or husband or son. Should a wife rebel against her husband, she runs the risk of losing land rights that belong to her husband, land that is her only means of survival. She may try going it alone, as a single woman, but there are proportionately very few jobs for women in African cities. (This is particularly true in South Africa under the political system of Apartheid.) Polygamy is still common in Africa. Relations among co-wives are seldom wholesome. Rivalry and insecurity abound. In addition, the arrival of any new daughter-in-law introduces an added strain in the relationship between the mother and her son. Mother and wife see themselves as competing for his love and income. Yet between mothers and daughters-in-law there is also an ever-present awareness that the two have a lot in common; that they will always be outsiders in the family lineage of their husbands. They share disadvantages; thus the young can always learn from the older woman. The son/husband is aware of the necessity for a healthy learning relationship between the two women, for he knows that soon, in her turn, his young wife will be fighting to secure her own children's position in the family structure. The whole relationship is governed by power struggle and intrigue. In all this, fathers-in-law keep their distance, since they are secure in terms of their power. As a result, they are well liked on all sides.

I have here painted a grim (but, I think, accurate) picture of the everyday life of African women, one which I have tried to capture in my novel, *And They Didn't Die*. However, I would like to qualify somewhat my above remarks by pointing out that the systems of oppression that govern the lives of African women are not monolithic. In fact, many African societies combine matriarchal and patriarchal practices. Although a matriarchal system by no means ensures any real social or political power for women, it does grant them more decision-making power in community and family life. For instance, among the Ashanti of Ghana, a woman enjoys inheritance and property rights, and older women are consulted in the making of community decisions. Although matriarchy has been undermined over the centuries by the dual onslaught of capitalism and patriarchy, historically the transition has been/is being accomplished only with tremendous struggle. Many African cultures support private ownership of land within a patriarchal structure, but the private ownership of property is incompatible with matriarchal law, which favors instead the communal ownership of land. Colonialists, of course, supported private ownership, reinforcing patriarchal tendencies and working to the disadvantage of the customary rights of women.

We see these complex relationships and power struggles among family members, between women and women, women and men, children and parents, reflected in much of the literature by contemporary African novelists, male and female. The character of Tsitsi in Patrick Chakaipa's novel *Garandichauya* is the "ideal wife." When her husband deserts her for another woman, she goes home and waits for almost a lifetime. The character Vida in Giles Kuimba's *Rurimi Inyoka* sticks to her post, too, even when she is taunted and maltreated by her mother-in-law. She remains reasonable and amiable even under the curse of childlessness, offering to leave her husband if she is to blame, but to stay with him if he is the culprit. MaNdlovu in Lenah Mazibuko's *Umzenzi Kakhalelwa* suffers the loss of all her children in infancy, but stays on in the home of her in-laws without complaining, working hard and acting as mediator between her husband and her mother-in-law. These characters opt for the path of martyrdom for lack of any alternatives; women who fail as "good wives" are treated very harshly.

Male authors are merciless against a woman character who fails to conform to traditional expectations. These characters commonly die for their mistakes. A quick review of the literature reveals that the most dreaded type of "difficult" woman is the domineering one, for instance, Julia in Dambudzo Marechera's *The House of Hunger*. The narrator of the novella describes her thus: "She snorted. Her painted fingernails gleamed like claws around her cigarette. She was probably thinking I would be easy prey; it saddened me to think that she had become one of those persons who depend for their sanity solely on the measure of their claws. The measure of the stains left behind." Charles Mungoshi's short stories often feature this type of woman, drawn larger-than-life as she overpowers her husband in both word and deed. In "Who Will Stop the Dark?" Zakeo's mother is one such woman; her dominance over Zakeo's father is a source of embarrassment for the young man. Yet the frustrations of a woman cursed with a feeble husband who, nevertheless, wields all the power, has all the power to change things, but will not or cannot, is understandable. Traditional belief structures did not conceive of "weak" men and strong women; or that, should a husband be weak, a powerful woman may easily drift into another relationship. Contemporary African male novelists, however, often plot such a narrative, then have the added pleasure of writing about the family dramas of adultery. And in African societies, the adulterous wife is more loathsome than the murderess.

The women most likely to be treated with admiration in African literature written by men are widows. It is interesting to investigate why this is so. The older widow in African culture may well have reached the point where she is content to remain at her in-laws, to assist her grown sons in sustaining their hold against newcomers and outsiders in the male-dominated power structure. In return for her help, she is looked after by those sons and their children. It is from this vantage point that a lot of books written by male writers offer us another one of their "positive" images of African womanhood: an older widow, propped high on a pedestal of power, virtue, conformity, success.

Much African literature simply recapitulates the sexist and misogynist ideologies that maintain the oppression of African women. Female characters incur vicious condemnation and punishment for their "crimes" – adultery, promiscuity, disobedience, a domineering nature – whereas male characters learn by their experiences, never die for their mistakes. Thus, the anguished cry of Nnu Ego in Emecheta's *The Joys of Motherhood*: "God, when will you create a woman who will be fulfilled in herself, a full human being, not anybody's appendage?"

But a number of African writers, primarily women, have rejected the strictures of such a punitive literature. Their writing has begun to address the problems confronted daily by African women – those of *self*-definition and *self*-determination. The married woman and the widowed woman, even the divorced woman, are traditionally defined by their relationship to men: father, husband, son. And so we African women writers are creating other representations of our sisters/ourselves, accurate and just portrayals of our everyday life in which the labor and achievements of women are recognized, their martyrdom and victimization condemned. In place of a punitive literature we are creating a liberating literature. We speak of mothers and wives, yes, but also of women who are breadwinners, teachers, farmers, nurses, politicians. These portrayals will in time help us to focus on the values that our societies should uphold and preserve. But the structures and attitudes that cripple us must be done away with, for in the context of our African struggles for freedom – freedom from imperialism, neocolonialism, and other forms of economic and racist oppression – we cannot condone the extremes of repression that our men have been willing to put us through. We must struggle against patriarchal power within the family and society.

Maxine Hong Kingston

The Novel's Next Step

I'm going to give you a head start on the book that somebody ought to be working on. The hands of the clock are minutes away from nuclear midnight. And I am slow, each book taking me longer to write. I didn't finish the story to stop the war in Vietnam until 1980. So let me set down what has to be done, and maybe hurry creation, which is about two steps ahead of destruction.

The protagonist has been born already; in fact, he's twenty-three years old and his name is Wittman Ah Sing, hero of *Tripmaster Monkey*. He has potential, having devised a fake book of political and artistic intentions to be improvisationally carried out. All the writer has to do is make Wittman grow up, and Huck Finn and Holden Caulfield will grow up. We need a sequel to adolescence—an idea of the humane beings that we may become. And the world would have a sequel.

How to write a novel that uses nonviolent means to get to nonviolent ends? We are addicted to excitement and crisis. We confuse "pacific" and "passive" and are afraid that a world without war is a place where we'll die of boredom. A tale about a society in which characters deal with one another nonviolently seems so anomalous that we've hardly begun to invent its tactics, its drama. There's a creative-writing adage that the loaded gun in an early chapter has to go off later on. How to break that rule? The loaded guns—and the first-strike and second-strike bombs —are ready. How to not shoot and not launch, and yet have drama? The writer needs to imagine the world healthy, nurturing young Wittman to be a good man, a citizen whose work improves life.

Suppose: After gathering everybody he knows and putting on a show, as he does in *Tripmaster Monkey*, Wittman Ah Sing and his wife, Taña, like many Californians of the sixties, go somewhere to start a commune. They will take along Percival and Paul Goodman's *Communitas* as their field guide. A good man, a good Buddhist, builds his *sangha*. Animals have been miraculously appearing and will help deconstruct the cities. Pheasants have been spotted flying low along the streets of Detroit. In Studio City, where I lived for a while, coyotes cross

Ventura Boulevard to hunt cats. We need more ideas like the junk-car reef off Honolulu; the crannies and surfaces of the sunken cars attract fish and barnacles. In British, Dutch, and Australian writing, there are stories about squatters illegally claiming empty houses and apartments. And Jimmy and Rosalynn Carter set an example of charity, repairing inner-city buildings with their own hands. (Is it better to restore cities, though, or to rethink them?)

As *Tripmaster Monkey* ends, Wittman Ah Sing decides to flee conscription. Having always lived in cities, he will not have it in him to go to the north woods and start a commune from scratch. Maybe I'll have him do what I did – go to Hawai'i on the way to Japan, a country he thinks has a strong peace movement. But he stops at the verge of America. His fellow draft dodgers are lighting out for Molokai and Kauai. "Go stay Kauai, FBI man no can find 'em." Most Hawaiians, however, patriotically enlist, as the poor and the minorities have done during all the American wars. Paradise turns out to be the staging area for Vietnam. The mountains echo with target practice. Tanks go around and around Oahu, and ships loaded with rockets leave the harbor. Soldiers, bandaged on shockingly various parts of their bodies, recuperate on the beaches. The peace demonstrators are few, only about ten pacifists and Quakers; Wittman and Taña join them.

The motley people of Hawai'i teach Wittman that a Chinese American is a *pake*; he is to be the uncle, then, in the calabash family of man. He studies strangers to see who his long-lost relatives might be. Every family talks-story about some lonely old ancestor who came across the sea and became *hanai* to them, "worked hard that *pake*," and took care of the entire family. Wittman identifies with Hawaiian men, who look somewhat like himself because they're part Chinese, but who are as macho physically as he is macho verbally. He is a tripping, traveling monkey and they are of the *aina*, the land, which they're losing. Vivid nature fluorescently gets through even to our city monkey. Sitting on the ground in silence with others, listening to the ocean under the night sky, he understands that the universe is made up of more silence than words. All he need do is stop talking, and he becomes one with everything and everybody else. (The silence will counterpoint the twelve-speaker blast-out in *The Fake Book*.) All of us lost land, and we migrate from country to country, vying with those who got there earlier. Forget territory. Let's make love, mate and mix with exotic peoples, and create the new humane being.

Because he has married Taña De Weese, blond and Caucasian, Wittman, who invents philosophies to catch up with his actions as well as vice versa, recommends interracial marriage as the way to integrate the planet. Hapa children of any combination are the most beautiful, and the Ah Sing–De Weeses adopt one. With its dark red skin and little blue-black eyes, their *hanai* baby looks like all babies, so they decide that it can be any race. Wittman, taking up the role of father, practices the principle that we ought to be able to learn to love any stranger.

There are male animals–hamsters and rabbits are two species I myself have witnessed–that have to be separated from the birthing females to stop them from eating the babies. Just so, older men, even war veterans, draft boys and send them to war. Nations have wars every generation and kill off young men. Why is this? Why doesn't Wittman have this instinct? Doesn't he know the difference between being fatherly and being motherly?

Sometimes strangers don't like being loved. Soon after arriving in Hawai'i, I worked in a community project, my portion of which was to get dropouts to drop in and learn how to read. Saul Alinsky lectured to us, "Burn it down," perhaps only quoting a slogan from Watts. The Hawaiians answered, "It's too beautiful to burn down." Then they beat up our two Vista workers, who were blacks sent by a church in the Midwest, and ran them out of town. My next community project was Sanctuary for AWOL soldiers. They were on R and R in paradise and did not want to go back to Vietnam. Wittman and Taña could teach reading in the front room and try to keep their two AWOLs from coming out of the back room. They'll take their kid with them and join the communal Sanctuary at the Church of the Crossroads, where everyone gathers–AWOL soldiers and sailors, servicemen's unionists, hippies, Yippies, sociologists, Quakers, Buddhists, Catholic Action, *kahunas*, reporters, infiltrators. Outside, the black chaplain from Schofield yells into a bullhorn for his men to give themselves up. Wittman directs the dropouts and the AWOLs in a performance of Megan Terry's *Viet Rock* that wins hearts and blows minds.

The Sanctuary in Honolulu was the latest setting up of a City of Refuge, a free zone that would give absolute security to fugitives. Such an idea has been thought up and tried by many civilizations–Phoenicians, Syrians, Greeks, Romans. Moses appointed six Levitical cities and "intaking cities," three on either side of the Jordan. Medieval and Renaissance churches were sacred precincts of asylum. On the Big Island of Hawai'i, stone deities and a wall mark off a jut of land that is the City of Refuge. If the fugitive could swim or run to the City, the priests protected him or her. Mark Twain wrote about crowds lining the way to the gate, cheering on a man whose pursuers were racing to catch him. You can hide under the rock that hid Queen Ka'ahumanu, revolutionary feminist breaker of *kapu*. The City of

Refuge is a desolate spot of black rock and salt water; fugitives could not have survived there without the cooperation of the community. Fictionally, it would be dramatic to set the Vietnam Sanctuary on the Big Island, but I want to tell the true history of places of peace, and how they were established during the worst of times. Sanctuary has evolved so that it can be set up in the middle of a secular city like Honolulu. Can Cities of Refuge last and grow without war conditions? Is there an Asian tradition of refugees attaining a sacred ground and claiming protection by its deity? I want to follow the evolution of a humane impulse and support the newest Sanctuary movement, harboring refugees in flight from repressive Central American regimes.

By carrying out visions of *aina* and *sangha*, Wittman, Monkey of 72 Transformations, becomes almost Hawaiian. (When he learns their music, he will be truly Hawaiian.) A human being is a thinking creature; whatever and whomever we know belong to us, and we become part of them. Learning the culture and history of the land we're living on, we take root in the earth; we have Native American ancestors. We are already part white from learning in school about pilgrims and pioneers. And we are getting better at being black because of ethnic studies and Alex Haley giving us roots. The Monkey, who is able to change into fish, birds, mammals, and buildings, can now realize himself as many kinds of people. The ancestors connect us tribally and globally and guide our evolution. We can make the planet a beneficent home for all.

The dream of the great American novel is past. We need to write the Global novel. Its setting will be the United States, destination of journeys from everywhere. Wittman and Taña cut out of California only to find themselves among more Americans. Everybody gathers and regathers, unable to get away from one another until we work out how to live peacefully together. The pheasants and coyotes are amongst the hunters. Refugees from Southeast Asia and South America are coming to the last place that you would think North Americans would make unlivable, the United States. We shut the borders, migrants drop from the sky, as in *The Satanic Verses*, a pioneer Global novel for which the author has risked life and art. The danger is that the Global novel has to imitate chaos: loaded guns, bombs, leaking boats, broken-down civilizations, a hole in the sky, broken English, people who refuse connections with others. How to stretch the novel to comprehend our times – no guarantees of inherent or eventual order – without having it fall apart? How to integrate the surreal, society, our psyches?

Start with the characters. Find out – invent – how those AWOL soldiers, who came from the Midwest and the South and went to Vietnam and back, make themselves whole. And how those black Vista workers become generous men. And how the Hawaiians save the *aina*. Another Global writer, Bharati Mukherjee, wrote about a Canadian orphanage that took in mutilated children from Korea, Cambodia, Central America. One of those children, Angela – soldiers had cut off her nipples and thrown her into a pit – has turned eighteen and is about to leave the orphanage. How does she grow up a whole woman? Wittman has to break open the Chinese-American consciousness that he built with such difficulty and be a world citizen. And Taña has to use the freedom the feminists have won. These struggles have got to result in happy endings for all. And readers must learn not to worship tragedy as the highest art anymore.

For inspiring the Global novel, I would read again these ancestral guides: nineteenth-century Russian novels on social experiments, the most famous being Tolstoy's utopian farm at the end of *Anna Karénina*. The most entertaining were about free love; a trio loves together, each with a room of his or her own. *Sensei and His People*, by Yoshie Sugihara and David Plath, about a commune that Japanese settlers started in Manchuria in the thirties. Paul Goodman's *Making Do*, to remind us of urban conditions and humanitarian values and goals. These books keep to classic form; the problems are not so chaotic nor outcomes so revolutionary that they explode fiction. Tolstoy did not foresee technology overwhelming the land and its people. The free lovers do not go much outside the house. Sensei's commune ignores the existence of native Manchurians. And making do, scraping along, squatting and cadging, leaves too much in place. A few people living cooperatively could make repercussions that slowly change society; such a novel ought to take a long time in the reading, teaching readers to enjoy the slowness.

You have to withstand about a hundred pages of chaos in Mario Vargas Llosa's *The War of the End of the World*, which seems to be a descendant of *Water Margin*, the eight-hundred-year-old saga that was Mao Zedong's favorite. Then the outlaws and outcasts build Sanctuary; Canudos is a community with no property, no money, no taxes, no hunger, and no marriage. The government of Brazil surrounds Canudos and blows it up. Vargas Llosa foretells this destruction from the beginning, explosions and prophesies flashing backward and forward in time. The Global novelist of the future has to imagine the commune winning so that there will be no war and no end of the world.

I have never tried writing a novel by looking at it as a whole first. I've never before given away the ending and the effects – how I want readers to react. Ideas for a Global novel are rushing in to fill some empty sets that have been tantalizing me for a long time. William Burroughs said, "There's no such thing as a great Buddhist novel." Kurosawa tried making a great Buddhist movie, *Kagemusha*, which is about sitting still as war strategy. Pauline Kael said that even Kurosawa can't make a good movie about not moving.

Once upon a time China had three Books of Peace. Those books were hidden and never found, or they were burned, their writers killed, their reciters' tongues cut out. But we can retrieve the Books of Peace by envisioning what could be in them–something like the intimations that I've written here. Should I not have the ability or the years, this which you're reading may have to be it–a minimalist Global novel–short enough so that the speedy reader can finish up using his or her own words and deeds.

IV.

"NO STATISTICS OF THE SOUL":

SYSTEMS OF OPPRESSION AND THE

STRUGGLE FOR A CULTURE

CONFERENCE PRESENTATIONS

MAY 12, 1990

Hilton Als

Elena Poniatowska

Agustín Gómez-Arcos

Jamaica Kincaid

Hilton Als

It Will Soon Be Here

The wall surrounding memory misremembered is clean and wide and high, similar in effect to the wall one finds in certain airports in other countries, clean and wide and high like that, banking in or letting go those who want to remember clearly or don't. Passengers – coming or going – in the field of memory are a tangle of arms and legs, hands, hearts, hair and minds that – if you do not stand too close or listen too clearly – speak a language that is remarkable in its similarities, its oppressive loneliness, its denial: What a horrible memory, and so forth. Regardless of where many of us believe we land – in that field encumbered by not too much baggage or entirely too much – we all come from the same place, which is a road rutted by experience so banal, nearly remarkable, that memory tricks us into remembrance of it again and again, as if experience alone were not enough. What are we to do with such a life, one in which we are not left alone to events – love, shopping, and so forth – but to the holocaust of feeling memory – misremembered or not – imposed on us?

Against that wall, which is clean and wide and high, we plummet disastrously at times, when we can no longer be – quite – the fascist-minded custodians of our own past that we'd like to be, as in: I don't remember, I can't, and so forth. In censoring our past we censor ourselves – a not remarkable observation; nor is the idea that the will to censorship begins, like some weird music, in the home, heard, most acutely, by the children, or the queer children, someone's mother must love most.

Misplacing or misremembering one's childhood is a way of allowing oneself the notion that that past did not exist, that it was not lived through in quite that way, that somehow it did not make one different than the rest, as in, I was the one in hellish bliss wearing my mother's garters behind the closed door, not being a boy; or, I was in my childhood bed with her and our legs were entwined and young ladies supposedly keep their legs away from one another, and closed, and so forth.

Some of us regard these memories as accidents, which is for the best if you want to forget them. And although some of us repeat them for a life, we do not cleave to them in childhood where we could at least begin to understand them and thus ourselves with not a modicum of disgust. We condemn ourselves to this disgust by not remembering.

Something else happens in the process of falling, again and again, against the clean, wide, and high wall of misremembering or not remembering at all. With the blood that eventually appears as the result of this repeated violence to the self, one attempts to write one's name – with a finger, or nearly broken tongue – but can barely make it out after doing so, it's just too late, as in, That is the way my parents spell my name, I believe, but I cannot pronounce it, and so forth.

For as long as my memory can remember, I existed characterless, within no memory at all. Or if I did exist it was in remembering the text of someone else's life – that is, in the devouring of biography. If there was a general rule to my thinking then it was: This is someone else and it is not me so I will remember this because of that; or: The subject's having done this means that I do not – no life bears repeating; or: This takes me out of what I am – a self. It was never, ever about a self that belonged to me – that is, myself which, for so long, I dreamt did not belong to me because it didn't. Or maybe doesn't still.

Here is his story: Once upon a time there was this boy who did not have breasts, but he saw them on nearly everyone that he knew and admired in his family. Often he would bury his face in his mother's breasts, feeling no distance and great distance from her and them all at the same time. This was before he spoke much; his mother was in the distance of speech – brown like that, and all engrossing. They lived in this world just on the other side of speech, where reflection lives inside of reflection, until one day this boy, who in looks and manner had often, favorably, been compared to a girl, was in the subway with his mother. While there, this boy and his mother saw two people they recognized from their neighborhood: an older woman who was the mother of a son, too. This woman was always accompanied by her son, as she was now, underground, except that her son's appearance in this instance was all different. Almost in direct imitation of his mother, the son was dressed in black shoes with princess heels, and flesh-colored hose through which dark hair sprouted, and a lemon-colored linen shift with grease spots on it, and a purple head scarf, and bangles. He carried a purse with no straps, out of which he removed, after little or no consultation with his mother, a compact and lipstick to dress his face, too. As the boy and his mother looked at their neighbor and her son, the boy's mother sort of brushed his eyes closed for an instant with the back of her hand and said something he had never heard before but thought he knew the meaning of. She said, "Faggot." This boy never forgot that other boy who wanted so to look like his mother. He did not even forget him after the terror of memory reinstigated this memory, something that he censored from his family because of the way in which his mother had used the word *faggot* in the filth of that underground station, where there was someone exercising the courage inherent in attempting to be something other than oneself or completely oneself.

Here is a terrible memory: The boy who was favorably compared to women was thought to be the same by a man he did not know. This man covered his mouth in a hallway that stank and stank. He removed this boy's trousers without removing his own, but this man opened and opened his zipper. When he opened his zipper things were very dark and stank and stank in there and felt larger than awful, terrifying and familiar. This man's hands went to parts of this boy's body the boy himself had never known. There was something that hurt him very deeply; there were his trousers down around his ankles and there was this man's hand on his mouth, which was as big as the memory of what his mother had said once in the underground station, and was saying again in his ear or maybe the man was. Together this man and the boy's mother said the word, *faggot*. For a while this was all the boy remembered, besides the pain and the smell, and his body disappearing. That was his motive behind turning all of this into a dream, which it wasn't.

The deepest shame often accompanies our will not to remember – shame which is not fleeting although we often treat memory that way, as though being revision-ists of our own past made much of the difference, as in, "Actually I believe my childhood to have been quite happy. We had a dog, a psychiatrist, a house, and what not," and so forth. But for the child, the queer child some mother must have loved most, this revision of history takes place even before there is a past to be had, once confronted by the idea that the parent may pull the following out of his or her wig or hat, "You are no son/daughter of mine," and so forth. To whom do we belong in this ruined kingdom we all want to belong to, regardless of how wrecked, how stultifying? To be central and apparently loved, one will do a great deal, even exercise, continually, the courage of shutting up, the conviction that yes I am just like you and everyone else or at least exhibit the desire to be. At home, in the face of the parent, self-censorship as the entry fee into the ruined kingdom of their existence, of lies and lies again, means a good-bye to the memory of all the cocks and cunts and hearts and minds that we embrace in our mouths, and our hearts, too, but spit out before we give ourselves a chance of naming them. If one chooses this, all of those others who fly but fall so disastrously against the clean and wide and high wall of memory misremembered may choose not to remember you, too, as in the boy who will not love the other boy because he has never loved a boy whose skin was somehow like mud to him; or who will not love anyone because that love means to remember a hate that consumes his heart; or produces such a memory of the mother saying, "What if your father saw you like that?"; or interferes too profoundly with being something other than himself, which is a Jew and beautiful. There are many stories like this but only one, too. Our recourse in re-inventing the love affair with no love, the memory misremembered or tossed altogether, is learning how to write our name – in blood or whatever – on that clean and wide and high wall which only learning to admit oneself to one's home, recumbent with memory, can destroy.

The first oppression was a conquest five hundred years ago. The conquerors disembarked in Vera Cruz and unsheathed their swords. With blood and fire, Spain founded New Spain, imposed its religion and customs. Brutally, Spain substituted one order for another, built a church on top of every pyramid. For the Indians, it must have been terrifying to see their gods of fertility, water, and war destroyed and only one god put in their place, a god that did not even use his powers, but died on the cross like a poor thing.

The idols remained behind the altars, and the rituals continued. From this first oppression derived not only all other systems of oppression, but the struggle for our culture as well, an ancient culture that springs from the earth at every instance and survives in spite of all that has been done to destroy it. The culture was not uprooted, only dispersed. That is why it springs out like ferns that are always invincible, always grow back.

Today, May 12, 1990, history marches much faster than we do. In Latin America, the Sandinista Front loses the elections in Nicaragua, and the first ones to be astonished are the Sandinistas themselves. Now we see that nothing is infallible, nothing is irreversible, nothing is unrenounceable, nothing is unconditional. Today, the world's eyes turn to Eastern Europe and the Soviet Union; Latin America, out of the game, stands alone. What can Latin America give to the world if it is not its raw materials, just as Africa? What can it give if it has no great political leaders; if among us there are no Mikhail Gorbachevs or Lech Walesas? For five hundred years, Latin America's spiritual values have been trampled on, its archaeological treasures vandalized. Our vision has always been the vision of the vanquished.

The painter Frida Kahlo, paralyzed from the waist down, wrote on her sickbed, "Feet? Why do I need them if I have wings to fly?"

At this moment, Mexico is fighting to keep its cultural roots from rotting in a swamp of consumerism and vulgarity and insecurity. But our pre-Hispanic culture continues to assert itself. Every day the newspapers tell us of yet another buried idol found among the rubble. The idols suddenly come back to life, making it impossible for us to forget our past, even if the plastic culture of Disneyland is so keen on making it disappear, as the Spaniards once tried to do.

A few years ago, a peasant leader seized the land for the people. After this reclamation, the government tried to take control of the land. When the people would not let themselves be evicted, the government pretended that it was giving them the land. In front of the authorities, the peasant leader told his people, "Do not say thank you. Don't be grateful. Yours is the land. Yours is the corn. Yours is the earth. It has always been yours from the beginning of time. You came to live on earth, not to die. You have a place on earth, damn it, yours is the red flower that grows with the blue flower. Now you must forget that your inheritance was only a net of holes."

The poet, essayist, and novelist Rosario Castellanos became indignant about the exploitation of the Chamula Indians, who suffer silently as they carry their heavy burden. Her two novels (called "indigenous novels") recreate both the language and customs of the Chamula Indians, but more than that, she helps us to see the profound abyss that divides rich and poor in our country, and Indians and whites. In this society, Indians are always at the service of whites. In Mexico, the Indians descend from the original inhabitants of the territory that was invaded. Why, we might ask, did Castellanos take such an interest in the Indians? Because as a woman, she could identify with their oppression. During the colonial period— so that they would not abandon the tasks "appropriate" to their sex—women were not taught to read or write. Like the Indians, we women have to struggle against a socially repressive system, but we also have to struggle against Latin American *machismo*.

Three hundred years ago, in the solitude of her cloister in the convent, Sor Juana de la Cruz—the greatest Mexican poet, according to Octavio Paz—lived the drama of a woman who must ask forgiveness for her passion for knowledge. Sor Juana wrote about another very saintly and candid nun in the convent who believed that knowledge belonged to the Inquisition and ordered Sor Juana to cease her study. And Sor Juana wrote: "I obeyed her for three months, for she was my superior, and did not open a book, but as to not studying, that lies beyond my will. I did it . . . I saw nothing without reflection, heard nothing without consideration even in the smallest and most common things." Women have a way of studying that is their own. Sor Juana philosophizes even in the kitchen and discovers some deep truths. And in the process, Sor Juana declares that if Aristotle had cooked, he might have written much more.

After three hundred years, conditions are not much different than those that forced Sor Juana to choose a convent. I was very moved by the stories told in a book called *I Dream a World*, a book of portraits and brief biographies by Brian

Lanker of black women who changed America. Janet Collins, prima ballerina, remembers a major choreographer telling her that she would make a wonderful ballerina if only he could paint her white. The poet Sonia Sanchez says that black children discover they are black through negative experiences, and that if she had children, she would rock them into blackness, humming and singing to them. Mothers in Mexico have to rock their baby girls into womanhood, a womanhood that means that if there is little money, it will all go to their brothers, for their education, even if the girls are brighter. Women in Mexico stop believing in themselves when they are very young because no one else believes in them.

Latin America invades, possesses, interferes, gets in through the smallest crack. Latin America is always out there beyond the window, watching, spying, ready to attack. The street enters through the doors and windows. People find their way in, look at you while you sleep, while you eat, while you make love. In the great North American cities, everybody has something to do, walking quickly, never turning their heads to look at their neighbors. This is especially true in New York. In Latin America, in Mexico, no one has anywhere to go. Thousands and thousands of people with nothing for themselves. Nothing, not a single opportunity. Their empty hands hang at their sides or tremble in front of their empty mouths or drop into their empty laps. They are waiting hands, without any use. All this human energy wasted. Thousands and thousands look, wait, doze, then wake up to wait again. Nobody needs them so nobody loves them. Nobody misses them. Nobody will miss them. They are not needed anywhere. They are nobody. They do not exist. So much to do in this world, and there is no place for them. So much energy lost.

In the United States, these people sit in a writer's head, in the back of her mind. In Europe, also, they sit there, waiting to be picked up as characters in a story, a novel. In Mexico, people sit in the front of our minds. They never go away. They are always waiting. And they are always displaying their sickness and their poverty. Doesn't it seem absurd to write?

But many of us continue to write, and about our country's politics. For we, too, live the politics of Mexico. It belongs to us. I am thinking especially of Rigoberta Menchú who, on April 21, 1988, upon her arrival in Guatemala, was detained, accused of political activities against her country, and forced into exile. She wrote of her experience in *I, Rigoberta Menchú*. I am thinking of Domitila Barrios de Chungara, the wife of a Bolivian miner, who tells the story of what the mines mean to the lives of the workers in her book, *Let Me Speak*. I am thinking of Alicia

Dujovne Ortiz and Elvira Orphée and Luisa Valenzuela, all of whom have written about the disappearances in their homeland, Argentina. And of Benita Galliana, who wrote about her experiences in the communist party in Mexico, how there was no one who even cared if she knew how to read or write and how they ordered her around, asking her to do exactly the same things she did at home, brew coffee and make sandwiches. We are still waiting for the book about the four hundred Mexican seamstresses who were crushed to death in the earthquake of 1985 because no one in the government remembered they existed. And we are still waiting for the book about the ones who survived, who rose out of the ashes to organize a new union. They mourn in a new way. They don't sew for a boss anymore, they do it for themselves. For them, the boss is no longer the lord of creation. They say "I" when they begin a sentence. Despite extreme poverty, they don't want to be creatures out of a Dickens novel anymore.

It is also important to remember that in our hierarchical Latin American societies, the needs and interests of different women *are* very different. I am thinking of the 1975 International Women's Conference in Mexico, with the president of the Mexican delegation addressing a delegate from the oppressed mining community, saying something like: "For just one moment, Señora, forget the suffering of your people, forget the massacres. We have talked enough about it. And we have done enough listening. Now it is time to talk about ourselves, about women, about feminism, about you and about me. We will talk about women." And the delegate responded with something like: "Fine, we'll talk about both. If you will permit me I will begin, Señora. A week ago, I met you. Each morning you arrive in a different outfit. I don't. Each day you arrive perfectly made up and with your hair done like someone who has time to step into an elegant beauty parlor and spend a bundle on it. I, however, don't and can't. I see that every day you have a chauffeur, and a car waiting at the door of this congress to take you back to your house. And of course, I don't. And from looking at you, I am sure that you live in a pretty swank house, in an equally swank neighborhood, right? We, however, the wives of miners, have only a small place we call home, and when our husbands die or get sick or the company fires them, we have ninety days to leave the house and then we are out on the streets. Now, Señora, tell me, do you have something in common with my situation? Do I have anything in common with your situation? Then what kind of equality are we going to talk about together?"

Latin American literature is vast and new, as vast and new as our great continent that is still undiscovered. We still adore the sun, one god to whom we give tribute. Many times our Indian ancestors, the ancient Mexicans, have been filled with terror as their gods of fertility were taken away. Many women writers have not changed the calendar; the center of their solar system is still Man and the rules of life still those dictated by Man. But an infinite variety of genders await us in the future.

To elaborate testimonies and to document the country as a witness, some women have willingly chosen to think of themselves as a fiction. We women still have to transform our own lives and literature into subversion. This is why Sandra Gilbert's and Susan Gubar's *The Madwoman in the Attic* is such an accurate definition of women writers. In the library of women's literature in Latin America, too many of our writers are suicides: Argentinian poet Alfonsina Storni, who walked into the waves and whose body the Mar del Plata returned to the shore; Antonieta Rivas Mercado, the Mexican novelist who shot herself with her lover's pistol in the curé's room of Notre Dame cathedral; the Argentinian Clarice Lispector, who burned half her face smoking in bed – an "accident," yes, but too powerful in metaphor to be ignored; the poet Enriqueta Ochoa, found drowned in her bathtub; the Chilean singer Violeta Parra, who killed herself; Julia de Burgos, a feminist from Puerto Rico, author of the remarkable poem entitled "Give Me My Number," who died on the streets of New York and ended up in the morgue with a number tied to her ankle because no one claimed the body. These women writers were in the opposition, if not against their political regime, at least their interior regime. Women writers in Latin America have given their lives in a greater proportion than male writers, and it is not because they are unstable; it is because society is out of balance, it is hostile to women. Some of these women were even afraid to declare themselves writers, as if saying so would annihilate their womanhood, transform them into freaks.

To make a human being feel like a freak: isn't that a very refined, a very sophisticated, form of repression?

Agustín Gómez-Arcos

Censorship, Exile, Bilingualism

What won't people do to acquire freedom, to practice it? Ask the slave, the oppressed, the creator: they know the answer.

In a democracy, it seems inappropriate to talk about freedom, to insist upon the topic. Inappropriate and absurd. In the same way that dictatorship breeds oppression, it is assumed that democracy nurtures freedom. A presumption. And even a definition. In short – an indisputable truth, but only to a certain point, like all indisputable truths. Seen with a creator's eyes (eyes that have the habit of seeing beyond the human and the divine, the political, the social, and even the moral), democracy ends up inevitably producing conformity – that type of mutilated freedom that some call "intellectual comfort" – whereas sooner or later, oppression breeds rebellion. And who, among artists, would deny that rebellion has more creative power than conformity? Only those who have no desire to change the world, those who adapt to arbitrarily chosen rules, without asking themselves for even a second if that freedom to choose hasn't been previously manipulated. The creative power of the rebellious is much more profound, more destabilizing, because it has an ideological charge that the simple aesthete is unaware of or ignores.

Bilingualism in writers, usually the direct result of censorship and exile, is, as I conceive it, not an elitist or aesthetic *parti pris*, but rather a pure act of rebellion, a jump into the void, whose danger seems doubly accentuated by the virginity of the tool it employs (a language different from the native tongue) and by the public to which it is directed, which isn't what is usually called a *natural public*, in other words, a public made up of readers that use the same linguistic signs of communication as the writer. This dangerous adventure of writing in a foreign language (a language that is very difficult to master and that forces the writer to be always a student, and, of course, to commit all types of excesses, assaults against others), this dangerous adventure, I repeat, is, in my understanding, the most exciting act of rebellion, the most enriching thing that a writer can do, forcing him or her to be twice as conscious, and twice as responsible for his or her voluntary freedom of expression. In short: censorship creates exile, exile creates bilingualism, and bilingualism freedom of expression – or, at least, its imperative necessity.

In certain cases (and allow me to use myself as an example), this fundamental freedom, attained by hard work, also takes on a certain liberal connotation. No longer natural, having not been learned from the crib or from a childhood of expensive and foreign boarding schools, this new wealth that wasn't assigned to you is attained by sheer struggle, by your fingernails, with the great many difficulties that mold character – those inherent in the language that you are learning, others in the very stock of the culture. In this way, this act of learning is transformed little by little into an authentic act of aggression, a war that must be won above everything else, a war in which the enemies are not only in front of you, blindly defending the virtues of the language that you are invading, but also behind you, in all those (people and institutions) that, not content with having expelled you from your own language, vent their anger by accusing you of having betrayed it. As if you were committing adultery with a language that is not your own "legitimate" language. To them, your act of liberty is illegal, and as a consequence, worthless. This freedom of expression becomes covert freedom, illegal freedom, and its quality (literary or human) is left questioned by the mere act of expressing oneself outside of the norm. It is a freedom beyond the law. A freedom that is outcast, or exiled.

Up until now, I have written and published ten novels in French; good or bad, this work is nonexistent for my country. The current Spanish democracy rejects it, as if it were an illegitimate child or (and I've thought about this a lot) a terrorist act against the country where I was born, and whose nationality I keep with pride. As if my past and my memory did not belong to me, or before they were mine, they were a common heritage shared with my fellow countrypeople that I have had the audacity to express in a foreign language.

Therefore, we speak of the freedom of expression in democracy as if of its child: that cunning daily censorship that, by not being official, "dares not speak its name." In some cases, like mine, the freedom to remember and recount, practiced in exile and in an exiled language, produces memories seen as aggressive acts aimed at the new order, an order which, if we judge its desire to hide history, to minimize it, and even to erase it, looks like a twin brother of the old order. Only the old order was called "dictatorial order," and this, the new order, is called "democratic." Just like dictatorship, democracy is a master of the art of emptying words of meaning, of transforming them into new decor for the opportunists. In short:

they both speak, and in the same way. Meanwhile, the rebellious word, the word in constant rebellion, continues without having rights to citizenship.

That's why it is essential that so many forms of oral expression, so many linguistic forms of communication, continue to exist. Without a doubt, human nature, in order to survive, to protect itself from itself and its capacity to breed oppression, to materialize its intentions beyond the limits (and the Law) of the cavern and the jungle, has created so many different languages, different clamors and screams so as to escape homogenization or global totalitarianism, and all attempts at domination through language.

Bilingualism could be the metaphor for this inherent need for free expression. The acquisition of another language adds supplementary material to what one already had; it enriches and distances it, strips it of localism, of folklore, transforms it into material that extends beyond linguistic barriers. There will never be a censorship strong enough to gag writers as long as they still have their capacity to learn and, consequently, to speak in a second or third language. Regimes of all types have shown that the monolinguistic prison is much more destructive for writers than the other prisons, the real ones. Censorship, in itself, is one of the most atrocious captivities. Whether explicit or subtle, the act of censorship is produced and reproduced day after day under both totalitarianism and democracy. In the former, the work considered subversive is prohibited by decree, in the latter it is silenced by unspoken agreement. Censorship changes its mask, but not its undertaking. Rather than censoring oneself, a person who loves freedom of expression can reach out for a second language, a language that gives the writer the power to scream that which the native tongue prohibits; an almost immeasurable wealth: that of expressing the inexpressible, a state of perpetual levitation.

The day that the French language put that possibility within my reach was without a doubt the most remarkable day of my life. That day I understood that no one in my own country, no institution, would ever have the power to silence me. I'm still unpublished in Spain. But I am read throughout the world, in diverse languages. My deepest conviction is that, for all the reasons I have stated, I would continue to be mute, silenced, if I were not bilingual.

About a month ago, I went to England with a friend. We spent time in London and the English countryside. Now I have millions of opinions about the English, but they are rather long opinions. Actually, these opinions are prejudices, but the reason they remain opinions is because I come from a poor country and I cannot back them up. For instance, I thought that it was horrible the way the English kept their countryside, that it was just a lot of hedges. It was too neat. It might reflect something about the culture, perhaps that they have problems with constipation. I, for instance, might be in the position of saying to them, "I bet you don't shit easily," and this might actually be true. But this can only remain my opinion.

This may be a good thing. I believe it is a good thing. One shouldn't have these prejudices. But a very interesting thing happened between my friend and me which I will now tell you about.

My husband is a composer and he often performs in public and he likes to wear a very nice shirt when he does. So I thought, well, I will take him back a present of a nice shirt. So I went to Turnbull and Asser to get him a nice shirt. Afterwards, we needed a tie to go with the shirt, and one of the salespersons showed us a lot of ties in different colors but all with the same pattern. And he described the ties in tones perhaps only the Pope uses when silently or privately praying to God. He said, "Look at these ties, they have the Prince of Wales crest on them. Aren't they beautiful? This pattern is very exclusive to us. The Prince of Wales has never allowed his crest to be used in this way. It's such a marvelous thing." Now, I was incredibly horrified and just said, "My God, we hate princes in my family. My husband would never wear a tie with the Prince of Wales crest on it." The man was truly upset, which I was glad about. I thought that he should know that there was at least one person in England at that moment who did not like the Prince of Wales.

Well, I thought that was the end of it, but I had not considered that, as odious as the idea of the Prince of Wales is to me, that this is in fact my friend's tradition. This is in fact her country. And she correctly realized that I was in fact horrified by this country and this experience, that I was close to things that, when described, had always mentally ended the sentence with "And then it all burned down." Westminster Abbey, for instance. We were in Westminster Abbey, and we saw all the tombs. And it was really amazing that it had all been kept. You know, such as the piece of stone that is used in coronations – and it is actually a very unattractive piece of stone. If one saw it in one's yard, one would be likely to put it out of the way. But it is a very precious thing to the English. It is part of the coronation ritual, a stone that had been taken from Scotland because the English had heard that every king of Scotland had been crowned on that stone. So the stone represents an incredible act of conquest, a symbolic conquest of the Scots. When I see the stone, I think how much like something of me that stone is, and the end of the sentence involving the stone is, "and then it was blown up, and they never saw it again." And so the end of every sentence for me in England is: "And then it vanished." Everything.

Now, as I said, my friend sensed this and so got quite upset about my insulting this man about his Prince of Wales tie. She said, "But you know, this is my culture and my tradition." She really made me feel that I should have some sympathy and respect for where she comes from, and I thought about it and came to the conclusion that she is right as far as it goes. But on the whole, I think that the end of all sentences about England for me is: "And it didn't exist anymore."

I am from Antigua. The Antigua that I knew, the Antigua in which I grew up, is not the Antigua you, a tourist, would see now. That Antigua no longer exists partly for the usual reason, the passing of time, and partly because the bad-minded people who used to rule over it, the English, no longer do so.

In the Antigua that I knew, we lived on a street named after an English maritime criminal, Horatio Nelson, and all the other streets around us were named after some other English maritime criminals. There was Rodney Street, there was Hood Street, there was Hawkins Street, and there was Drake Street. There were flamboyant trees and mahogany trees lining East Street. Government House, the place where the Governor, the person standing in for the Queen, lived, was on East Street. Government House was surrounded by a high white wall – and to show how cowed we must have been, no one ever wrote bad things on it; it remained clean and white and high. There was the library on lower High Street, above the Department of the Treasury, and it was in that part of High Street that all colonial government business took place. In that part of High Street, you could cash a check at the Treasury, read a book in the library, post a letter at the post office, appear before a magistrate in court. It was in that same part of High Street that you could get a passport in another government office. In the middle of High Street was the Barclays Bank. The Barclay brothers, who started Barclays Bank,

were slave-traders. That is how they made their money. When the English outlawed the slave trade, the Barclay brothers went into banking. It made them even
richer. It's possible that when they saw how rich banking made them, they gave
themselves a good beating for opposing an end to slave trading (for surely they
would have opposed that), but then again, they may have been visionaries and
agitated for an end to slavery, for look at how rich they became with their banks
borrowing from (through their savings) the descendants of the slaves and then
lending back to them. But people just a little older than I am can recite the name of
and the date the first black person was hired as a cashier at this very same Barclays
Bank in Antigua. Do you ever wonder why some people blow things up? I can
imagine that if my life had taken a certain turn, there would be the Barclays Bank,
and there I would be, both of us in ashes. Do you ever try to understand why
people like me cannot get over the past, cannot forgive and cannot forget? There
is the Barclays Bank. The Barclay brothers are dead. The human beings they
traded, the human beings who to them were only commodities, are dead. It should
not have been that they came to the same end, and heaven is not enough of a
reward for one and hell enough of a punishment for the other. People who think
about these things believe that every bad deed, even every bad thought, carries
with it its own retribution. So you see the queer thing about people like me?
Sometimes we hold your retribution.

And then there was another place, called the Mill Reef Club. It was built by
some people from North America who wanted to live in Antigua but who seemed
not to like Antiguans (black people) at all, for the Mill Reef Club declared itself
completely private, and the only Antiguans (black people) allowed to go there
were servants. People can recite the name of the first Antiguan (black person) to
eat a sandwich at the clubhouse and the day on which it happened; people can
recite the name of the first Antiguan (black person) to play golf on the golf course
and the day on which the event took place. In those days, we Antiguans thought
that the people at the Mill Reef Club had such bad manners, like pigs. There they
were, strangers in someone else's home, and then they refused to talk to their
hosts or have anything human, anything intimate, to do with them. And what
were these people from North America, these people from England, these people
from Europe, with their bad behavior, doing on this little island? For they so enjoyed behaving badly, as if there were pleasure immeasurable to be had from not
acting like a human being. Let me tell you about a man. Trained as a dentist, he
took it on himself to say he was a doctor, specializing in treating children's

nesses. No one objected – certainly not us. He came to Antigua as a refugee (running away from Hitler) from Czechoslovakia. This man hated us so much that he would send his wife to inspect us before we were admitted into his presence, and she would make sure that we didn't smell, that we didn't have dirt under our fingernails, and that nothing else about us – apart from the color of our skin – would offend the doctor.

Then there was a headmistress of a girls' school, hired through the colonial office in England and sent to Antigua to run this school, which only in my lifetime began to accept girls who were born outside a marriage; in Antigua it had never dawned on anyone that this was a way of keeping black children out of this school. This woman was twenty-six years old, not too long out of university, from Northern Ireland, and she told these girls over and over again to stop behaving as if they were monkeys just out of trees. No one ever dreamed that the word for any of this was *racism*. We thought these people were so ill-mannered, and we were so surprised by this, for they were far away from their home, and we believed that the farther away you were from your home the better you should behave. We thought they were un-Christian-like; we thought they were small-minded; we thought they were like animals, a bit below human standards as we understood these standards to be. We felt superior to all these people; we thought that perhaps the English among them who behaved this way weren't English at all, for the English were supposed to be civilized, and this behavior was so much like that of an animal, the thing we were before the English rescued us, that maybe they weren't from the real England at all but from another England, one we were not familiar with, not at all from the England we were told about, not at all from the England we could never be from, the England that was so far away, the England that not even a boat could take us to, the England that, no matter what we did, we could never be of. We felt superior, for we were so much better behaved and we were full of grace, and these people were so badly behaved and they were completely empty of grace. We were taught the names of the kings of England. In Antigua, the twenty-fourth of May was a holiday – Queen Victoria's official birthday. We didn't say to ourselves, Hasn't this extremely unappealing person been dead for years and years? Instead, we were glad for a holiday.

I cannot tell you how angry it makes me to hear people from North America tell me how much they love England, how beautiful England is, with its traditions. All they see is some frumpy, wrinkled-up person passing by in a carriage waving at a crowd. But what I see is the millions of people, of whom I am just one, made

orphans: no motherland, no fatherland, no gods, no mounds of earth for holy
ground, no excess of love which might lead to the things that an excess of love
sometimes brings, and worst and most painful of all, no tongue. For isn't it odd
that the only language I have in which to speak of this crime is the language of the
criminal who committed the crime? And what can that really mean? For the language of the criminal can contain only the goodness of the criminal's deed. The
language of the criminal can explain and express the deed only from the criminal's
point of view. It cannot contain the horror of the deed, the injustice of the deed,
the agony, the humiliation inflicted on me. When I say to the criminal, "This is
wrong, this is wrong, this is wrong," or "This deed is bad, and this other deed is
bad, and this one is also very, very bad," the criminal understands the word *wrong*
in this way: it is wrong when "he" doesn't get his fair share of the profits from the
crime just committed; he understands the word *bad* in this way: a fellow criminal
betrayed a trust. That must be why, when I say, "I am filled with rage," the
criminal says, "But why?" And when I blow things up and make life generally unlivable for the criminal, the criminal is shocked, surprised. But nothing can erase
my rage – not an apology, not a large sum of money, not the death of the criminal
– for this wrong can never be made right, and only the impossible can make me
still: can a way be found to make what happened not have happened?

I attended a school named after a Princess of England. Years and years later, I
read somewhere that this Princess made her tour of the West Indies (which included Antigua, and on that tour she dedicated my school) because she had fallen
in love with a married man, and since she was not allowed to marry a divorced
man she was sent to visit us to get over her affair with him. How well I remember
that all of Antigua turned out to see this Princess person, how every building that
she would enter was repaired and painted so that it looked brand-new, how every
beach she would sun herself on had to look as if no one had ever sunned there before, and how everybody she met was the best Antiguan body to meet, and no one
told us that this person we were putting ourselves out for on such a big scale, this
person we were getting worked up about as if she were God Himself, was in our
midst because of something so common, so everyday: her life was not working
out the way she had hoped, her life was one big mess.

Have you ever wondered to yourself why it is that all people like me seem to
have learned from you is how to imprison and murder each other, how to govern
badly, and how to take the wealth of our country and place it in Swiss bank accounts? Have you ever wondered why it is that all we seem to have learned from

you is how to corrupt our societies and how to be tyrants? You will have to accept that this is mostly your fault. Let me just show you how you looked to us. You came. You took things that were not yours, and you did not even, for appearances' sake, ask first. You could have said, "May I have this, please?" and even though it would have been clear to everybody that a yes or no from us would have been of no consequence you might have looked so much better. Believe me, it would have gone a long way. I would have had to admit that at least you were polite. You murdered people. You imprisoned people. You robbed people. You opened your own banks, and you put our money in them. The accounts were in your name. The banks were in your name. There must have been some good people among you, but they stayed home. And that is the point. That is why they are good. They stayed home. But still, when you think about it, you must be a little sad. The people like me, finally, after years and years of agitation, made deeply moving and eloquent speeches against the wrongness of your domination over us, and then finally, after the mutilated bodies of you, your wife, and your children were found in your beautiful and spacious bungalow at the edge of your rubber plantation – found by one of your many house servants – you say to me, "Well, I wash my hands of all of you, I am leaving now," and you leave, and from afar you watch as we do to ourselves the very things you used to do to us. And you might feel that there was more to you than that, you might feel that you had understood the meaning of the Age of Enlightenment; you loved knowledge, and wherever you went you made sure to build a school, a library. But then again, perhaps as you observe the debacle in which I now exist, the utter ruin that I say is my life, perhaps you are remembering that you had always felt people like me cannot run things, people like me will never grasp the idea of Gross National Product, people like me will never be able to take command of the thing the most simple-minded among you can master, people like me will never understand the notion of rule by law, people like me cannot really think in abstractions, people like me cannot be objective, we make everything so personal. You will forget your part in the whole setup, that bureaucracy is one of your inventions, that Gross National Product is one of your inventions, and all the laws that you know mysteriously favor you. Do you know why people like me are shy about being capitalists? Well, it's because we, for as long as we have known you, *were* capital, like bales of cotton and sacks of sugar, and you were the commanding, cruel capitalists, and the memory of this is so strong, the experience so recent, that we can't quite bring ourselves to embrace this idea that you think so much of. As for what we were like before we met you, I no longer care. No periods of time over which my ancestors held sway, no documentation of complex civilizations, is any comfort to me. Even if I really came from people who were living like monkeys in trees, it was better to be that than what happened to me, what I became after I met you.

Christa Wolf

The Sense and Nonsense of Being Naive

Translated by Jan van Heurck

Editor's note: This essay was Wolf's contribution to an anthology published in East Germany in 1974 and edited by Gerhard Schneider, the "S" whom Wolf addresses in the opening sentence.

Dear S., simple as this request of yours may seem, it is giving me trouble. Maybe if I look for the reasons why, I can still comply. From the start, I felt no urge to write this little piece, but once I promised I would, you had the right to expect me to deliver it on time. Besides, as children we are taught that we ought sometimes to make ourselves do things we do not feel like doing, and I suppose I thought this was a good opportunity. The results – the usual mess of notes on my desk, the usual opening paragraphs stacked in piles of varying thickness all over the floor – did not this time give me a feeling of impatience and confidence, but rather of failure. The only thing that stopped me from calling off the job prematurely was the title I came up with – a title that is bound to strike you as odd, as it does me – but that seemed to open a way for me to talk about my subject in general – hence, evasive – terms.

By then I had realized that you are after information that I am determined not to reveal to you, and that this discrepancy is the real source of my reluctance, and is bound to remain so. Have you really any idea what you are asking? Telling the story behind any work of literature means no more and no less than giving an account of the whole preceding period of one's life; tracing back to their origin the roots of themes one regards as peculiarly one's own, however timidly one may have broached them; indicating their development, separating them from outside influences, and thus protecting the tracks which lead to one's own self. But who *could* and, above all, who would *want* to do that? The result would be hints, no more – we nearly always have to make do with them – and *then* how in heaven's name could they be filtered out from the rest?

Besides, shouldn't certain things be kept under wraps out of love for one's fellow human beings? "Tell me about the first thing you wrote!" you asked me. In the first place, there is no such animal. Thinking back one keeps remembering still earlier efforts, tried at still earlier ages – plans of novels and plays which were never more than half or three-quarters carried out, diaries, occasional verse on political and private themes, emotion-drenched letters exchanged with girlfriends, all the way back to the fairy tales one made up as a child, fantasies of revenge and other fantasies, daydreams and night dreams, and tall tales intended for practical use: those all-important preliminary forms of naive artistic composition that it can be devastating for a child to be deprived of, and that sometimes can develop into a need to express oneself by writing. And all this still does not tell us much. You, as a reader for a publishing house, know that the need to express oneself in writing is quite widespread, as is the sensitivity to basic experiences of the sort everybody has to go through: feelings of weakness and helplessness, anxiety, pain, anger, shame, pride, pity, grief, happiness, despair, jubilation, triumph. Concerned parents do not mind your feeling these things but would prefer you not to feel them too intensely, lest as a result you become – God forbid! – permanently prone to fanciful notions and extravagant emotion.

But a childhood caught between the commonplace in private life and fanaticism in public[1] may find no other outlet than a secret eccentricity and the effort to counteract it by choosing a straightforward profession: that of schoolteacher, for instance, which is what I used to list as my job when filling out forms, until I reached the age of twenty-one. After that, I spent years on the fringes of an occupation for which it never even occurred to me to presume I had the ability, due in part to the fact that the very young seldom are able to write prose. The true cause of my inhibition to write, which I may talk of on another occasion, of course could not be overcome without deep turmoil, or overnight. In short, you yourself must know how a lukewarm urge can evolve into a compulsion that sets itself above all the commandments – simply because it affords the means to be at least temporarily in harmony with oneself.

I had no thought of anyone reading my stuff. On the contrary, my early work was tucked away in a safe hiding place, for it involved highly intimate matters whose ambivalence was evident from the fact that they could neither be completely revealed nor remain unspoken. This shameful inner conflict – which was not as innocuous as it may sound – set off a perpetual-motion machine of the kind that produces, in an unascertainable percentage of cases, the product you referred to in your inquiry as "the first thing I wrote."

But the writer herself does not use that term, *my first work*. If she did, her cause would already be lost: she would find herself precariously between two stages of naiveté and would have to be careful not to step down too heavily on a floor that might be incapable of supporting her weight. At this point she would also face the first in a long series of questions of conscience: whether this first work which had the luck or misfortune to get published was written with publication *in mind*, and whether this intention changed her attitude toward an activity she had been intimately familiar with in the past. In my case, the answer to both questions must be yes, and where the second is concerned, I say it with regret. The transition from amateur to professional changes an author. One change is a loss of naiveté in the sense of innocence. The later you notice the changes, the more dangerous they can get, and only by vigorous and ruthless countermeasures can you obviate them to some degree.

You can see for yourself how the land lies, the moment I even try to entertain thoughts of your request. There is no need for you to leap to your own defense. I understand perfectly well what you really want to know – the usual things: "What was your first published work?" (Answer: the *Moskauer Novelle* – not counting book reviews and literary essays.) "When was it published?" (Answer: 1961.) "Where and in what circumstances was it written?" (In the East German town of Halle on the Saale River, on a quiet street called Amselweg, Blackbird Road, through which there wafted the stink of synthetic chemicals from the factories in Leuna, and from the Buna rubber plants; at a light-colored desk that had been moved in front of a window to afford me a view of our balcony and a slightly rank garden where our children were playing noisily with the neighbors' children. I could tell you the names of the neighbors and the names of my children and describe them to you as well, but I have forgotten what season of the year I saw outdoors when I looked up from the desk.) But your main question would be: "Where did you get the material for your story?" In other words, which parts are taken from "real life" and which are "invented"? Where can the curious reader find the "autobiographical nucleus"? Because everybody knows that, generally speaking, it is the author's own life she works up into literature. This ploy to inveigle me into unwilling, unimportant, and misleading confessions I reject on the grounds that the labor of "working things up" is worthwhile only if the work cannot be destroyed later by someone carelessly spilling the beans. "Well then, can you at least tell us whether some of your characters had real-life models, and if so, which ones?" (No comment.) "How old were you when you wrote this story?" (Almost thirty.) "Were you familiar with Moscow?" (Not familiar enough, as you can easily tell from my story, provided you know Moscow better than I did – and in fact I now know it better myself, although I do not feel any urge to write about it.) "Then can you tell us a couple of your chief motives for writing this story?"

Your impertinent questions – even if I have only been imagining their impertinence – met a barrier so reliable that for days I could not think of a thing to say, and I was about to call it quits when, unfortunately, I got the idea of rereading that story I wrote fourteen years ago, which you are now asking me to talk about against my will. I need hardly tell you that it was as painful to read as I had imagined it would be. Nor need I say that I do not propose, in this essay, to put myself through the justly grueling task of poking fun at my story for its lack of formal skill, which must be obvious to everyone – its awkward sentences, the images that do not come off, the wooden dialogue, the naturalistic descriptions – all the things that you run across even in good books and that people half correctly believe belong to the "craft of writing," which anyone can learn if he or she has a mind to. What disturbed me more is a tendency to closedness and perfection in the formal structure, the way the characters are amalgamated into a plot that unfolds like clockwork – even though I know that the events and feelings which underlie parts of the tale could not be more violent and obscure.

This finished-off quality reveals something I had almost begun to forget: how well I had absorbed my university courses in German literature, and all those articles, which often covered the whole page without a break, about uses and disadvantages, realism and formalism, progress and decadence in literature and art – absorbed them so well that, without my realizing it, my vision was colored by them and I was moving far away from a realistic manner of seeing and writing.

Observing this, I began to feel interested in that first story of mine after all, quite independently of your question. How, I wondered, could a woman almost thirty years old, who had been far from untouched and unmoved by the agitated and agitating events of this century, write, nine years past its midpoint, a tract of this kind? I mean "tract" in the sense of a religious tract written to propagate a faith – because there is no denying that this story of a love affair between a German woman and a Russian man shows a certain pious naiveté in the way it stays neatly within prescribed borders and does not allow confusion to spread outside the psychological zone. Of course, renunciation is not something that merits our scorn; only it need not be given a moral motivation when the prevailing rules dictate it anyhow: remember, we are talking about 1959.

But do not be afraid that this is going to turn into self-incrimination or an attempt to get myself off the hook on the grounds of incompetence. Hermann Paul's dictionary defines the original meaning of the word *naive* as "innate, natural" – and indeed, that urge to express oneself by writing which I mentioned earlier may well be described as "natural" and "naive." But the word *talent* (from Latin *talentum*, deriving in turn from the Greek) referred originally not to a quality but to a unit of weight and money. After its appearance in the parable in Matthew 25:14 where a man gives "talents" to his servants, "talent" took on the figurative meaning of a capital sum from which one is supposed to make a profit. Thus, it is up to the person herself – should even a few ounces of this talent have been "entrusted" to her – whether she lets them go to waste or makes them grow. Talent turns into a trial, a challenge, a thorn whose point can on occasion be broken off.

This, by the way, is what must have happened to my story. As it traveled down from my head through my arm, my hand, my pen, and my typewriter onto the paper, it seems to have undergone a transformation, as literature inevitably must – but a loss of energy as well. Apparently, my fear of dangerous explosives led to the use of controlling devices, building components that could be linked together to form a story. This is the birth of fable – fable in the ancient sense of "idle talk," as opposed to a truthful account. Fabulous creatures find a good home in it, a dry and reliable shelter, if they will take a little trouble to fit; and they learn to get on fabulously together and beget a convenient moral.

Of course, I would not deny the eminent relations between literature and social morality. But an author's social morality should not be limited to hiding from her society all she can of what she knows about it. I say this despite the fact that not so long ago – how quickly we forget! – a lot of carbon copies, produced from prefabricated formulas, were circulating under the label "sticking to the Party line." And we – by "we" I mean present company included – got in the habit of using the label "Party line" in a very careless way.

To get back to the subject at hand: maybe I did not know any better than to write a "tract." In any case, it strikes me that my mixed feelings on rereading my story derived from the almost complete *absence* of mixed feelings in the text itself. Faith and fidelity, love, friendship, generosity, straightforwardness – aren't these the same pure, unequivocal emotions, unmenaced by hidden pits and hidden motives, which touch us in children but amuse us in adults, because they are signs of naiveté? Naiveté, that is, not as Friedrich Schiller uses the word, but in its plain sense, in the sense it most commonly has today: simplemindedness? But what is so shocking about this that I feel I must struggle to convert my hopeless dismay into a wholesome dismay?

What is so shocking is this: the fact that I did not know better–anyhow, not *much* better–and that I *could* and *should* have known better. By 1959, after all, it was possible to turn up a few facts about the real background of life in a Soviet family, or the problematic relationship of two peoples, one of whom only fourteen years earlier was still trying to enslave, even exterminate, the other; it is not enough just to assign one side a bad conscience and make the other side look generous. In fact, conscience is not enough if it takes no other form than *bad* conscience–nor are the most pious intentions if they are presented as goals already achieved. Moreover, even in a love story you cannot get by with showing no more than a few idyllic glimpses of an event such as–for instance–the 20th Communist Party Congress in Moscow. I could go on with this unworkable attempt to crawl back inside my story and keep interrupting it with heckling cries, malicious remarks, and demands for improvement–if it were not that my knowledge of self-censorship has grown over the past fourteen years and would not let me sustain the tone.

Just "knowing better" is not enough. How simple it would be if extrinsic factors were all that hindered us from telling everything we know. But although it is true that people write in order to say what previously was unknown, every literature (including the work of great authors) proves the reverse as well: that it is used to conceal. The writer's struggle with herself, which goes on between the lines and behind the sentences–this struggle to reach the limit of what she can say and perhaps cross beyond it at an unforeseeable point, only to discover that she cannot do it after all, that she is not *allowed* because she is unable to violate with impunity a self-imposed taboo compared to which the dictates of outside censors seem insignificant: this tension is what gives writing its fascination and, once we have discovered it, gives reading its fascination, too, even if the reader does not have to be consciously aware of what moves him or her so deeply, beyond the fate of the characters.

So now we can tackle naiveté from another angle. A certain measure of self-deception (of naiveté) seems necessary to life; we continually draw on it as it is continually replenished. That this measure must be greater when we are young than later, when disillusionments–not regrettably–have sobered us, is something

I cannot deny. *But* thirty is an age when one can no longer claim to be young, and I would give a lot to know some of the reasons why people of my generation took so long to grow up – a fact that I expect has escaped you no more than it has me.

Of course, I would have resisted that allegation fourteen years ago, but now I think I know what I am talking about. Just listen to the members of my generation sometime. Notice which topics they almost never bring up and which tend to trigger emotional outbursts when they do come up. This will tell you something about those deposits embedded in our life histories that we have not been able to come to terms with and that interfere with our becoming independent adults. Of course, when I wrote my story, I believed what I said: that the inner "conversion" of my generation had now "come to pass." And it is quite true that our conscious ideas did undergo the radical change which necessarily was the first step in this conversion. The change was a deeply unsettling experience that encompassed the whole of the personality, and anyone who seriously bore in mind the atrocities we were all appointed to commit and barely escaped through no merit of our own could easily have been destroyed by the aftershock, like the man who rode on horseback across Lake Constance and only afterward realized he could have fallen through the ice at any time. It is only to be expected that many of our generation carry a residue of deep insecurity, an almost ineradicable self-distrust – albeit often unconscious and glossed over by restless activity – which is bound to express itself in their social behavior, including their literature.

For our deep and persistent horror at the barbarism that emanated from our country and that we denied for so long is not enough to complete our conversion; nor is any new sobriety that applies only to past history. We may have recognized, repented, and amended the errors in our thinking, after much effort, and we may have radically altered our attitudes and opinions, our entire view of the world – and yet our *style* of thinking was not to be changed so quickly, still less certain reaction and behavior patterns that have become engrained in people as children and continue to structure the way their character relates to the surrounding world: the habit of trusting those in authority, for instance; the compulsion to idolize or submit to others, the tendency to deny reality, the tendency to zealous intolerance.

Of course, all of this can be explained, but for once I would like to *read* the explanations. Our old, overblown self-esteem, with a deep sense of inferiority at the root of it, was deservedly destroyed and could not simply be replaced by a new, readymade self-esteem. But in order to survive, people eagerly latched onto inadequate substitutes – a new blind religious zeal, for instance, and the arrogant claim that now they had found, once and for all, the only correct and only workable truth – at a time when, I need hardly tell you, dialectical thinking was what was really needed, especially from socialists. In fact, the *Moskauer Novelle* – which I am still discussing – bears witness to all this by the touching efforts it makes to use rationality to ward off the subterranean threats of passion or grief, and by claiming and presupposing changes which, in fact, it had yet to be proved had taken place. The story is not completely successful at either attempt and thus produces those holes and ruptures that give cause for hope after all.

I am sure you will believe me when I say that what I am writing here is neither a complaint nor an accusation, but more an exercise in self-communication – a preliminary, abstract formulation of problems that remain to be dealt with concretely in literature. Prose is one of those genres that depend on coolheadedness and self-command and which thus seem to have no use for naiveté. At the same time, like all so-called art, prose feeds off that store of primordial behavior whose groundwork is laid in our childhood. It requires spontaneous, direct, no-holds-barred reaction, thought, feeling, and action; an unself-conscious – that is, after all, a "naive" – and unbroken connectedness to oneself and one's personal history – those very things that our generation has forfeited.

This contradiction is itself one of the things that determines how we live, and how we write, too. We can ignore or deny it, belittle or cover it up, brace ourselves against it, lament it or curse it. We can run away from it, taking refuge in the unproductive, mechanical processes of life, or we can be broken by it without even knowing it. Whatever tricks we put ourselves through, there is only one way to relate to our times in a creative and unforced manner, and that is by working through this conflict which affects more than one generation and thus provides the raw material for role models. Persistent, unflinching work is needed on those complexes, rooted in the past, that it hurts to touch: not so as to tie society's resources to the past unnecessarily, but to make them productive in the present. This task, if carried out consistently, could lead to literary discoveries of a kind we do not expect.

Fourteen years is only an accidental time span, after all. How can we guess how near or how far the day may be before we disbelieve the things we are saying today – for instance, what I have written in these pages? That is how it should be. If our hopes were destroyed the moment they arise, all production would stop, and with it, hope itself; whereas nowadays, when our every word must pass knottier and more severe tests than in the past, our work indeed may be more arduous and wearisome, but by no means has it become impossible. New kinds of information require new resolutions and techniques if they are to be brought into play effectively. So far, we are still left speechless when we hear on the news that the United States' twelve-year "military involvement" in Indochina simply "ended punctually at 5 a.m." one morning, after 6.6 million tons of bombs costing more than 30 billion marks had been dropped on Vietnam, Laos, and Cambodia, "with scant success." In a case like this, an old-fashioned word like *madness* is not much good to us, and it will take some hard work to get the quotation marks out of sentences like the above. Yet, to act decisively–in any way that goes beyond the merely mechanical–requires us to recover that basic trust in ourselves that we have lost.

And so I will end–to my surprise and yours–with a word in praise of folly. That folly I mean which has many faces, some of them perfectly consistent with insight and experience. That folly which nourishes great experiments but lets frivolousness, cynicism, and resignation wither away. Which enables us to build houses, plant trees, bring children into the world, write books–to *act*, as clumsily and imperfectly as ever we may. Such action, in any case, is wiser than surrender to the multiform, often hard-to-recognize, perfect techniques of destruction.

Patrick McGrath

$\mathcal{P}oe's\ \mathcal{D}ank\ \mathcal{V}aults$

Montresor invites Fortunato into the vaults of his palazzo beneath Venice during the carnival, ostensibly to seek his advice on some Amontillado he's just bought. He gets Fortunato drunk on the way through the cellars and then chains him to a wall in a remote crypt. Then he bricks him up. Why? It's in the first line: "The thousand injuries of Fortunato I had borne as I best could, but when he ventured upon insult, I vowed revenge."

This is "The Cask of Amontillado." Montresor has suffered a thousand injuries, but it takes an *insult* for him to vow revenge. The thousand injuries were somehow less than insults, smaller than insults – slights, then. Imagined slights: our narrator is paranoid. Nothing he says can be trusted. So when he says that Fortunato is vindictive, we will be inclined to believe the opposite – or that it's *he*, Montresor, who is the vindictive one. This is what the unreliable narrator does, permits the writer to construct fictions in which two diametrically opposed meanings can be contained in the same statement.

Many commentators have taken the breakdown of logical and ontological categories as the essential motor of the gothic genre. In Poe's tale no direct access to the real or implicit meaning of Montresor's words can be given, because it is Montresor who narrates. The reader has no way of verifying his suspicions. The madman bricks up his victim in a foul-smelling crypt in the deepest and dankest parts of his cellars and leaves him there to rot, but it's the reader who's walled up by Poe in this hermetic tale, immured in Montresor's insanity.

Elsewhere in Poe we experience this same effect, this sudden vertiginous grasping at the *matter* of the tale only to come up clutching handfuls of metaphor "untenanted by any tangible form." Roderick Usher's mind, like Montresor's, is as much a reflection of his house as his house is a reflection of his mind; when the one fissures, the other fissures also – "and the deep and dank tarn closed sullenly and silently over the fragments of the House of Usher." In this tale, climate, landscape, architecture, genealogy, and psychology all seem to bleed into one another until it's impossible to distinguish a figure from its metaphors. A sort of coalescence of elements results, even as a movement of regression is occurring, a falling back into a state of primal unity – a death, in other words. Again we have the dissolution and fusion of discrete conceptual categories, the gothic collapsing the terms of all oppositions it encounters, always negating, always choosing ruin over sound structure, darkness over light, sickness over health.

Poe worked a psychological terrain and, apart from a few grotesques, did not deal with biological monstrosity. Elsewhere in the genre, however, the monster is the figure that most graphically provokes uncertainty about the order of things. The vampire, which makes its first literary appearance around 1800, is biologically anomalous, characterized by an inability to rot and a fatal susceptibility to sunlight. Such an impossible being represents a potent zone of contradiction, standing in opposition to the culture's ruling metaphors of nature and the self. It articulates the hidden against the social, the repressed against the spoken, and our fascination with it is part of what gives the genre its vitality and resilience. Rationality's Other, the monster typically inhabits the realm of the imagination, or intoxication, or nightmare or madness or art, speaking a living language of difference that denies daylight logic. The disposal of the monster finally stamps the work as conservative or subversive.

Several parties conspired in the birth of the gothic, among them the aesthetic theory that the Horrid and the Terrible were legitimate sources of the Sublime; the cult of Nature, which came to full flower in de Sade (who himself considered the tale of terror a product of revolutionary upheaval: in 1800 he wrote, "there was nobody left who had not experienced more misfortunes in four or five years than could be depicted in a century by literature's most famous novelists: it was necessary to call upon hell to arouse interest"); and a long-standing cultural appetite for the gentle melancholy of ruins, which began acquiring rather morbid overtones. The best of the first wave is Matthew Lewis's *The Monk*. This fine novel energetically tracks the spiritual collapse of Ambrosio, a bad priest, his rape of a lovely virgin in the dank vaults of a church, and his eventual damnation. On its publication in 1796 it caused an uproar, Lewis (aged twenty) and his publisher were indicted, and *The Monk* was expurgated. Thus in its very infancy did the gothic display its subversive inclinations.

Like Lewis's Ambrosio, Poe's monsters are moral monsters: addicts, neurotics, and paranoids for the most part, and in them we see the entire gothic tradition pivoting on a point midway between the first wave, the old classical gothic of dripping cellars and haunted houses and clanking chains; and its modern expression, the gothic of pathological personality, characterized by transgressive tendencies and extreme distortions of perception, affect, and the moral sense. In Poe, the *mind*, rather than the body, or the house, displays the features of the old gothic sites: darkness, complexity, mystery, suspicion, evil, inversion, contradiction, decay. In Poe the mind is a dank vault, a space where terror and unreason hold sway, passion is transformed into disgust, love turns to hatred, and good engenders evil. In an associative or allegorical sense, such inversions challenge the structures of order, system, and identity, and this, finally, is what the gothic is always about: transgression, and death. These are its perennial themes. In Poe, as in Freud, as in the best, subversive gothic work, the dank vault is where the corpses and the outlaws live, it's where the dirt goes.

Zoë Wicomb

Tracing the Path from National to Official Culture

Taking its cue from the Sechaba Festival of Culture recently held in Glasgow [1990] – a miscellany of political discussion and diverse cultural events – this paper does not move manfully toward resolution. Instead, I want to speak rather generally on an aspect of African National Congress (ANC) cultural activity more accustomed to genuflection than discussion or analysis. I am referring to the festival phenomenon of dancers scantily clad in animal skins and ethnic micro-skirts, complete with drums. Displays of this kind are presented as South African national culture; in Glasgow, where it was sedately applauded by European trade unionists in four-piece suits, a Scottish clansman followed with bagpipes. (Thanks to Hugh Trevor-Roper's work on the invention of tradition in Scotland, we may note that the clansman's ancient ethnic kilt was in fact invented in the early nineteenth century.)

Discussion at the Sechaba conference demonstrated that we have come a long way from the received view of culture as "the best that is known and thought," but this notion seems to have been replaced by a sort of common-sense view of culture as something which simply is the way people live and a reflection of these ways of living in drama, poetry, dance, and so on. This reflectionist model has, of course, been demolished by Raymond Williams, who points out that culture "is never a form in which people happen to be living, at some isolated moment, but a selection and organization, of past and present."[1] To speak of cultural renewal, then, is to discuss how, what, and on what basis we select and organize, and as a point of departure in such a discussion, I would choose from any number of genres. The example of the dancers, however, offers up in stark relief the issues of nation and tradition that are clearly implicated in the notion of culture. It is these notions and their confluence in material practice that I wish to investigate.

Cultural renewal cannot be a switch from old to new, but rather a continuous process of assessment and criticism. And this would involve assessing the very forums in which such commentary occurs. If criticism takes place within the general relations of all cultural work, then the conference where we debate the subject is itself an instance of cultural reproduction. We may be angry about the things speakers say in such situations, but we have to guard against creating an atmosphere where such things can't be said. Edward Said's observation that "all intellectual or cultural work occurs...on some very precisely mapped-out and permissible terrain, which is ultimately contained by the State,"[2] is pertinent, for even in the case of an emergent order, the palimpsestic map already exists and institutions stand at the ready to install their sacred calves. Cultural renewal demands that we study the map, however faint it may be, explore the terrain, and check its relation to the democratic principle.

That these extravagances of "traditional" dance are offered in the name of a national culture is clear from the context in which they are found. I have seen these displays both at home and in Britain, accompanying ANC political speeches, so that it is reasonable to assume that the visual information of the performance is intended to illustrate or support the linguistic information. Speakers have expounded on the new democratic order of the ANC's legal, political, and cultural positions, but relations between the visual and the textual information can produce meanings that contradict the apparent political messages. For instance: Albie Sachs announcing that gender equality will be enshrined in the constitution. At the same event, we are confronted with a band of fully dressed male musicians fronted by women in skimpy "traditional" dress with nothing to do but click their fingers and gyrate to the gaze of the audience. Similarly, in Glasgow, Mendi Msimange persuasively explaining how tribal killings are a construction by conservative elements in the government, and giving an account of a highly industrialized, urbanized society engaged in a culture of resistance. The accompanying visual information foregrounds tradition as the Sechaba performers leap onto the stage. Or there is Govan Mbeki recommending that we develop, alongside the particular culture, a universal culture (of which Shakespeare is quoted as an example), a distinction made in the interest of both cultural diversity and internationalism. The accompanying display is one of the traditional dances in animal skins.

A democratic movement cannot afford to neglect its imagery. It is inevitable that we re-read the political message at the intersection of image and text and find that all is not well. And here it is appropriate to speak of image, since the visual display of actual performers in such contexts becomes an image of South African performance and invites us to image South African culture in terms of traditional dancers. The logo used by the Sechaba Festival offers an example. Taken from the ANC journal, *Sechaba*, which means nation, the image is an adaptation of the journal's logo: a spear and shield held by a black male in loincloth more or less segue into a paintbrush and the outline of Africa, which also becomes a palette. What is suggested is the fusion of cultural activity with warfare, so that nationhood (represented as a product of struggle), tradition, and cultural activity are bonded in this image. (That nationhood is so often represented as unambiguously male is an issue I have no time to address in this paper.)

It is now commonplace to speak of meaning being generated by context, and the very coexistence of the performance with the political speech points to its ritual function of illustrating or affirming the speech. It is this affiliation of certain forms that raises the specter of a path between national and official culture. Cultural practice is not simply derived from, or a reflection of, an otherwise constituted social order, but is itself a major element in the constitution of that order. If culture is, as Raymond Williams describes, "a *signifying system* through which necessarily (though among other means) a social order is communicated, reproduced, experienced, and explored,"[3] this convergence means that we cannot dismiss questionable practices repeatedly promoted as examples of a national culture, precisely because such practices *constitute* the social and political order.

I do not wish to dismiss the notion of a national culture. Clearly a need for such a notion has been created by colonization and Apartheid's strategies of division. But it is worth noting that the meanings of the terms *nation* and *culture* are transformed when they are welded together to form the popular phrase *national culture*. The pluralism implicit in the separate terms – where nation refers to a whole country and culture means the way we live as well as all our diverse forms of expression – is lost as hegemony creeps into the meaning of the combined form. From the rhetoric of the liberation movement we gather that a national culture never simply exists; it is always something that has to be forged, a process, something in the making. However, in the fixed syntagm of the combined form, both the process of forging a culture and the inherent cyclical nature of that process is suppressed. It is interesting to note that terms like *women's culture* or *black culture* never become bonded in this way, precisely because in a white patriarchal society such cultures can never be hegemonic. The adjectival function of woman or black is retained, but national becomes in a sense nominalized, to assert that the cultural form in question is naturally welded to the nation.

There is, of course, nothing natural about it. Those in power decide on cultural expressions that are deemed suitable for export. We could say that a national culture is indeed synonymous with export culture; that it refers not so much to how we see ourselves, but rather to how we wish others to see us; that is, we promote a particular image of ourselves that we offer as representative. If we press the relation between cultural production and the market economy, we arrive at something like Outspan, the name for oranges not eaten at home (where our children die of vitamin deficiency), but rather packaged for foreign consumption. However, we know that Outspan oranges are chosen for their size, color, and wholesomeness. That qualifying criteria are not discussed seems to be inherent in the fixed syntagm of national culture. Which practices, for instance, are excluded and why?

Benedict Anderson's interpretation of nationalism as an imagined political community is persuasive: "*imagined* because the members of even the smallest nation will never know most of their fellow-members, meet them, or even hear of them, yet in the minds of each lives the image of their communion."[4] But Anderson makes an important distinction between imagining or creating and inventing or fabricating. The notion of simultaneity, or temporal coincidence, is necessary for representing the kind of imagined community that is the nation. Members of the community then must be aware that the things they do are being replicated simultaneously by others whose existence they do not doubt. By way of analogy, Anderson refers to the structure of the "old-fashioned" novel in which characters who do not know each other are interrelated through a narrative. Simultaneity is enacted as these various characters affect each other without realizing that their actions link them together. It follows that a national culture will embody that simultaneity: that we imagine everyone wanting to sing "Nkosi Sikelel i'Afrika" on particular occasions. But just as a nation is an imagined community, a national culture as communal expression is imagined. And here slippage so easily occurs: the narrative that demonstrates simultaneity becomes the master narrative; to regard a particular expressive form as the national culture—always by the agencies and institutions of an authoritative order—is also about limiting the imagination, about becoming official. The institutions of church, universities, the ANC cultural office, and so forth, will make pronouncements on culture that will also be about exclusion and differentiation, the most obvious and necessary being those expressions that support an old repressive order. Edward Said refers to culture as a "system of exclusions legislated from above... by which such things as anarchy, disorder, irrationality, inferiority, bad taste, and immorality are identified, then deposited outside the culture and kept there by the power of the State and its institutions."[5] To instate a popular form like a traditional dance may be an attempt to draw in the culturally disenfranchised, but the term *popular* masks obvious exclusions: the dance can be performed only by strong, young, black people.

If we look at the tradition in whose name such a performance is defended, further problems arise. Under colonial rule, cultural practices were stifled so that the period is characterized by rupture. Since the fabric of society has changed under the pressures of urbanization and industrialization, it is inaccurate to haul up practices of the past in the name of an authentic tradition, when tradition itself is bound up with temporality and reliant on a temporal continuum. Historians like Jeff Guy and Sandra Burman have commented on institutions like *lobola*, or bride-wealth, which "no longer fulfills the same function as it did in precapitalist societies; it is only at the most superficial level that it can be seen as the perpetuation of a traditional social feature."[6] In the precapitalist context, bride-wealth based on productive female labor brought security and respect to women; in the post-colonial context, it necessarily becomes commodified as part of a wider system of accumulation based on wage-labor and thus can be read as the demeaning sale of women. "Traditional" dances like *Iqhawe*, marked by "traditional" dress, drums, singing, and sexually provocative movement, can be analyzed in the same way. In the past, when sexuality was celebrated within the parameters of agrarian codes, the dance would have evolved as a desirable form that allowed the young to pick their future partners. Such a dance as export culture, however, no longer serves that function but, more importantly, *can* no longer serve that function in a society reared on "Dallas" and "Dynasty" in which sexuality is commodified and fetishized through multinational capital. In other words, the *Iqhawe* is not and cannot be *Iqhawe:* participants do not choose sexual partners at these political events; it is a representation of a form of the past and as such must forfeit its claim to authenticity.

If we take the meaning of a work to be determined by its context, not only of production but also of reception, then we have to attend to how meaning is produced for a "Dallas"-fed audience among which racist views of black hypersexuality still abound and where Otherness is reinforced by the dance. Which is not the same as saying that our practices must be circumscribed by European perceptions of us; but rather that, as Njabulo Ndebele so admirably shows in his fiction, affirmative statements about our undervalued culture require thoughtful negotiation with negative stereotypes.

If a culture has been arrested, hybridized, and tipped into alien trappings, then tradition becomes a hypothetical notion. We have to imagine how certain practices would have developed, or whether they would have been retained at all. To haul up traditions through the centuries is to do what the anthropologist Johannes Fabian accuses European anthropologists of—"denial of coevalness," or believing that we do not experience time as the European does.[7] Europe "others" people by assuming that they exist in a kind of eternal present, an assumption that has allowed anthropologists to codify and classify customs and manners of non-Europeans in ways that fixed them in time. Since tradition is not a monolith dragged along through the ages, the idea of keeping it alive or reviving it is one that must be problematized. Williams cites tradition as "an instance of cultural reproduction in action . . . a selection and reselection of elements of the past."[8] Only certain elements of the past are retained; others are gladly dropped, and various groups would ideally select which ones and how according to their own interests. We should therefore be looking at the criteria for retaining, dropping, modifying, or reviving certain practices and asking questions about such criteria.

One criterion that is openly acknowledged and insisted upon is, of course, that the national culture must be founded upon resistance to the old order. And a close look at the process of establishing the national culture goes some way toward explaining its criteria. It is inevitable that a subordinate culture should be in dialogue with the official culture of the regime, in other words, react against it in order to transform not only the official forms but also the oppressed people's self-perception. So if the dominant culture undervalues our way of life, our customs, our clothes, and our language with the result that we have distanced ourselves from these forms, a resistance culture reacts by boldly reclaiming these cultural expressions and, gloriously indifferent to dominant perceptions, inflects them with the politics of resistance. Or reacts by rehabilitating forms like the miners' gumboot dance that previously had been given a degrading function by the repressive system. But this process surely must continue; attempts at arresting it at this stage turn the reactive (that which opposed an unjust system) into reactionary (that which opposes further change). Such a movement from reactive to reactionary parallels the shift from a national culture that is an imaginary entity which fires our will to be free, into an official culture that is an ossification, an attempt to fix certain forms, to authorize and validate them as *the* desirable, correct forms. The process, of course, will continue regardless; the cycle will repeat itself: the official culture can only lead to a new culture of resistance as the unofficial voices struggle to be heard.

If resistance is endemic to culture, then the slide into official culture can only be avoided by acknowledging this fact and by gathering the notion of resistance into the concept of a national culture. There is clearly a need to imagine a community with common aspirations, but it is unrealistic for such a national culture to aspire to a common expressive form. A national culture does find its material form in the highly symbolic national anthem, but there can be only one such anthem. To instate a traditional performance as artistic expression of such comradeship will always be what a dominant group imagines to be a legitimate expression for the subordinate. That is what our discourse about culture ought to confront; an emerging democratic order must acknowledge the fact that even within such an order there are power relations at play. And the reflectionist model of cultural expression, that it simply mirrors what we experience, conveniently conceals the relationship between culture and power.

It is the reflectionist model that allows the documentary to be privileged by the democratic movement as the desirable cultural form, and, according to this model, the traditional dance can be read as documenting the past. However, a look at photography, which in South Africa has become synonymous with documentation, offers an example of how the question of power is evaded. The documentary does, of course, play the important political function of providing information in a state of emergency, or of presenting information that conflicts with that put out by a repressive regime. But it is important to remember that in support of its lies, the regime too relies on this medium. In a recent issue of *Creative Camera*, Neville Dubow, professor of fine art at the University of Capetown, writes of photographic practice as if it could be nothing other than documenting the violence in South Africa. He refers to "standards of technical excellence" that presumably allow the photographer to record more accurately. As a new direction, he commends David Goldblatt's *The Transported of Kwandebele*, a work that required the photographer to make a daily grinding bus journey with the people of the Kwandebele homeland to their place of employment. He took photographs during the journey, and his collaborator collected statements from the people. The work, we are told, is an accurate documentation of their lives, a cultural form that reflects the real world of Apartheid. The camera, jolted during the journey, testifies to the authenticity of the experience.[9]

Now I do not want to be rude about well-meaning projects, but in the wider world of fine-art photography, technical excellence has long since been superseded by manipulating the medium in order to explore it as ideological tool. Radical feminists, for instance, have used photography to expose the myth of the camera's objectivity and to upset the belief in vision as a privileged means of access to truth. Goldblatt's work about Kwandebele will undoubtedly be interesting in that it will tell us more about the photographer and his curious experience, an experience that is not and can never be the experience of the people he purports to tell us about. The work conflates the two, and so suppresses its reproduction of power relations.

Strategies for writing can also be discussed in terms of power relations. In their work on Kafka called "What Is a Minor Literature?" Félix Guattari and Gilles Deleuze pooh-pooh the dream of so many literary movements to assume the status of a major literature, "to offer themselves as a sort of state language, an official language."[10] They use the spatial metaphor of territorialization that they believe characterizes literature produced by an oppressed or marginalized people written in the language of the oppressors. For Kafka, as a member of a Jewish minority, the available choices were, first, to enrich Prague German artificially, in other words, to infuse the language with Jewish mysticism – Kabbala and alchemy. Deleuze and Guattari call this an attempt at symbolic reterritorialization that they say "accentuates its break from the people and will find its political result only in . . . the 'dream of Zion.'"[11] The second choice is reterritorialization through dialect or patois, a vernacular language filled with archaisms to which the writer will try to give a contemporary sense. Kafka chose deterritorialization. He wrote in Prague German and exploited the very poverty of the deterritorialized language, pushing it further in the direction of deterritorialization, to "tear out of Prague German all the qualities of underdevelopment that it has tried to hide."[12] There are obviously problems with Deleuze and Guattari's references to the poverty of Prague German. But if we leave aside such misconceptions about a language being poor and read their description as a metaphor for the political inflection of language, then the notion of territorialization seems to me a useful one to apply, not only to literary but to all cultural practice in the new emerging South Africa.

If we look at Apartheid's project in geographical terms, that is, at the establishment and underdevelopment of the homelands in the name of maintaining indigenous cultures, then deterritorialization becomes more than a metaphor. A truly national state, the abolition of an unjust geography, would coincide with abolishing notions of master narrative, of so-called truthful documentation, of turning minor vernacular forms into major official ones.

In terms of the geographical metaphor, the Kwandebele project and the privileging of traditional dance as an expression of national culture can be seen as acts of reterritorialization. Since the dance is itself a reworking of tradition that seeks to conceal that transformation, coming clean or coming to terms with such transformations seems essential. We can no longer ignore popular cultural fusions or the obvious hybridizations popularized through the new media networks. The technological revolution has given all cultures an internationalist aspect; conservative forces have drawn on this aspect to forge the popular culture as represented, for instance, on television or syndicated magazines from *True Love* to *Tribute*. Rather than pursue "authenticity," a radical culture would engage with such representations, expose the poverty in their glossy images of the corporate black, intervene in their presentation, and *re*-present in ways that explore and challenge power relations. We may have to give up beloved notions of correct forms for expressing a national culture, but such radical cultural practices, which necessarily will constitute a new social order, will also prevent the perilous slide into official culture.

Harold A. Bascom

Apata

I was raised in a coastal village in Guyana in which the standard for beauty was measured against the Euro-Caucasian profile and skin hue. Being dark-skinned was a life sentence. I remember well my elder brothers and their friends squatting before the village church at night and talking about women. For them, having "class" meant landing a girl with skin the color of vanilla ice cream. The dark-skinned dreamt of having a light-skinned mate to "pass them off." It was even believed that a dark-skinned man who landed a high-level, white-collar position should seek to acquire a light-skinned spouse to enhance his prestige in social circles. And it was considered an achievement to return from Europe with a white wife. Into such a society I was born and grew up – though not at all stupid – under the Union Jack.[1]

I am burnt-umber dark. From a very young age, cognizance of the politics of skin pigmentation came forcibly down on me. *Dark* was not the word that was used to make many a dark-skinned native feel less than human. That word was *black*, accompanied by a scornful twisting of the lips. For many of us, it was cringing time when the light-skinned chose to sing:

> If you're white, you see the light,
> If you're brown, you stick around...
> But if you're black – stay back!

And sadly, many a dark-skinned man, woman, and child believed the rhyme and accepted subservience throughout their lives. Nonetheless, some dark-skinned individuals damned the ditty and dared to see the light. It was, however, a task to be dark-skinned and successful.

My primary school years were very significant. Somehow there was always that "Sir" or "Miss" who preferred to cuddle and encourage the light-skinned child. As a result, light-skinned students stood to gain better grades. We dark-skinned children, on the other hand – shunned and often afraid to speak up – stood the greatest chance of being shunted into the "dunce" section of the class. (A friend of mine, dark and scorned, found solace as a truant between the old tombs of the school church's cemetery. He later drifted into a life of crime and was shot dead trying to escape the law in a hospital cemetery not far from the sighing Atlantic.)

Things being that way, the light-skinned were likely to win the scholarships, the white-collar jobs, and subsequently, the high political offices; the dark-skinned – the pick, shovel, and a job in the road repair gang. For many "unbleached" individuals, it was easier to dream, to live for the present than for a questionable future.

And then there was Clement Cuffy (also known as Michael Durant). The story exploded in the newspapers in 1959. I was eight years old. Cuffy was a twenty-two-year-old black criminal who, according to police and the press, stole a Winchester semiautomatic rifle (along with a thousand rounds of high-speed ammunition) from the white mining prospector he worked for in the hinterlands and robbed a village post office. The British Guiana Police Force mounted an investigation and an unprecedented manhunt for the post-office robber.

After some eight to nine months, Cuffy was traced to a bush camp near my coastal village. Surrounded by the dragnet, Cuffy was called upon to surrender. Instead, he opened fire; the police returned it; one corporal was killed and a constable severely wounded. Clement Cuffy escaped. The story made headlines the morning after: the search for "outlaw" Clement Cuffy began in earnest, and it was hailed as the greatest manhunt in the annals of British Guiana, involving hundreds of police personnel.

In flashback I see myself, eight years old, standing day after day on the bridge that led from the public road and over a trench to our front lot, watching police lorries rushing past to the manhunt area and, many hours later, speeding back from Parika, the village next to the area. And for me every lorry whizzing back carried dead or wounded policemen. I remember being shown the picture of Clement Cuffy, and twenty-three years later, thumbing through yellowing back issues of newspapers and old police reports, finding this "mug shot" of Cuffy: "DESCRIPTION: age 22/ negro/ 5'7"/ medium build/ broad shoulders/ extra thick lips/ high cheek bones/ ears very close to the head." Eventually Cuffy was captured; he had three wounds in his leg, received during his various encounters with the police, from which he subsequently died.

• • •

Cut to the 1970s. I am now a young man. I want to write a novel. All around me I see a lack of belief in ourselves as Guyanese, a lack of belief in ourselves as a people, a lack of pride in our everyday lives and in our very existence. For many of my people, our Guyanese heritage is something to be denied. The few locally written stage plays are structured along colonialist lines: lead/central characters speak "standard" English; lesser characters (servants, maids, gardeners) speak in the local dialect, which is often written in such a way as to make those characters sound ridiculous, rendering them menial and comic. In the majority of stage plays produced during this time, local actors and actresses receive accolades for speaking "round mouth" (as mimicked, high-brow English enunciation is still referred to).

I could not accept this and became even more determined to write a novel. Friends cautioned against it. Who would publish a novel *about* Guyana in a close-to-the-true Guyanese vein? There is nothing that promises fictional adventure in this drab existence. (It was during this time that the Guyanese writer Shiek Sadeek, who later died overseas where he had fled in hopes of recognition, had been forced to self-publish his second full-length novel *The Malali Makers*, a local story written in a Spillane-ish framework complete with first-person P.I. slanguage.) The major objection to my proposed novel, however, was: one must be living abroad in order to publish a "real" book.

But determined I was. I looked to my childhood for the subject matter for the novel that would prove them wrong. I looked into myself and there was Clement Cuffy and in his wake three hundred armed policemen led by white and mulatto officers. Here was a local who was not perceived as just another cutlass-wielding native criminal by the colonial authorities. Here was a man branded "kill crazy" and yet who stood out as a lone black man who dared to pit himself against the colonial system. I looked into myself, and there was Clement Cuffy looking back at me with his mean dark face and his telescopic rifle... and in his heart, still, that resolve *to be*. And my novel, *Apata,* was born.

Eduardo Galeano

The Dictatorship and Its Aftermath

Translated by Mark Fried

The Symbols

A lot of ash has fallen on this purple land. During the twelve years of military
dictatorship, Liberty was only the name of a plaza and a prison. In that prison –
the principal cage for political prisoners – it was against regulation to draw preg-
nant women, birds, butterflies, or stars; the prisoners could not whistle, laugh,
sing, walk quickly, nor greet one another without permission. But then, except for
the jailers and the exiles, everyone was a prisoner: three million prisoners, even if
the jails seemed to hold only a few thousand. One out of every eighty Uruguayans
had a hood tied over his head; but invisible hoods covered the rest as well, condemned to isolation and noncommunication, even if they were spared the torture.
Fear and silence became a mandatory way of life. The dictatorship, enemy of all
that grows and moves, paved over the grass it could trap in the plazas and cut
down or painted white all trees within range.

The Model

With slight variations, a similar model of repression and inoculation against the
forces of social change was applied in several Latin American countries during the
1970s. To enforce the Pan-American doctrine of national security, the military
acted as occupying armies in their own countries, as the armed wing of the International Monetary Fund and the system of privilege that the fund embodies and
perpetuates. The guerrilla threat provided the alibi for state terrorism, which then
mobilized to cut workers' salaries in half, crush unions, and suppress critical
thought. By spreading mass terror and uncertainty, they hoped to impose a reign
of the deaf-mute. The computer at the Joint Chiefs of Staff of the Armed Forces

placed all Uruguayan citizens into one of three categories, A, B, or C, according to the degree of threat they posed to the proposed military kingdom of the sterile. Without the Certificate of Democratic Faith, emitted by that computer and delivered by the police – specialists in Democracy, having taken courses from Dan Mitrione, U.S. Professor of Torture Techniques – one could neither obtain employment nor keep it. Even to have a birthday party, police authorization was required. Every house was a cell; every factory, every office, every school became a concentration camp.

The Aggression

The dictatorship demolished the system of education and in its place imposed a system of ignorance. By the brutal substitution of professors and programs, they sought to domesticate students and oblige them to accept both a barracks morality, which considers sex a "hygienic outlet" or "marital duty," and a mummified culture, which considers "natural" the right of property over things and people, as well as the duty of women to obey men, children to obey parents, the poor to obey the rich, blacks to obey whites, and civilians to obey the military.

The order was given to dismember and detongue the country. All ties of solidarity and creativity that brought Uruguayans into contact with one another were a crime; a conspiracy, all that brought them into contact with the world; and subversive, any word that did not lie. All who took part were punished – political and union activists *and* whoever did not denounce them.

The Response

And nevertheless, Uruguayan culture managed to keep breathing, inside the country and out. In all its history it never received higher praise than the ferocious persecution it suffered during those years. Uruguayan culture remained alive and was able to respond with life to the machinery of silence and death. It stayed alive in those who remained and those of us who had to leave, in the words that passed from hand to hand, from mouth to mouth, like contraband, hidden or disguised; in the actors who spoke today's truth through Greek theater, and in those who were forced to wander about the world like errant jesters; in the troubadours who sang defiantly in exile and at home; in the scientists and artists who did not sell their souls; in the insolent carnival musicians and in the newspapers that died and were reborn; in the cries scrawled on the streets and in the poems scrawled in the jails on cigarette papers.

But if by culture we mean a way of being and of communicating, if culture contains all the symbols of collective identity we express in everyday life, then the resistance was not limited to these outward signs. It was much broader and deeper.

In the final days of the dictatorship, Obdulio Varela, a popular soccer player who knows well the people and the land, offered a bitter summation: "*We have grown selfish,*" Obdulio said at the beginning of 1985. "*We no longer see ourselves in others. Democracy is going to be difficult.*"

And yet, the Uruguayan people knew how to respond with solidarity in spite of the system of dismemberment. There were many ways of finding each other and of sharing – though it be little, though it be nothing – which also formed part, a radiant part, of Uruguay's cultural resistance during those years and which flowered above all among the poorest of the working class. And I am referring not only to the great street demonstrations, but also to less spectacular events like soup kitchens and housing cooperatives and other works of imagination and anger which confirmed that solidarity is inversely proportional to income level. Or to put it à la Martín Fierro, the fire that really heats comes from below.

The Damage

There are no statistics of the soul. There is no way to measure the depth of the cultural wound. We know that Uruguay exports shoes to the United States and that nevertheless Uruguayans now buy five times fewer shoes than twenty years ago. But we cannot know to what extent they have poisoned our insides, to what extent we have been mutilated in our consciousness, our identity, and our memory.

There are a few facts, it's true, that are plain to see – circumstances caused, or at least worsened, by the dictatorship and by the economic policies in whose service it turned Uruguay into a vast torture chamber. For example, there are books that can help us to know and to understand ourselves and that could contribute a great deal toward the recuperation of the country's culture. But if the price of just one of those books is equivalent to one-seventh or one-eighth of the monthly salary earned by many Uruguayans, then *censorship by price is functioning just as efficiently as censorship by the police did before*. The circulation of Uruguayan books has fallen by five or six times; people do not read, not because they don't want to, but because they can't afford to.

The impossibility of return is another fact. There is no damage comparable to the drain of human resources that the country has been suffering for years and that the dictatorship multiplied. Of those of us who went into exile for having, as one functionary put it, "ideological ideas," some have been able to return. Some, I say, not all, or even close to all. Of the hundreds of thousands whom the system has condemned – and continues to condemn – to seek beyond the borders their daily bread, how many can return? *Sick with sterility, the system performs a curious alchemy: it converts the keys of progress into a national malady.* The high cultural level of Uruguayan workers, which could and should be a factor that encourages development, is turned against the country insofar as it facilitates the departure of the population. Now we have a democracy, a civilian government instead of a military dictatorship; but the system is the same, and economic policy remains essentially unchanged.

Business freedom – enemy of human freedom – usurpation of wealth, usurpation of life: this economic policy has had cultural consequences that are quite evident. *The encouragement of consumption, the consumer squandering that reached paroxysm during the dictatorship, not only led to an asphyxiating six-fold increase in the foreign debt, it also discouraged creativity. The speculative urge not only empties us of material wealth, it empties us of ethical values and, therefore, of cultural values, because it derides productivity and confirms the old suspicion that those who work are fools.* In addition, the avalanche of foreign merchandise that destroys local industry and pulverizes wages, the readjustment of the economy to adapt to the foreign market, and the abandonment of the domestic market *imply, culturally speaking, self-hate*: the country spits in the mirror and adopts the ideology of impotency as its own.

"Sorry, it's made here," a shopkeeper told me when he sold me a can of meat, the day after my return. After twelve years of exile, I confess that I did not expect this. And when I mentioned it to my friends, they blamed "the Process." Neither did I expect the dictatorship to be called *Process. The language was, and perhaps still is, sick from fear.* We have lost the healthy custom of calling a spade a spade.

The Task

Our land of free men and women is hurt but alive. The military dictatorship that for twelve years forced it to shut up, to lie, to distrust, was unable to sour its soul. *"They weren't able to turn us into them,"* a friend told me, after the years of terror. And I believe it.

But fear survives disguised as prudence. Be careful, be careful: democracy is fragile, and it will break if you jostle it. From the point of view of the owners of an unjust system, one that strikes fear in order to perpetuate itself, all creative audacity is thought to be a terrorist provo-

cation. A responsible government is an immobilized government; its duty is to keep the *latifundios* and the repressive machinery intact, to forget the dictatorship's crimes, and to pay punctually the interest on the foreign debt. The officers left the country in ruins, and in ruins it remains. In the villages, the old people water flowers among the tombs.

And the young people? The policy of collective mutilation was aimed above all at them. The dictatorship tried to drain them of their conscience and of everything else. The system that denies them work and obliges them to leave is directed against them, above all against them. Will they be creative enough, insolent enough, and tough enough to confront the system that denies them? Will they realize in time that, for the country to remain democratic, it cannot remain paralyzed? Or will the oxygen of Liberty make them repent their youth and keep the fear of ghosts in their hearts? Will they embrace with fatal resignation the destiny of sterility and solitude that those specters offer the country? Or will they act to transform it – even if they do it all wrong – using their capacity for enthusiasm and beautiful madness? Will the country be a fountain of life or an elephant cemetery?

Nadine Gordimer

Living in the Interregnum

THE WILLIAM JAMES LECTURE, 1982

> Police files are our only claim to immortality.
> – Milan Kundera, *The Book of Laughter and Forgetting*

I live at six thousand feet in a society whirling, stamping, swaying with the force of revolutionary change. The vision is heady – the image of the demonic dance – and accurate, not romantic: an image of actions springing from emotion, knocking deliberately aside. The city is Johannesburg, the country South Africa, and the time the last years of the colonial era in Africa.

It's inevitable that nineteenth-century colonialism should finally come to its end there, because there it reached its ultimate expression, open in the legalized land- and mineral-grabbing, open in the labor exploitation of indigenous peoples, open in the constitutionalized, institutionalized racism that was concealed by the British under the pious notion of uplift, the French and the Portuguese under the sly notion of selective assimilation. An extraordinarily obdurate crossbreed of Dutch, German, English, French in the South African white settler population produced a bluntness that unveiled everyone's refined white racism: the flags of European civilization dropped, and there it was unashamedly, the ugliest creation of man, and they baptized the thing in the Dutch Reformed Church, called it *Apartheid*, coining the ultimate term for every manifestation, over the ages, in many countries, of race prejudice. Every country could see its semblances there; and most peoples.

The sun that never set over one or other of the nineteenth-century colonial empires of the world is going down finally in South Africa. Since the black uprisings of the mid-seventies, coinciding with the independence of Mozambique and Angola, and later that of Zimbabwe, the past has begun to drop rapidly out of sight, even for those who would have liked to go on living in it. Historical coordinates don't fit life any longer; new ones, where they exist, have couplings not to the rulers, but to the ruled. It is not for nothing that I chose as an epigraph for my novel *July's People* a quotation from Gramsci: "The old is dying, and the new cannot be born; in this interregnum there arises a great diversity of morbid symptoms."[1]

In this interregnum, I and all my countrymen and women are living. Ten thousand miles from home, I speak to you out of it. I am going, quite frequently, to let events personally experienced as I was thinking toward or writing this paper interrupt theoretical flow, because this interaction – this essential disruption, this breaking in upon the existential coherence we call concept – is the very state of being I must attempt to convey. I have never before spoken publicly from so personal a point of view. Apart from the Joycean reasons of secrecy and cunning – to which I would add jealous hoarding of private experience for transmutation into fiction – there has been for me a peculiarly South African taboo. In the official South African consciousness, the ego is white; it has always seen all South Africa as ordered around it. Even the ego that seeks to abdicate this alienation does so in an assumption of its own salvation that in itself expresses ego and alienation. And the Western world press, itself overwhelmingly white, constantly feeds this ego from its own. Visiting journalists, parliamentarians, congressmen, and congresswomen come to South Africa to ask whites what is going to happen there. They meet blacks through whites; they rarely take the time and trouble, on their own initiative, to encounter more than the man who comes into the hotel bedroom to take away the empty beer bottles. With the exception of films made clandestinely by South African political activists, black and white, about resistance events, most foreign television documentaries, while condemning the whites out of their own mouths, are nevertheless preoccupied with what will happen to whites when the Apartheid regime goes. I have shunned the arrogance of interpreting my country through the private life that, as Theodor Adorno puts it, "drags on only as an appendage of the social process,"[2] in a time and place of which I am a part. Now I am going to break the inhibition or destroy the privilege of privacy, whichever way you look at it. I have to offer you myself as my most closely observed specimen from the interregnum; yet I remain a writer, not a public speaker: nothing I say here will be as true as my fiction.

There is another reason for confession. The particular segment of South African society to which I belong, by the color of my skin, whether I like it or not, represents a crisis that has a particular connection with the Western world, to which you in this audience belong. I think that may become self-evident before I arrive at the point of explication; it is *not*, I want to assure you, the old admitted complicity in the slave trade or the price of raw materials.

I have used the term *segment* in defining my place in South African society because within the white section of that society – less than one-fifth of the total population now, predicted to drop to one-seventh by the year 2000[3] – there is a segment pre-occupied, in the interregnum, neither by plans to run away from nor merely by ways to survive physically and economically in the black state that is coming. I cannot give you numbers for this segment, but in measure of some sort of faith in the possibility of structuring society humanly, in the possession of skills and intellect to devote to this end, there is something to offer the future. *How* to offer it is our preoccupation. Since skills, technical and intellectual, can be bought in markets other than those of the vanquished white power, although they are important as a commodity ready to hand, they do not constitute a claim on the future.

That claim rests on something else: how to offer *one's self.*

In the eyes of the black majority which will rule, whites of former South Africa will have to redefine themselves in a new collective life within new structures. From the all-white Parliament to the all-white country club and the separate "white" television channels, it is not a matter of blacks taking over white institutions, it is one of conceiving of institutions – from nursery schools to government departments – that reflect a societal structure vastly different from that built to the specifications of white power and privilege. This vast difference will be evident even if capitalism survives, since South Africa's capitalism, like South Africa's whites-only democracy, has been unlike anyone else's. For example, free enterprise among us is for whites only, since black capitalists may trade only, and with many limitations on their "free" enterprise, in black ghettos. In cities the kind of stores and services offered will change when the lifestyle of the majority – black, working class – establishes the authority of the enfranchised demand in place of the dictated demand. At present the consumer gets what the producer's racially estimated idea of his place in life decrees to be his needs.

A more equitable distribution of wealth may be enforced by laws. The hierarchy of perception that white institutions and living habits implant throughout daily experience in every white, from childhood, can be changed only by whites themselves, from within. The weird ordering of the collective life, in South Africa, has slipped its special contact lens into the eyes of whites; we actually *see* blacks differently, which includes *not seeing*, not noticing their unnatural absence, since there are so many perfectly ordinary venues of daily life – the cinema, for instance – where blacks have never been allowed in, and so one has forgotten that they could be, might be, encountered there.

I am writing in my winter quarters, at an old deal table on a veranda in the sun; out of the corner of my eye I see a piece of junk mail, the brochure of a chain bookstore, assuring me of constantly expanding service and showing the staff of a newly opened branch – Ms. So-and-So, Mr. Such-and-Such, and (one black face) "Gladys." What a friendly, informal form of identification in an "equal opportunity" enterprise! Gladys is seen by fellow workers, by the photographer who noted down names, and – it is assumed – readers, quite differently from the way the white workers are seen. I gaze at her as they do . . . She is simply "Gladys," the convenient handle by which she is taken up by the white world, used, and put down again, like the glass the king drinks from in Rilke's poem.[4] Her surname, her African name, belongs to Soweto, which her smiling white companions are less likely ever to visit than New York or London.

The successfully fitted device in the eye of the beholder is something the average white South African is not conscious of, for Apartheid is above all a habit; the unnatural seems natural – a far from banal illustration of Hannah Arendt's banality of evil. The segment of the white population to which I belong has become highly conscious of a dependency on distorted vision induced since childhood; and we are aware that with the inner eye we have "seen too much to be innocent."[5] But this kind of awareness, represented by white guilt in the 1950s, has been seen by us off into the sunset, since, as Czeslaw Milosz puts it, "guilt, which is so highly developed in modern man . . . saps his belief in the value of his own perceptions and judgments,"[6] and we have need of ours. We have to believe in our ability to find new perceptions, and our ability to judge their truth. Along with weeping over what's done, we've given up rejoicing in what Günter Grass calls headbirths,[7] those Athenian armchair deliveries of the future presented to blacks by whites.

Not all blacks even concede that whites can have any part in the new that cannot yet be born. An important black leader who does, Bishop Desmond Tutu,[8] defines that participation:

. . . what I consider to be the place of the white man in this – popularly called the liberation struggle. I am firmly non-racial and so welcome the participation of all, both black and white, in the struggle for the new South Africa which must come whatever the cost. But I want . . . to

state that at this stage the leadership of the struggle must be firmly in black hands. They must determine what will be the priorities and the strategy of the struggle.

Whites unfortunately have the habit of taking over and usurping the leadership and taking crucial decisions—largely, I suppose, because of the head start they had in education and experience...of this kind. The point is that however much they want to identify with blacks it is an existential fact...that they have not really been victims of this baneful oppression and exploitation...It is a divide that can't be crossed and that must give blacks a primacy in determining the course and goal of the struggle. Whites must be willing to follow.[9]

Blacks must learn to talk; whites must learn to listen—wrote the black South African poet Mongane Wally Serote, in the seventies.[10] This is the premise on which the white segment to which I belong lives its life at present. Does it sound like an abdication of the will? That is because you who live in a democracy are accustomed to exerting the right to make abstract statements of principle for which, at least, the structures of practical realization exist; the symbolic action of the like-minded in signing a letter to a newspaper or the lobbying of Congress is a reminder of constitutional rights to be invoked. For us, Tutu's premise enjoins a rousing of the will, a desperate shaking into life of the faculty of rebellion against unjust laws that has been outlawed by the dying power, and faculties of renewal that often are rebuffed by the power that is struggling to emerge. The rider Desmond Tutu didn't add to his statement is that although white support is expected to be active, it is also expected that whites' different position in the still-standing structures of the old society will require actions that, while complementary to those of blacks, must be different from blacks'. Whites are expected to find their own forms of struggle, which can only sometimes coincide with those of blacks.

That there can be, at least, the coincident cooperation is reassuring; that, at least, should be a straightforward form of activism. But it is not; for in this time of morbid symptoms there are contradictions within the black liberation struggle itself, based not only, as would be expected, on the opposing ideological alignments of the world outside, but also on the moral confusion of claims—on land, on peoples—from the precolonial past in relation to the unitary state the majority of blacks and the segment of whites are avowed to. So, for whites, it is not simply a matter of follow-the-leader behind blacks; it's taking on, as blacks do, choices to be made out of confusion, empirically, pragmatically, ideologically, or idealistically about the practical moralities of the struggle. This is the condition, imposed by history in those areas of action where black and white participation coincides.

I am at a public meeting at the Johannesburg City Hall one night, after working at this paper during the day. The meeting is held under the auspices of the Progressive Federal Party, the official opposition in the all-white South African parliament. The issue is a deal being made between the South African government and the kingdom of Swaziland whereby three thousand square miles of South African territory and 850,000 South African citizens, part of the Zulu "homeland" KwaZulu, would be given to Swaziland. The principal speakers are Chief Gatsha Buthelezi, leader of 5.5 million Zulus, Bishop Desmond Tutu, and Mr. Ray Swart, a white liberal and a leader of the Progressive Federal Party. Chief Buthelezi has consistently refused to take so-called independence for KwaZulu, but – although declaring himself for the banned African National Congress – by accepting all stages of so-called self-government up to the final one, has transgressed the nonnegotiable principle of the African National Congress, a unitary South Africa. Bishop Tutu upholds the principle of a unitary South Africa. The Progressive Federal Party's constitution provides for a federal structure in a new, nonracial South Africa, recognizing as de facto entities the "homelands" whose creation by the Apartheid government the party nevertheless opposes. Also on the platform are members of the Black Sash, the white women's organization that has taken a radical stand as a white ally of the black struggle; these women support a unitary South Africa. In the audience of about two thousand, a small number of whites is lost among exuberant, ululating, applauding Zulus. Order – and what's more, amicability – is kept by Buthelezi's marshals, equipped, beneath the garb of a private militia drawn from his tribal Inkatha movement, with Zulu muscle in place of guns.

What is Bishop Tutu doing here? He doesn't recognize the "homelands."

What are the Black Sash women doing here? They don't recognize the "homelands."

What is the Progressive Federal Party doing – a party firmly dedicated to constitutional action only – hosting a meeting where the banned black liberation salute – and battle cry – "Amandla! Awethu!": "Power – to the people!" – is shaking the columns of municipal doric, and a black man's tribal army instead of the South African police is keeping the peace? What am I doing here, applauding Gatsha Buthelezi and Ray Swart? I don't recognize the "homelands" nor do I support a federal South Africa.

I was there – *they* were there – because, removed from its areas of special interest (KwaZulu's "national" concern with land and people belonging to the Zulus), the issue was yet another government device to buy off surrounding states that give shelter to South African freedom fighters, and create support for a proposed "constellation" of southern African states gathered protectively around the present

South African regime; finally, to dispossess black South Africans of their South African citizenship, thus reducing the ratio of black to white population.

Yet the glow of my stinging palms cooled; what a paradox I had accommodated in myself! Moved by a display of tribal loyalty when I believe in black unity, applauding a "homelands" leader, above all, scandalized by the excision of part of a "homeland" from South Africa when the "homelands" policy is itself the destruction of the country as an entity. But these are the confusions blacks have to live with, and if I am making any claim to accompany them beyond Apartheid, so must I.

The state of interregnum is a state of Hegel's "disintegrated consciousness,"[11] of contradictions. It is from its internal friction that energy somehow must be struck, for us whites; energy to break the vacuum of which we are subconsciously aware, for however hated and shameful the collective life of Apartheid and its structures has been to us, there is, now, the unadmitted fear of being without structures. The interregnum is not only between two social orders but also between two identities, one known and discarded, the other unknown and undetermined. Whatever the human cost of the liberation struggle, whatever "Manichean poisons,"[12] must be absorbed as stimulants in the interregnum, the black knows he or she will be at home, at last, in the future. The white who has declared himself or herself for that future, who belongs to the white segment that was never at home in white supremacy, does not know whether he or she will find a home at last. It is assumed, not only by racists, that this depends entirely on the willingness of blacks to let whites in; but we, if we live out our situation consciously, proceeding from the Pascalian wager that the home of the white African exists, know that this depends also on our finding our way there out of the perceptual clutter of curled photographs of master and servant relationships, the 78 rpms of history repeating the conditioning of the past.

A black man I may surely call my friend because we have survived a time when he did not find it possible to accept a white's friendship, and a time when I didn't think I could accept that he should decide when that time was past, said to me this year, "Whites have to learn to struggle." It was not an admonition but a sincere encouragement. Expressed in political terms, the course of our friendship, his words and his attitude, signify the phasing out or passing usefulness of the extreme wing of the black consciousness movement, with its separatism of the past ten years, and the return to the tenets of the most broadly based and prestigious of black movements, the banned African National Congress: nonracialism, belief that race oppression is part of the class struggle, and recognition that it is possible for whites to opt out of class and race privilege and identify with black liberation.

My friend was not, needless to say, referring to those whites, from Abram Fischer to Helen Joseph and Neil Aggett,[13] who have risked and in some cases lost their lives in the political struggle with Apartheid. It would be comfortable to assume that he was not referring, either, to the articulate outriders of the white segment, intellectuals, writers, lawyers, students, church and civil rights progressives, who keep the whips of protest cracking. But I know he *was*, after all, addressing those of us belonging to the outriders on whose actions the newspapers report and the secret police keep watch, as we prance back and forth ever closer to the fine line between being concerned citizens and social revolutionaries. Perhaps the encouragement was meant for us as well as the base of the segment—those in the audience but not up on the platform, young people and their parents' generation, who must look for some effective way, in the living of their own personal lives, to join the struggle for liberation from racism.

For a long time, such whites have felt that we are doing all we can, short of violence—a terrible threshold none of us is willing to cross, though aware that all this may mean is that it will be left to blacks to do so. But now blacks are asking a question to which every white must have a personal answer, on an issue that cannot be dealt with by a show of hands at a meeting or a signature to a petition; an issue that comes home and enters every family. Blacks are now asking why whites who believe Apartheid is something that must be abolished, not defended, continue to submit to army call-up.

We whites have assumed that army service was an example of Czeslaw Milosz's "powerlessness of the individual involved in a mechanism that works independently of his will."[14] If you refuse military service your only options are to leave the country or go to prison. Conscientious objection is not recognized in South Africa at present; legislation may establish it in some form soon, but if this is to be, is working as an army clerk not functioning as part of the war machine?

These are reasons enough for all—except a handful of men who choose prison on religious rather than on political grounds—to get into the South African army despite their opposition to Apartheid.[15] These are not reasons enough for them to do so, on the condition on which blacks can accept whites' dedication to mutual liberation. Between black and white attitudes toward struggle there stands the overheard remark of a young black woman: "I break the law because I am alive."

We whites have still to thrust the spade under the roots of our lives; for most of us, including myself, struggle is still something that has a place. But for blacks it is everywhere or nowhere.

> What is poetry which does not save Nations or people?
> – Czeslaw Milosz, *Selected Poems*

I have already delineated my presence here on the scale of a minority within a minority. Now I shall reduce my claim to significance still further. A white; a dissident white; a white writer. If I were not a writer, I should not have been invited here at all, so I must presume that although the problems of a white writer are of no importance compared with the liberation of 23.5 million black people, the peculiar relation of the writer in South Africa as interpreter, both to South Africans and to the world, of a society in struggle, makes the narrow corridor I can lead you down one in which doors fly open on the tremendous happening experienced by blacks.

For longer than the first half of this century the experience of blacks in South Africa was known to the world as it was interpreted by whites. The first widely read imaginative works exploring the central fact of South African life – racism – were written in the 1920s by whites, William Plomer and Sarah Gertrude Millin.[16] If blacks were the subjects but not the readers of books written about them, then neither whites nor blacks read much of what have since become the classics of early black literature – the few works of Herbert and Rolfes Dhlomo, Thomas Mofolo, and Sol Plaatje.[17] Their moralistic essays dealt with contemporary black life, but their fiction was mainly historical, a desperate attempt to secure, in art forms of an imposed culture, an identity and history discounted and torn up by that culture.

In the 1950s, urban blacks – Ezekiel Mphahlele, Lewis Nkosi, Can Themba, Bloke Modisane, following Peter Abrahams – began to write in English only, and about the urban industrial experience in which black and white chafed against one another across color barriers.[18] The work of these black writers interested both black and white at that improvised level known as intellectual, in South Africa: *aware* would be a more accurate term, designating awareness that the white middle-class establishment was not, as it claimed, the paradigm of South African life, and white culture was not the definitive South African culture. Somewhere at the black writers' elbows, as they wrote, was the joggle of independence coming to one colonized country after another, north of South Africa. But they wrote iron-ically of their lives under oppression; as victims, not fighters. And even those black writers who were political activists, such as the novelist Alex La Guma and the poet Dennis Brutus, made of their ideologically channeled bitterness not more than the Aristotelian catharsis, creating in the reader empathy with the oppressed rather than rousing rebellion against repression.

The fiction of white writers also produced the Aristotelian effect – and included in the price of hardback or paperback a catharsis of white guilt, for writer and reader. (It was at this stage, incidentally, that reviewers abroad added their dime's worth of morbid symptoms to our own by creating "courageous" as a criterion of literary value for South African writers.) The subject of both black and white writ-ers – the actual entities of South African life instead of those defined by separate entrances for white and black – was startlingly new and important; whatever any writer, black or white, could dare to explore there was considered ground gained for advance in the scope of all writers. There had been no iconoclastic tradition; only a single novel, William Plomer's *Turbott Wolfe*, written thirty years before, whose understanding of *what our subject really was* was still a decade ahead of our time when he phrased the total apothegm: "The native question – it's not a question, it's an answer."[19]

In the 1970s black writers began to give that answer – for themselves. It had been vociferous in the consciousness of resistance politics, manifest in political ac-tion – black mass organizations, the African National Congress, the Pan-Africanist Congress, and others – in the 1960s. But except at the oral folk-literature level of "freedom" songs, it was an answer that had not come, yet, from the one source that had never been in conquered territory, not even when industrialization con-scripted where military conquest had already devastated: the territory of the sub-conscious, where a people's own particular way of making sense and dignity of life – the base of its culture – remains unget-at-able. Writers, and not politicians, are its spokespeople.

With the outlawing of black political organizations, the banning of freedom songs and platform speeches, there came from blacks a changed attitude toward culture, and toward literature as verbal, easily accessible culture. Many black writers have been in conflict – and challenged by political activists: are you going to fight or write? Now they were told, in the rhetoric of the time: there is no conflict if you make your pen our people's weapon.

The Aristotelian catharsis, relieving black self-pity and white guilt, was clearly not the mode in which black writers could give the answer black resistance required from them. The iconoclastic mode, though it had its function where race fetishists had set up their china idols in place of "heathen" wooden ones, was too ironic and detached, other-directed. Black people had to be brought back to themselves. Black writers arrived, out of their own situation, at Brecht's discovery: their audience needed to be educated to be *astonished at the circumstances under which they function.*[20] They began to show blacks that their living conditions are their story.

South Africa does not lack its Chernyshevskys to point out that the highroad of history is not the sidewalks of fashionable white Johannesburg's suburban shopping malls any more than it was that of the Nevsky Prospekt.[21] In the bunks of migratory laborers, the 4 a.m. queues between one-room family and factory, the drunken dreams argued round braziers, is the history of blacks' defeat by conquest, the scale of the lack of value placed on them by whites, the degradation of their own acquiescence in that value; the salvation of revolt is there, too, a match dropped by the builders of every ghetto, waiting to be struck. The difficulty, even boredom, many whites experience when reading stories or watching plays by blacks in which, as they say, "nothing happens," is due to the fact that the experience conveyed is not "the development of actions" but "the representation of conditions,"[22] a mode of artistic revelation and experience for those in whose life dramatic content is in its conditions.

This mode of writing was the beginning of the black writer's function as a revolutionary; it was also the beginning of a conception of himself differing from that of the white writer's self-image. The black writer's consciousness of himself as a writer comes now from his participation in those living conditions; in the judgment of his people, that is what makes him a writer—the authority of the experience itself, not the way he perceives it and transforms it into words. Tenets of criticism are accordingly based on the critic's participation in those same living conditions, not on his ability to judge how well the writer has achieved "the disposition of natural material to a formal end that shall enlighten the imagination"— this definition of art by Anthony Burgess would be regarded by many blacks as arising from premises based on white living conditions and the thought patterns these determine: an arabesque of smoke from an expensive cigar.[23] If we have our Chernyshevskys we are short on Herzens. Literary standards and standards of human justice are hopelessly confused in the interregnum. Bad enough that in the case of white South African writers some critics at home and abroad are afraid to reject sensationalism and crass banality of execution so long as the subject of a work is "courageous." For black writers the syllogism of talent goes like this: all blacks are brothers; all brothers are equal; therefore you cannot be a better writer than I am. The black writer who questions the last proposition is betraying the first two.[24]

As a fellow writer, I myself find it difficult to accept, even for the cause of black liberation to which I am committed as a white South African citizen, that a black writer of imaginative power, whose craftsmanship is equal to what he has to say, must not be regarded above someone who has emerged – admirably – from political imprisonment with a scrap of paper on which there is jotted an alliterative arrangement of protest slogans. For me, the necessity for the black writer to find imaginative modes equal to his existential reality goes without question. But I cannot accept that he must deny, as proof of solidarity with his people's struggle, the torturous inner qualities of prescience and perception that will always differentiate him from others and that make of him – a writer. I cannot accept, either, that he should have served on him, as the black writer now has, an orthodoxy – a kit of emotive phrases, an unwritten index of subjects, a typology.

The problem is that agitprop, not recognized under that or any other name, has become the first contemporary art form that many black South Africans feel they can call their own. It fits their anger; and this is taken as proof that it is an organic growth of black creation freeing itself, instead of the old shell that it is, inhabited many times by the anger of others. I know that agitprop binds the artist with the means by which it aims to free the minds of the people. I can see, now, how often it thwarts both the black writer's common purpose to master his art and revolutionary purpose to change the nature of art, create new norms and forms out of and for a people re-creating themselves. But how can my black fellow writer agree with me, even admit the conflict I set up in him by these statements? There are those who secretly believe, but few who would assert publicly, with Gabriel García Márquez: "The writer's duty – his revolutionary duty if you like – is to write well."[25] The black writer in South Africa feels he has to accept the criteria of his people because in no other but the community of black deprivation is he in possession of selfhood. It is only through unreserved, exclusive identification with blacks that he can break the alienation of having been Other for nearly 350 years in the white-ordered society, and only through submitting to the beehive category of "cultural worker," programmed, that he can break the alienation of the artist-elitist in the black mass of industrial workers and peasants.

And, finally, he can toss the conflict back into my lap with Camus' words: "Is it possible...to be in history while still referring to values which go beyond it?"

The black writer is "in history," and its values threaten to force out the transcendent ones of art. The white, as writer and South African, does not know his place "in history" at this stage, in this time.

There are two absolutes in my life. One is that racism is evil—human damnation in the Old Testament sense, and no compromises, as well as sacrifices, should be too great in the fight against it. The other is that a writer is a being in whose sensibility is fused what Lukács calls "the duality of inwardness and outside world," and he must never be asked to sunder this union.[26] The coexistence of these absolutes often seems irreconcilable within one life, for me. In another country, another time, they would present no conflict because they would operate in unrelated parts of existence; in South Africa now they have to be coordinates for which the coupling must be found. The morality of life and the morality of art have broken out of their categories in social flux. If you cannot reconcile them, they cannot be kept from one another's throats, within you.

For me, Lukács's "divinatory-intuitive grasping of the unattained and therefore inexpressible meaning of life"[27] is what a writer, poorly evolved for the task as he or she is, is made for. As fish that swim under the weight of many dark fathoms look like any other fish but on careful examination are found to have no eyes, so writers, looking pretty much like other human beings, but moving deep under the surface of human lives, have at least some faculties of supra-observation and hyper-perception not known to others. If a writer does not go down and use these—why, he's just a blind fish. *Exactly*—says the new literary orthodoxy: he doesn't see what is happening in the visible world, among the people, on the level of their action, where battle is done with racism every day. On the contrary, say I, he brings back with him the thematic life-material that underlies and motivates their actions. "Art ...lies at the heart of all events," Joseph Brodsky writes.[28] It is from there, in the depths of being, that the most important intuition of revolutionary faith comes: the people know what to do, before the leaders. It was from that level that the yearning of black schoolchildren for a decent education was changed into a revolt in 1976; their strength came from the deep silt of repression and the abandoned wrecks of uprisings that sank there before they were born. It was from that level that an action of ordinary people for their own people made a few lines low down on a newspaper page, the other day: when some migrant contract workers from one of the "homelands" were being laid off at a factory, workers with papers of permanent residence in the "white" area asked to be dismissed in their place, since the possession of papers meant they could at least work elsewhere, whereas the migrant workers would be sent back to the "homelands," jobless.

"Being an 'author' has been unmasked as a role that, whether conformist or not, remains inescapably responsible to a given social order."[29] Nowhere in the world is Susan Sontag's statement truer than in South Africa. The white writer has to make the decision whether to remain responsible to the dying white order – and even as dissident, if he goes no further than that position, he remains *negatively* within the white order – or to declare himself positively as answerable to the order struggling to be born. And to declare himself for the latter is only the beginning; as it is for whites in a less specialized position, only more so. He has to try to find a way to reconcile the irreconcilable within himself, establish his relation to the culture of a new kind of posited community, nonracial but conceived with and led by blacks. I have entered into this commitment with trust and a sense of discovering reality, coming alive in a new way – I believe the novels and stories I have written in the last seven or eight years reflect this – for a South Africa in which white middle-class values and mores contradict realities has long become the unreality, to me. Yet I admit that I am, indeed, determined to find my place "in history" while still referring as a writer to the values that are beyond history. I shall never give them up.

Can the artist go through the torrent with his precious bit of talent tied up in a bundle on his head? I don't know yet. I can only report that the way to begin entering history out of a dying white regime is through setbacks, encouragements and rebuffs from others, and frequent disappointments in oneself. A necessary learning process...

I take a break from writing.

I am in a neighboring black country at a conference on Culture and Resistance. It is being held outside South Africa [in Gaborone, Botswana] because exiled artists and those of us who still live and work in South Africa cannot meet at home. Some white artists have not come because, not without reason, they fear the consequences of being seen, by South African secret police spies, in the company of exiles who belong to political organizations banned in South Africa, notably the African National Congress; some are not invited because the organizers regard their work and political views as reactionary. I am dubbed the blacks' darling by some whites back home because I have been asked to give the keynote address at a session devoted to literature; but I wonder if those who think me favored would care to take the flak I know will be coming at me from those corners of the hall where black separatists group. They are here not so much out of democratic right as out of black solidarity, paradoxically, since the conference is in itself a declaration that in the conviction of participants and organizers the liberation struggle and post-Apartheid culture are nonracial. There is that bond of living conditions that lassos all blacks within a loyalty containing, without constraining or resolving, bitter political differences.

Do I think white writers should write about blacks?

The artless question from the floor disguises both a personal attack on my work and an edict publicly served upon white writers by the same orthodoxy that prescribes for blacks. In the case of whites, it proscribes the creation of black characters – and by the same token, flipped head-to-tails, with which the worth of black writers is measured: the white writer does not share the total living conditions of blacks, therefore he must not write about them. There are some whites – not writers, I believe – in the hall who share this view. In the ensuing tense exchange I reply that there are whole areas of human experience, in work situations – on farms, in factories, in the city, for example – where black and white have been observing one another and interacting for nearly 350 years. I challenge my challenger to deny that there are things we know about each other that are never spoken, but are there to be written – and received with the amazement and consternation, on both sides, of having been found out. Within those areas of experience, limited but intensely revealing, there is every reason why white should create black and black white characters. For myself, I have created black characters in my fiction; whether I have done so successfully or not is for the reader to decide. What's certain is that there is no representation of our social reality without that strange area of our lives in which we have knowledge of one another.

I do not acquit myself so honestly a little later, when persecution of South African writers by banning is discussed. Someone links this with the persecution of writers in the Soviet Union, and a young man leaps to reply that the percentage of writers to population is higher in the Soviet Union than in any other part of the world and that Soviet writers work "in a trench of peace and security."

The aptness of the bizarre image, the hell for the haven he wishes to illustrate, brings no smiles behind hands among us; beyond the odd word-substitution is, indeed, a whole arsenal of tormented contradictions that could explode the conference.

Someone says, out of silence, quietly and distinctly: "Bullshit."

There is silence again. I don't take the microphone and tell the young man: there is not a contrast to be drawn between the Soviet Union's treatment of writers and that of South Africa, *there is a close analogy – South Africa bans and silences writers just as the Soviet Union does, although we do not have resident censors in South African publishing houses and dissident writers are not sent to mental hospitals. I am silent. I am silent because, in the debates of the interregnum, any criticism of the communist system is understood as a defense of the capitalist system which has brought forth the pact of capitalism and racism that is Apartheid, with its treason trials to match Stalin's trials, its detentions of dissidents to match Soviet detentions, its banishment and brutal uprooting of communities and individual lives to match, if not surpass, the gulag. Repression in South Africa has been and is being lived through; repression else-where is an account in a newspaper, book, or film. The choice, for blacks, cannot be distanced into any kind of objectivity: they believe in the existence of the lash they feel. Nothing could be* less than better *than what they have known as the "peace and security" of capitalism.*[30]

I was a coward and no doubt often shall be one again, in my actions and state-ments as a citizen of the interregnum; it is a place of shifting ground, forecast for me in the burning slag heaps of coal mines we children used to ride across with furiously pumping bicycle pedals and flying hearts, in the Transvaal town where I was born.

And now the time has come to say I believe you stand on shifting ground with me, across ten thousand miles, not because I have brought it with me, but because in some strange pilgrimage through the choices of our age and their consequences the democratic left of the Western world has arrived by many planned routes and plodding detours at the same unforeseen destination. It seems to be an abandoned siding. There was consternation when, early this year, Susan Sontag had the great courage and honesty publicly to accuse herself and other American intellectuals of the left of having been afraid to condemn the repression committed by communist regimes because this was seen as an endorsement of America's war on Vietnam and collusion with brutish rightist regimes in Latin America.[31] This moral equivo-cation draws parallel with mine at the writer's congress, far away in Africa; she has given me the courage, at second hand, to confess. Riding handlebar to handle-bar across the coal slag, both equivocations reveal the same fear. What is its mean-ing? It is fear of the abyss, of the greater interregnum of human hopes and spirit where against Sartre's socialism as the "horizon of the world" is silhouetted the chained outline of Poland's Solidarity, and all around, in the ditches of El Salvador, in the prisons of Argentina and South Africa, in the roofless habitations of Beirut, are the victims of Western standards of humanity.

I lie and you lie not because the truth is that Western capitalism has turned out to be just and humane, after all; but because we feel we have nothing to offer, now, except the rejection of it.

Because communism since 1917 has turned out not to be just or humane either, has failed this promise even more cruelly than capitalism, have we to tell the poor and dispossessed of the world there is nothing else to be done than to turn back from the communist bosses to the capitalist bosses? In South Africa's rich capitalist state stuffed with Western finance, fifty thousand black children a year die from malnutrition and malnutrition-related diseases, while the West piously notes that communist states cannot provide their people with meat and butter. In two decades in South Africa, three million black people have been ejected from the context of their lives, forcibly removed from homes and jobs and "resettled" in arid, undeveloped areas by decree of a white government supported by Western capital. It is difficult to point out to black South Africans that the forms of Western capitalism are changing toward a broad social justice in the example of countries like Sweden, Denmark, Holland, and Austria, with their mixed welfare economies, when all black South Africans know of Western capitalism is political and economic terror. And this terror is not some relic of the colonial past; it is being financed *now* by Western democracies – concurrently with Western capitalist democracy's own evolution toward social justice.

The fact is, black South Africans and whites like myself no longer believe in the ability of Western capitalism to bring about social justice where we live. We see no evidence of that possibility in our history or our living present. Whatever the Western democracies have done for themselves, they have failed and are failing, in their great power and influence, to do for us. This is the answer to those who ask, "Why call for an alternative left? Why not an alternative capitalism?" Show us an alternative capitalism working from without for real justice in our country. What are the conditions attached to the International Monetary Fund loan of approximately $1 billion that would oblige the South African government to stop population removals, to introduce a single standard of unsegregated education for all, to reinstate millions of black South Africans deprived of citizenship?[32]

If the injustices of communism cannot be reformed, must we assume that those of capitalism's longer history, constantly monitored by the compassionate hand of liberalism, can be? Must we accept that the workers of the Third World may hope only to be manipulated a little for their betterment and never to attain worker self-rule because this has been defeated in Poland by those very people in power who professed to believe in it? The dictum I quoted earlier carried, I know, its supreme irony: most leaders in the communist world have betrayed the basic intuition of democracy, that "the people know what to do"—which is perhaps why Susan Sontag saw communism as fascism with a human face. But I think we can, contrary to her view, "distinguish" among communisms, and I am sure, beyond the heat of an extemporary statement, so does she. If the United States and Sweden are not Botha's South Africa, was Allende's Chile East Germany, though both were in the socialist camp? We must "distinguish" to the point where we take up the real import of the essential challenge Susan Sontag leveled—to love truth enough, to pick up the blood-dirtied, shamed cause of the left and attempt to re-create it in accordance with what it was meant to be, not what sixty-five years of human power-perversion have made of it. If, as she rightly says, once we did not understand the nature of communist tyranny—now we do, just as we have always understood at first hand the nature of capitalist tyranny. This is not a Manichaean equation—which is god and which the devil is not a question the evidence could decide, anyway—and it does not license withdrawal and hopelessness. We have surely learned by now something of where socialism goes wrong, which of its precepts are deadly dangerous and lead, in practice, to fascist control of labor and total suppression of individual freedom. Will the witchcraft of modern times not be exorcised, eventually, by this knowledge? If fascist rule is possible within the framework of communist society, does this not mean we must apply the kind of passion that goes into armaments research to research a socialism that progressively reduces that possibility? Let the West call us traitors once again, and the East deride us as revisionists. Is it really inconceivable that socialism can ever be attained without horrors? Certainly Lech Walesa and his imprisoned followers don't find it so.

As for capitalism, whatever its reforms, its avowed self-perpetuation of advancement for the many by creation of wealth for the few does not offer any hope to fulfill the ultimate promise of equality, the *human* covenant man entered into with himself in the moment he did the impossible, stood up, a new self, on two feet instead of four. In the interregnum in which we coexist, the American left—disillusioned by the failure of communism—needs to muster with us of the Third World—living evidence of the failure of capitalism—the cosmic obstinacy to believe in and work toward the possibility of an alternative left, a democracy without economic or military terror. If we cannot, the possibility itself will die out, for our age, and who knows when, after what even bloodier age, it will be rediscovered.

There is no forgetting how we could live if only we could find the way. We must continue to be tormented by the ideal. Its possibility must be there for peoples to attempt to put into practice, to begin over and over again, wherever in the world it has never been tried, or has failed. This is where your responsibility to the Third World meets mine. Without the will to tramp toward the possibility, no relations of whites, of the West, with the West's formerly subject peoples can ever be free of the past, because the past, for them, was the jungle of Western capitalism, not the light the missionaries thought they brought with them.

Chinua Achebe

Postscript: James Baldwin

Editor's note: This address was presented at the memorial service for James Baldwin on 16 December 1987, University of Massachusetts, Amherst.

Since James Baldwin passed away in his adopted home, France, on the last day of November 1987, the many and varied tributes to him, like the blind men's versions of the elephant, have been consistent in one detail – the immensity, the sheer prodigality of endowment.

When my writing first began to yield small rewards in the way of free travel, UNESCO came along and asked where would I like to go. Without hesitation I said: U.S.A. and Brazil. And so I came to the Americas for the first time in 1963.

My intention, which was somewhat nebulous to begin with, was to find out how the Africans of the diaspora were faring in the two largest countries of the New World. In UNESCO files, however, it was stated with greater precision. I was given a fellowship to enable me to study literary trends and to meet and exchange ideas with writers.

I did indeed make very many useful contacts: John O. Killens, Langston Hughes, Ralph Ellison, Paule Marshall, LeRoi Jones, and so on; and for good measure, Arthur Miller. They were all wonderful to me. And yet there was no way I could hide from myself or my sponsors my sense of disappointment that one particular meeting could not happen because the man concerned was away in France. And that was the year of *The Fire Next Time!*

Before I came to America I had discovered and read *Go Tell It on the Mountain* and been instantly captivated. For me it combined the strange and familiar in a way that was entirely new. I went to the United States Information Service Library in Lagos to see what other material there might be *by* or *on* this man. There was absolutely nothing. So I offered a couple of suggestions and such was the persuasiveness of newly independent Africans in those days that when next I looked in at the library they had not only Baldwin but Richard Wright as well.

I had all my schooling in the educational system of colonial Nigeria. In that system Americans, when they were featured at all, were dismissed summarily by our British administrators as loud and vulgar. Their universities, which taught such subjects as dishwashing, naturally produced the half-baked noisy political agitators, some of whom were now rushing up and down the country because they had acquired no proper skills.

But there was one American book that the colonial educators considered of sufficient value to be exempted from the general censure of things American and actually be prescribed reading in my high school. It was the autobiography of Booker T. Washington, *Up from Slavery*.

This bizarre background probably explains why my first encounter with Baldwin's writing was such a miraculous experience. Nothing that I had heard or read or seen quite prepared me for the Baldwin phenomenon. Needless to say my education was entirely silent about W.E.B. Du Bois, who as I later discovered had applied *his* experience of what he called "the strange meaning of being black" in America to ends and insights radically different from Washington's.

A major aspect of my re-education was to see (and what comfort it gave me!) that Baldwin was neither an aberration nor was he likely to be a flash in the pan. He brought a new sharpness of vision, a new energy of passion, a new perfection of language to battle the incubus of race which Du Bois had prophesied would possess our century – which prophecy itself had a long pedigree through the slave revolts back into Africa where, believe it or not, a seventeenth-century Igbo priest-king Eze Nri had declared slavery an abomination. I say *believe it or not* because this personage and many others like him in different parts of Africa do not fit the purposes of your history books.

When at last I met Jimmy in person in the jungles of Florida in 1980 I actually greeted him with *Mr. Baldwin, I presume!* You should have seen his eyes dancing, his remarkable face working in ripples of joyfulness. During the four days we spent down there I saw how easy it was to make Jimmy smile; and how the world he was doomed to inhabit would remorselessly deny him that simple benediction.

Baldwin and I were invited by the African Literature Association to open its annual conference in Gainesville with a public conversation. As we stepped into a tremendous ovation in the packed auditorium of the Holiday Inn, Baldwin was in particularly high spirits. I thought the old preacher in him was reacting to the multitude.

He went to the podium and began to make his opening statements. Within minutes a mystery voice came over the public address system and began to hurl racial insults at him and me. I will see that moment to the end of my life. The happiness brutally wiped off Baldwin's face; the genial manner gone; the eyes flashing in defiant combativeness; the voice incredibly calm and measured. And the words of remorseless prophecy began once again to flow.

One of the few hopeful examples of leadership in Africa was terminated abruptly two months ago [October 1987]. Captain Thomas Sankara, leader of Burkina Faso, was murdered in his fourth year of rule by his second-in-command. The world did not pay too much attention to yet another game of musical chairs by power-hungry soldiers in Africa. In any event, Sankara was a brash young man with Marxist leanings who had recently had the effrontery to read a lecture to a visiting head of state who happened to be none other than President Mitterrand of France himself. According to press reports of the incident, Mitterrand, who is a socialist veteran in his own right, rose to the occasion. He threw away his prepared speech and launched into an hour-long counterattack in which he must have covered much ground. But perhaps the sting was in the tail: "Sankara is a disturbing person. With him it is impossible to sleep in peace. He does not leave your conscience alone."[1]

I have no doubt that Mitterrand meant his comment as praise for his young and impatient host. But it was also a deadly arraignment and even conviction. Principalities and powers do not tolerate those who interrupt the sleep of their consciences. That Baldwin got away with it for forty years was a miracle. Except of course that he didn't get away; he paid dearly every single day of those years, every single hour of those days.

What was his crime that we should turn him into a man of sadness, this man inhabited by a soul eager to be loved and to smile? His demands were so few and so simple.

His bafflement, childlike – which does not mean simpleminded but deeply profound and saintly – comes across again and again and nowhere better perhaps than in his essay "Fifth Avenue, Uptown."

Negroes want to be treated like men: a perfectly straightforward statement containing only seven words. People who have mastered Kant, Hegel, Shakespeare, Marx, Freud, and the Bible find this statement utterly impenetrable.[2]

This failure to comprehend turns out to be, as one might have suspected, a willful, obdurate refusal. And for good reason. For let's face it, that sentence, simple and innocent-looking though it may seem, is in reality a mask for a profoundly subversive intent to reorder the world. And the world, viewed from the high point of the pyramid where its controllers reside, is working perfectly well and sitting firm.

Egypt's Pharaoh, according to the myth of the Israelites, faced the same problem when a wild-eyed man walked up to him with a simple demand, four words long: "Let my people go!" We are not told that he rushed off to his office to sign their exit visa. On the contrary.

So neither history nor legend encourages us to believe that a man who sits on his fellow will some day climb down on the basis of sounds reaching him from below. And yet we must consider how so much more dangerous our already very perilous world would become if the oppressed everywhere should despair altogether of invoking reason and humanity to arbitrate their cause. This is the value and the relevance, into the foreseeable future, of James Baldwin.

As long as injustice exists, whether it be within the American nation itself or between it and its neighbors; as long as a tiny cartel of rich, creditor nations can hold the rest in iron chains of usury; so long as one-third or less of humankind eats well and often to excess while two-thirds and more live perpetually with hunger; as long as white people who constitute a mere fraction of the human race consider it natural and even righteous to dominate the rainbow majority whenever and wherever they are thrown together; and – the oldest of them all – the discrimination by men against women, as long as it persists, the words of James Baldwin will be there to bear witness and to inspire and elevate the struggle for human freedom.

Notes

Philomena Mariani

1. Robert Bly, *Iron John: A Book About Men* (Reading, Mass.: Addison-Wesley, 1991), pp. 2-3.

2. Remark by Paul Weyrich, Moral Majority spokesperson, quoted in Leslie Bennetts, "Conservatives Join on Social Concerns," *The New York Times*, 30 July 1980, p. 1.

3. Robert Bly, *Iron John*, pp. 22-23.

4. Ibid., p. 17.

5. Ibid., pp. 4, 18, 19, 165, 185.

6. Ibid., p. 16.

7. Ibid., p. 24.

8. Ibid., p. 25.

9. Ibid., pp. 21-22.

10. Ibid., p. 6.

11. Ibid., pp. 169-170.

12. Angela Carter, *The Sadeian Woman and the Ideology of Pornography* (New York: Pantheon, 1978), pp. 5-6.

13. For the canonical texts of the culture-of-dependency school, see Ken Auletta, *The Underclass* (New York: Random House, 1982), George Gilder, *Wealth and Poverty* (New York: Basic Books, 1981), Lawrence M. Mead, *Beyond Entitlement: The Social Obligations of Citizenship* (New York: Free Press, 1986), Charles A. Murray, *Losing Ground: American Social Policy, 1950-1980* (New York: Basic Books, 1984), and Shelby Steele, *Content of Our Character: A New Vision of Race in America* (New York: St. Martin's Press, 1990). For the mobilization against feminism and multiculturalism in the academy, see Allan Bloom, *The Closing of the American Mind* (New York: Simon and Schuster, 1987), Dinesh D'Souza, *Illiberal Education: The Politics of Race and Sex on Campus* (New York: Free Press, 1991), Roger Kimball, *Tenured Radicals: How Politics Has Corrupted Higher Education* (New York: Harper and Row, 1990), and Camille Paglia, "Ninnies, Pedants, Tyrants and Other Academics," *The New York Times Book Review*, 5 May 1991. See as well Michael Novak, "Homosexuality: A Social Rot," *Conservative Digest* 5, no. 1 (January 1979), for an early précis of conservative views on the restoration of the "male principle." Finally, for an excellent discussion of the relationship between right-wing religious organizations and their New Right counterparts, see Rosalind Pollack Petchesky, "Antiabortion, Antifeminism, and the Rise of the New Right," *Feminist Studies* 7, no. 2 (Summer 1981): 206-246. Petchesky's article helped immeasurably in framing my own arguments.

14. Petchesky, "Antiabortion, Antifeminism, and the Rise of the New Right," p. 224.

bell hooks

1. Ivan Van Sertima, *They Came Before Columbus* (New York: Random House, 1976).

2. Plinio Apuleyo Mendoza and Gabriel García Márquez, *The Fragrance of Guava*, trans. Ann Wright (London: Verso, 1983), p. 31.

3. Manlio Argueta, *One Day of Life*, trans. Bill Brow (New York: Vintage, 1983), pp. 199-200.

4. Ibid., p. 215.

5. See *Literature in Exile*, ed. John Glad (Durham, N.C.: Duke University Press, 1990), p. 60.

6. Angela Carter, *The Sadeian Woman and the Ideology of Pornography* (1978; New York: Pantheon, 1988), p. 13.

7. Ama Ata Aidoo, *Our Sister Killjoy* (London: Longman, 1977), p. 6.

8. Nawal El Saadawi, preface to the 1983 edition of *Woman at Point Zero*, trans. Sherif Hetata (London: Zed Books).

9. Gustavo Gutiérrez, *On Job: God-Talk and the Suffering of the Innocent*, trans. Matthew J. O'Connell (Maryknoll, N.Y.: Orbis Books, 1987).

10. *Literature in Exile*, p. 123.

11. Antonio Faundez, *Learning to Question: A Pedagogy of Liberation* (New York: Continuum, 1989), p. 11.

12. Thich Nhat Hanh and Daniel Berrigan, *The Raft Is Not the Shore: Conversations Toward a Buddhist/Christian Awareness* (Boston: Beacon Press, 1975).

13. James H. Cone, *My Soul Looks Back* (Maryknoll, N.Y.: Orbis Books, 1982), p. 12.

Homi K. Bhabha

1. Tom Wolfe, *The Bonfire of the Vanities* (New York: Farrar, Straus and Giroux, 1987), p. 7.

2. Jean-Paul Sartre, preface to Frantz Fanon, *The Wretched of the Earth*, trans. Constance Farrington (New York: Grove Press, 1963), p. 24.

Michelle Cliff

1. Zoë Wicomb, quoted in "To Soweto, with Love," *The Village Voice*, 20 February 1990, p. 26.

2. Roberto Fernández Retamar, "Caliban: Notes Toward a Discussion of Culture in Our America," in *Caliban and Other Essays*, trans. Edward Baker (Minneapolis: University of Minnesota Press, 1989), p. 16.

3. Gayatri Chakravorty Spivak, "Three Women's Texts and a Critique of Imperialism," *Critical Inquiry* 12, no. 1 (Autumn 1985): 249.

4. Nancy R. Harrison, *Jean Rhys and the Novel as Women's Text* (Chapel Hill: University of North Carolina Press, 1988), p. 128.

5. See Susanne Everett, *The Slaves* (New York: Putnam, 1978), p. 65.

6. Elizabeth Hess, "Out of Body," *The Village Voice*, 8 December 1987, p. 119.

7. It is a dreadful irony that Ana Mendieta's own life ended with her body imprinted on a New York City street, after falling from the thirty-fourth floor of her husband's apartment building. Her husband was acquitted of wrongdoing. The year was 1985; the artist was thirty-six years old.

Anton Shammas

1. *The New York Times*, 25 November 1987, p. A7.

2. Gilles Deleuze and Félix Guattari, *Kafka: Toward a Minor Literature*, trans. Dana Polan (Minneapolis: University of Minnesota Press, 1986), p. 16.

3. Michelle Cliff, *The Land of Look Behind* (Ithaca, N.Y.: Firebrand Books, 1985), p. 12.

4. Deleuze and Guattari, *Kafka*, pp. 17, 19.

5. Walter Benjamin, "The Storyteller," in *Illuminations*, ed. Hannah Arendt, trans. Harry Zohn (New York: Schocken Books, 1968), pp. 83-109.

Luisa Valenzuela

1. Jean Baudrillard, *La transparence du mal: Essai sur les phénomènes extrêmes* (Paris: Galilée, 1990), p. 88; translation mine.

Leslie Marmon Silko

1. See Leslie Marmon Silko, *Storyteller* (New York: Seaver Books, 1981).

2. In Simon J. Ortiz, *Howbah Indians* (Tucson: Blue Moon Press, 1978).

3. See Simon J. Ortiz, "The Killing of a State Cop," in *The Man to Send Rain Clouds*, ed. Kenneth Rosen (New York: Viking Press, 1974), pp. 101-108.

Lynne Tillman

1. M. M. Bakhtin, *The Dialogic Imagination*, ed. Michael Holquist (Austin: University of Texas Press, 1981), p. 354.

2. Gilles Deleuze and Félix Guattari, *Kafka: Toward a Minor Literature*, trans. Dana Polan (Minneapolis: University of Minnesota Press, 1986), p. 16.

3. Ibid., p. 26.

4. Ibid., p. 17.

5. Ford Madox Ford, *The Bodley Head Ford Madox Ford*, vol. 1 (London: The Bodley Head, 1971), p. 323.

6. Edward Said, "Ignorant Armies Clash by Night," *The Nation*, 11 February 1991, p. 163.

Jessica Hagedorn

1. *The New York Times*, 7 May 1989, Section 2, p. 1.

2. Trinh T. Minh-ha, *Woman, Native, Other* (Bloomington: Indiana University Press, 1989), p. 19.

Ama Ata Aidoo

1. See Cheikh Anta Diop, *The Cultural Unity of Black Africa: The Domains of Patriarchy and of Matriarchy in Classical Antiquity* (1959; Chicago: Third World Press, 1963); Martin Bernal, *Black Athena: The Afroasiatic Roots of Classical Civilization* (New Brunswick, N.J.: Rutgers University Press, 1987); Ivan Van Sertima, ed., *Black Women in Antiquity* (London: Transaction Books, 1988); and any of the volumes of *The Journal of African Civilizations*, edited by Ivan Van Sertima, a true labor of love which Sertima has kept going for years out of Rutgers University with no reward or recognition.

2. See Sara El-Gammal, "Soon to Be as Good as Old," *The Herald* (Harare), 15 February 1991.

3. See Thomas L. Hodgkin, *Nationalism in Colonial Africa* (London: Muller, 1956), and Claude Ake, *Revolutionary Pressures in Africa* (London: Zed Press, 1978).

Ana Castillo

1. These and the following passages are a tapestry woven from Gloria Anzaldúa's *Borderlands/ La Frontera: The New Mestiza* (San Francisco: Spinsters, 1987), Cherríe Moraga's *Loving in the War Years: Lo que nunca pasó por sus labios* (Boston: South End Press, 1983), and my own novel, *The Mixquiahuala Letters* (New York:

Doubleday, 1992).

2. Gloria Anzaldúa discusses this point in an excellent chapter of *Borderlands* entitled "How to tame a wild tongue."

3. Ivan Argüelles, "Contributors Advice," *Caliban*, no. 4 (1988): 81.

4. An excellent example of this is found in the work of the poet Alurista. He further imbues language with ancient and contemporary meanings; I would call him a "mytholinguist."

5. Octavio Paz, *Children of the Mire: Modern Poetry from Romanticism to the Avant-Garde*, trans. Rachel Phillips (Cambridge, Mass.: Harvard University Press, 1974), p. 161.

6. Anzaldúa, *Borderlands*, p. 43.

7. Ibid.

8. Ibid., p. 19.

9. Moraga, *Loving in the War Years*, p. ii.

10. Ibid., pp. 90-143.

11. Anzaldúa, *Borderlands*, p. 21.

12. Carmen Tafolla, *To Split a Human* (San Antonio: Mexican-American Cultural Center, 1985), p. 59.

13. Castillo, *The Mixquiahuala Letters*, p. 113.

14. Moraga, *Loving in the War Years*, p. 113.

15. Ibid., p. 112.

16. Anzaldúa, *Borderlands*, p. 21.

17. Castillo, *The Mixquiahuala Letters*, p. 73.

18. Sigrid Weigel, "Double Focus: On the History of Women's Writing," trans. Harriet Anderson in *Feminist Aesthetics*, ed. Gisela Ecker (Boston: Beacon Press, 1985), p. 72. I have found this article immensely insightful and helpful in viewing my own works and my life as a woman writer.

19. Ibid., p. 73.

Alix Kates Shulman

1. *The New York Times*, 16 September 1981, p. C25.

2. Norman Mailer, *The Prisoner of Sex* (Boston: Little, Brown, 1971), p. 228.

3. Alice Walker, *Meridian* (New York: Harcourt

Brace Jovanovich, 1976), pp. 205-206.

Lauretta Ngcobo

1. That the dowry functions in this way becomes clear in cases in which the man has not paid a dowry: his children will belong to his wife's people and will take his wife's name. If a man pays the dowry, his children belong to him and take his name. Should he die, his people are most anxious that his widow remarry within the family (and without further dowry payment). In this way, they ensure that the children remain within the husband's family, both biologically and socially.

Christa Wolf

1. *Editor's note*: Wolf is referring to her childhood in the Nazi period.

Zoë Wicomb

1. Raymond Williams, *Culture* (London: Fontana Press, 1981), p. 184.
2. Edward Said, *The World, the Text, and the Critic* (Cambridge, Mass.: Harvard University Press, 1983), p. 169.
3. Williams, *Culture*, p. 13.
4. Benedict Anderson, *Imagined Communities: Reflections on the Origin and Spread of Nationalism* (London: Verso, 1983), p. 15.
5. Said, *The World, the Text, and the Critic*, p. 11.
6. Jeff Guy, "Gender Oppression in Southern Africa's Precapitalist Societies," in *Women and Gender in Southern Africa to 1945*, ed. Cherryl Walker (Cape Town: David Philip, 1990), p. 44.
7. Johannes Fabian, *Time and the Other: How Anthropology Makes Its Object* (New York: Columbia University Press, 1983), p. 35.
8. Williams, *Culture*, p. 187.
9. Neville Dubow, "Photography in South Africa," *Creative Camera* (August-September 1990): 38.
10. Gilles Deleuze and Félix Guattari, *Kafka: Toward a Minor Literature*, trans. Dana Polan

(Minneapolis: University of Minnesota Press, 1986), p. 27.
11. Ibid., p. 19.
12. Ibid., p. 26.

Harold A. Bascom

1. *Editor's note*: Bascom is here making reference to a novel by Barbadian writer Austin Clarke entitled *Growing Up Stupid Under the Union Jack*.

Nadine Gordimer

1. [In a slightly different translation in] *Selections from the Prison Notebooks of Antonio Gramsci*, ed. and trans. Quintin Hoare and Geoffrey Nowell Smith (London: Lawrence and Wishart, 1971), p. 276.
2. Theodor Adorno, "Cultural Criticism and Society," in *Critical Sociology: Selected Readings*, ed. Paul Connerton (Harmondsworth: Penguin, 1976), p. 271.
3. Total population, 1980, 23.7 million, of which 4.5 million are white. *Survey of Race Relations in South Africa 1981*, ed. M. Horrell (Johannesburg: South African Institute of Race Relations, 1982), p. 52.
4. Rainer Maria Rilke, "Ein Frauenschicksal" (A Woman's Fate), in *Selected Poems of Rainer Maria Rilke*, trans. C. F. MacIntyre (Berkeley: University of California Press, 1978), p. 73.
5. Edmundo Desnoes, *Memories of Underdevelopment* (Harmondsworth: Penguin, 1971), p. 104.
6. Czeslaw Milosz, *Native Realm: A Search for Self-Definition*, trans. Catherine S. Leach (New York: Doubleday, 1968), p. 125.
7. Günter Grass, *Headbirths, or, The Germans Are Dying Out*, trans. Ralph Manheim (New York: Harcourt Brace Jovanovich, 1982).
8. In 1984, the second South African to win the Nobel Prize for Peace.
9. Bishop Desmond Tutu, letter to *Frontline* (Johannesburg) 2, no. 5 (April 1982): 4.
10. Paraphrased from the poem "Ofay-watcher, throbs–phase," in *Yakhal' Inkomo* (Johannes-

burg: Renoster, 1972), pp. 50-51.

11. See Lionel Trilling, *Sincerity and Authenticity* (Cambridge, Mass.: Harvard University Press, 1972), p. 114.

12. Czeslaw Milosz, "The Accuser," in *Bells in Winter* (New York: Ecco Press, 1978), p. 62.

13. Dr. Neil Aggett, Transvaal organizer of the African Food and Canning Workers' Union, was detained on 27 November 1981, and died in detention on 5 February 1982. Though the inquest brought evidence of extraordinary brutality and torture during his detention, the magistrates found his death not caused by any act or omission on the part of the police.

14. Milosz, *Native Realm*, p. 120.

15. This changed as the decade progressed. See author's "Letter from Johannesburg 1985," in *The Essential Gesture: Writing, Politics & Places* (New York: Knopf, 1988), pp. 301-310.

16. William Plomer, *Turbott Wolfe* (London: Hogarth Press, 1925; reprint, Johannesburg: Donker, 1980). Sarah Gertrude Millin, *God's Step-Children* (London: Constable, 1924; reprint: Johannesburg: Donker, 1986).

17. The Dhlomo brothers are among the major black South African writers of this century, though their legacy has been largely ignored until recently. Rolfes Dhlomo wrote mainly in Zulu, but for his one novel in English see R.R.R. Dhlomo, *An African Tragedy* (Lovedale: Lovedale Press, 1928). For Herbert Dhlomo see H.I.E. Dhlomo, *Collected Works*, ed. N. Visser and T. Couzens (Johannesburg: Ravan Press, 1985).

18. For representative works of the time by these writers, see Ezekiel Mphahlele, *Down Second Avenue* (1959; London: Faber, 1971); Lewis Nkosi, *Home and Exile* (1965; London: Longman, 1983); Can Themba, *The Will to Die* (London: Heinemann, 1972), and *The World of Can Themba*, ed. E. Patel (Johannesburg: Ravan Press, 1982); Bloke Modisane, *Blame Me on History* (1963; Johannesburg: Donker, 1986); Peter

Abrahams, *Mine Boy* (1946; London: Heinemann, 1975).

19. Paraphrased from Plomer, *Turbott Wolfe* (1925), p. 122.

20. Walter Benjamin, "What Is Epic Theater?" in *Illuminations*, ed. Hannah Arendt, trans. Harry Zohn (New York: Schocken Books, 1968), p. 150.

21. Nikolai G. Chernyshevsky, *Polnoye sobraniye sochinenii* (St. Petersburg, 1906), vol. 8. Paraphrased from the translated quotation, "The highroad of History is not the sidewalk of the Nevsky Prospekt," in Tibor Szamuely, *The Russian Tradition*, ed. Robert Conquest (London: Secker and Warburg, 1974), p. 122.

22. Benjamin, "What Is Epic Theater?," p. 150.

23. Anthony Burgess, "Creativity," *The Observer* (London), 9 May 1982, p. 27.

24. For an account of the renewal of aesthetic preoccupations in black writing in the mid-1980s, see "The Essential Gesture," in Gordimer, *The Essential Gesture*, pp. 285-300.

25. Gabriel García Márquez in conversation with Plinio Apuleyo Mendoza in *The Fragrance of Guava*, trans. Ann Wright (London: Verso, 1983), p. 59.

26. Georg Lukács, *The Theory of the Novel*, as quoted by Walter Benjamin in *Illuminations*, p. 99.

27. Ibid.

28. Joseph Brodsky, "Homage to Yalta," in *A Part of Speech* (New York: Farrar, Straus and Giroux, 1980), p. 12.

29. Susan Sontag, *Under the Sign of Saturn* (New York: Farrar, Straus and Giroux, 1980), p. 14.

30. *Star* (Johannesburg), 4 August 1982.

31. Text of speech by Susan Sontag, 6 February 1982, Town Hall, New York, published as "Communism and the Left," *The Nation*, 27 February 1982, pp. 230-231.

32. The IMF loan was given to South Africa in 1982. The United States has a 20 percent slice under the weighted voting system of the IMF

and so outvoted all loan opponents combined.
The United States consequently surely has cor-
responding responsibility for how the money
South Africa receives is spent. Is there any evidence that this responsibility is being taken up?

Chinua Achebe

1. *The New York Times*, 23 August 1987, p. 10.
2. James Baldwin, "Fifth Avenue, Uptown," first
published in *Esquire* (July 1960); reprinted in
The Price of the Ticket (New York: St. Martin's
Press, 1985), p. 211.

Selected Bibliography

Achebe, Chinua. *Anthills of the Savannah*. London: Heinemann, 1987.

———. *Arrow of God*. London: Heinemann, 1964.

———. *Girls at War and Other Stories*. London: Heinemann, 1972.

———. *Hopes and Impediments: Selected Essays, 1965-1987*. Garden City, N.Y.: Anchor, 1988.

———. *A Man of the People*. Garden City, N.Y.: Anchor, 1967.

———. *Morning Yet on Creation Day: Essays*. Garden City, N.Y.: Anchor, 1975.

———. *No Longer at Ease*. New York: Ballantine, 1960.

———. *Things Fall Apart*. 1959; New York: Ballantine, 1983.

———. *The Trouble with Nigeria*. London: Heinemann, 1984.

———. *The University and the Leadership Factor in Nigerian Politics*. Enugu, Nigeria: ABIC Books, 1988.

Aidoo, Ama Ata. *Anowa*. Harlow: Longman, 1970.

———. *Changes*. London: The Women's Press, 1991.

———. *The Dilemma of a Ghost*. Harlow: Longman, 1965.

———. *The Eagle and the Chickens and Other Stories*. Edited by Irene Staunton. Enugu, Nigeria: Tana Press, 1986.

———. *Images of Africa in the 1980s, 1990s, and at Century's End*. In progress.

———. *No Sweetness Here*. Garden City, N.Y.: Doubleday, 1970.

———. *Our Sister Killjoy: or, Reflections from a Black-Eyed Squint*. London: Longman, 1977.

———. *Someone Talking to Sometime*. Harare, Zimbabwe: College Press, 1985.

Alegría, Claribel. *Family Album: Three Novellas*. Translated by Amanda Hopkinson. London: The Women's Press, 1990.

———. *Luisa in Realityland*. Translated by Darwin J. Flakoll. Willimantic, Conn.: Curbstone Press, 1987.

——— (and Darwin J. Flakoll). *Nicaragua, la revolucion sandinista: Una cronica politica, 1855-1979*. Mexico City: Ediciones Era, 1982.

———. *They Won't Take Me Alive: Salvadorean Women in Struggle for National Liberation*. Translated by Amanda Hopkinson. London: The Women's Press, 1987.

———. *Woman of the River*. Translated by Darwin J. Flakoll. Pittsburgh: University of Pittsburgh Press, 1989.

Als, Hilton. *Three Books of the Negress*. New York: Farrar, Straus and Giroux, forthcoming.

Atwood, Margaret. *Bluebeard's Egg*. Toronto: McClelland and Stewart, 1981.

———. *Bodily Harm*. Toronto: McClelland and Stewart, 1981.

———. *Cat's Eye*. New York: Doubleday, 1989.

———. *Dancing Girls and Other Stories*. Toronto: McClelland and Stewart, 1977.

———. *The Edible Woman*. Boston: Little, Brown, 1969.

———. *The Handmaid's Tale*. Boston: Houghton Mifflin, 1986.

———. *Lady Oracle*. New York: Simon and Schuster, 1976.

———. *Life Before Man*. New York: Simon and Schuster, 1979.

———. *Second Words: Selected Critical Prose*. Toronto: Anansi, 1982.

———. *Surfacing*. New York: Simon and Schuster, 1972.

———. *True Stories*. New York: Simon and Schuster, 1981.

Baldwin, James. *Another Country*. New York: Dial

Press, 1962.

——. *Blues for Mister Charlie*. New York: Dial Press, 1964.

——. *The Devil Finds Work: An Essay*. New York: Dial Press, 1976.

——. *The Evidence of Things Not Seen: An Essay*. New York: Holt, Rinehart, and Winston, 1985.

——. *The Fire Next Time*. New York: Dial Press, 1963.

——. *Giovanni's Room*. New York: Dial Press, 1956.

——. *Go Tell It on the Mountain*. New York: Knopf, 1953.

——. *Going to Meet the Man*. New York: Dial Press, 1965.

——. *Just Above My Head*. New York: Dial Press, 1974.

——. *No Name in the Street*. New York: Dial Press, 1972.

——. *Nobody Knows My Name: More Notes of a Native Son*. New York: Dial Press, 1961.

——. *Notes of a Native Son*. Boston: Beacon Press, 1955.

——. *One Day, When I Was Lost: A Scenario. Based on Alex Haley's "The Autobiography of Malcolm X."* New York: Dial Press, 1972.

——. *The Price of the Ticket: Collected Nonfiction, 1948-1985*. New York: St. Martin's Press, 1985.

——. *Tell Me How Long the Train's Been Gone: A Novel*. New York: Dial Press, 1968.

Bascom, Harold A. *Apata: The Story of a Reluctant Criminal*. London: Heinemann, 1986.

Bhabha, Homi K., ed. *Nation and Narration*. London: Routledge, 1990.

Carter, Angela. *The Bloody Chamber and Other Stories*. New York: Harper and Row, 1978.

——. *Come Unto these Yellow Sands*. Newcastle-upon-Tyne: Bloodaxe Books, 1985.

——. *Fireworks: Nine Profane Pieces*. London: Quartet Books, 1974.

——. *Heroes and Villains*. New York: Simon and Schuster, 1969.

——. *The Infernal Desire Machines of Dr. Hoffman*.

New York: Penguin, 1982.

——. *Love: A Novel*. London: Hart-Davis, 1971.

——. *Nights at the Circus*. London: Chatto and Windus, 1984.

——. *Nothing Sacred: Selected Writings*. London: Virago, 1982.

——. *The Passion of New Eve*. London: Virago, 1982.

——. *The Sadeian Woman and the Ideology of Pornography*. 1978; New York: Pantheon, 1988.

——. *Saints and Strangers*. New York: Viking, 1986.

——. *The War of Dreams*. New York: Harcourt Brace Jovanovich, 1972.

Castillo, Ana. *Massacre of the Dreamers: Reflections on Mexican-Indian Women in the U.S.: 500 Years After the Conquest*. Albuquerque: University of New Mexico Press, 1992.

——. *The Mixquiahuala Letters*. 1986; New York: Doubleday, 1992.

——. *Sapogonia*. Tempe, Ariz.: Bilingual Review Press, 1990.

——. *Women Are Not Roses*. Houston: Arte Publico Press, 1984.

Cliff, Michelle. *Abeng: A Novel*. Trumansberg, N.Y.: The Crossing Press, 1984.

——. *Bodies of Water*. New York: Dutton, 1990.

——. *Claiming an Identity They Taught Me to Despise*. Watertown, Mass.: Persephone Press, 1980.

——. *The Land of Look Behind*. Ithaca, N.Y.: Firebrand Books, 1985.

——. *No Telephone to Heaven*. New York: Dutton, 1987.

Dujovne Ortiz, Alicia. *El agujero en la tierra: Novela*. Caracas: Monte Avila Editores, 1983.

——. *Le bonne Pauline*. Paris: Mercure de France, 1980.

——. *Buenos Aires*. Seyssel: Champ Vallons, 1984.

——. *El Buzon de la esquina*. Buenos Aires: Calicanto Editorial, 1977.

——. *Mon arbre, mon amant*. Paris: Mercure de France, 1982.

——. *Recetas, florecillas y otros contentos*. Buenos Aires: Editorial Rayuela, 1973.

——. *La sourire des dauphins*. Paris: Gallimard, 1989.

El Saadawi, Nawal. *God Dies by the Nile*. London: Zed Books, 1985.

——. *Death of an Ex-Minister*. Translated by Shirley Eber. London: Methuen, 1987.

——. *The Hidden Face of Eve: Women in the Arab World*. Translated by Sherif Hetata. London: Zed Books, 1980.

——. *Memoirs of a Woman Doctor: A Novel*. Translated by Catherine Cobham. San Francisco: City Lights Books, 1989.

——. *Two Women in One*. Translated by Osman Nusairi and Jana Gough. London: Al-Saqi, 1985.

——. *Woman at Point Zero*. Translated by Sherif Hetata. London: Zed Books, 1983.

Galeano, Eduardo. *The Book of Embraces*. Translated by Cedric Belfrage. New York: W. W. Norton, 1991.

——. *Days and Nights of Love and War*. New York: Monthly Review Press, 1983.

——. *Guatemala: Occupied Country*. Translated by Cedric Belfrage. New York: Monthly Review Press, 1969.

——. *Memory of Fire*. Vol. 1: *Genesis*. Vol. 2: *Faces and Masks*. Vol. 3: *Century of the Wind*. Translated by Cedric Belfrage. New York: Pantheon, 1985-1988.

——. *Open Veins of Latin America: Five Centuries of the Pillage of a Continent*. Translated by Cedric Belfrage. New York: Monthly Review Press, 1973.

——. *Voces de nuestro tiempo*. San Jose: Editorial Universitaria Centroamericana, 1981.

Gómez-Arcos, Agustín. *Ana Non*. Paris: Stock, 1977.

——. *Bestiaire*. Paris: Le Pré aux clercs, 1986.

——. *A Bird Burned Alive*. Translated by Anthony and Marie-Luce Pugh. 1984; London: Chatto and Windus, 1988.

——. *The Carnivorous Lamb*. Translated by William Rodarmor. Boston: Godine, 1984.

——. *L'Enfant pain*. Paris: Seuil, 1983.

——. *L'Enfant miraculée*. Paris: Fayard, 1981.

——. *L'Homme à genoux*. Paris: Julliard, 1989.

——. *Maria República*. Paris: Stock, 1976.

——. *Marruecos*. Madrid: Mondadori, 1991.

——. *Pré-Papa; ou Roman de fées*. Paris: Stock, 1979.

——. *Scène de chasse furtive*. Paris: Stock, 1978.

Gordimer, Nadine. *Burger's Daughter*. London: Jonathan Cape, 1979.

——. *The Conservationist*. New York: Viking, 1974.

——. *The Essential Gesture: Writing, Politics & Places*. Edited by Stephen Clingman. London: Jonathan Cape, 1980.

——. *July's People*. New York: Viking, 1981.

——. *The Lying Days*. London: Virago, 1983.

——. *Occasion for Loving*. London: Virago, 1983.

——. *Some Monday for Sure*. London: Heinemann, 1976.

——. *Something Out There*. London: Jonathan Cape, 1984.

——. *A Sport of Nature: A Novel*. New York: Knopf, 1987.

Hagedorn, Jessica. *Dangerous Music*. San Francisco: Momo's Press, 1975.

——. *Dogeaters*. New York: Pantheon, 1990.

——. *Pet Food and Tropical Apparitions*. San Francisco: Momo's Press, 1981.

Head, Bessie. *A Bewitched Crossroad: An African Saga*. New York: Paragon House Publishers, 1984.

——. *The Collector of Treasures, and Other Botswana Village Tales*. London: Heinemann, 1977.

——. *Maru: A Novel*. London: Gollancz, 1971.

——. *A Question of Power: A Novel*. New York: Pantheon, 1974.

——. *Serowe, Village of Rainwind*. London: Heinemann, 1981.

——. *When Rain Clouds Gather*. London: Heinemann, 1968.

——. *A Woman Alone*. London: Heinemann,

1990.

hooks, bell. *Ain't I a Woman: Black Women and Feminism.* Boston: South End Press, 1981.

____. *Feminist Theory from Margin to Center.* Boston: South End Press, 1984.

____. *Talking Back: Thinking Feminist, Thinking Black.* Boston: South End Press, 1989.

____. *Yearning: Race, Gender, and Cultural Politics.* Boston: South End Press, 1990.

Indiana, Gary. *Horse Crazy.* New York: Grove Press, 1989.

____. *Scar Tissue and Other Stories.* New York: Calamus Books, 1987.

____. *White Trash Boulevard.* New York: Hanuman Books, 1988.

Islas, Arturo. *Migrant Souls: A Novel.* New York: Morrow, 1990.

____. *The Rain God: A Desert Tale.* Palo Alto, Calif.: Alexandrian Press, 1984.

Kincaid, Jamaica. *Annie John.* New York: Farrar, Straus and Giroux, 1985.

____. *At the Bottom of the River.* New York: Farrar, Straus and Giroux, 1983.

____. *Lucy.* New York: Farrar, Straus and Giroux, 1990.

____. *A Small Place.* New York: Farrar, Straus and Giroux, 1988.

Kingston, Maxine Hong. *China Men.* New York: Knopf, 1980.

____. *Tripmaster Monkey: His Fake Book.* New York: Knopf, 1989.

____. *The Woman Warrior: Memoirs of a Girlhood Among Ghosts.* New York: Knopf, 1976.

McGrath, Patrick. *Blood and Water and Other Tales.* New York: Poseidon Press, 1988.

____. *The Grotesque: A Novel.* New York: Poseidon Press, 1989.

____. *Spider.* New York: Poseidon Press, 1990.

Mosley, Walter. *Devil in a Blue Dress.* New York: W. W. Norton, 1990.

____. *A Red Death.* New York: W. W. Norton, 1991.

Mukherjee, Bharati. *Darkness.* New York: Penguin, 1985.

____ (and Clark Blaise). *Days and Nights in Calcutta.* Garden City, N.Y.: Doubleday, 1977.

____. *Jasmine.* New York: Grove Press, 1989.

____. *The Middleman and Other Stories.* New York: Grove Press, 1988.

____. *The Tiger's Daughter.* Boston: Houghton Mifflin, 1972.

____. *Wife.* 1975; New York: Penguin, 1987.

Munif, Abdelrahman. *Cities of Salt.* Translated by Peter Theroux. New York: Vintage, 1989.

____. *Hina Tarakna al-Jisr* (When We Left the Bridge). Beirut: Al-Muassasah al-Arabiyah, 1985.

Ngcobo, Lauretta. *And They Didn't Die: A Novel.* New York: Braziller, 1991.

____. *Cross of Gold: A Novel.* London: Longman, 1981.

Poniatowska, Elena. *Ay vida, no me mereces! Carlos Fuentes, Rosario Castellanos, Juan Rolfo: La literatura de la onda.* Mexico City: Mortiz, 1985.

____. *Dear Diego.* Translated by Katherine Silver. New York: Pantheon, 1986.

____. *La "flor de lis."* Mexico City: Ediciones Era, 1988.

____. *Hasta no verte, Jesus mio.* Mexico City: Ediciones Era, 1969.

____. *Massacre in Mexico.* Translated by Helen Lane. 1971; New York: Viking, 1975.

____. *De noche vienes.* 2d ed. Mexico City: Editorial Grijalbo, 1979.

Rushdie, Salman. *Grimus: A Novel.* London: Gollancz, 1975.

____. *Haroun and the Sea of Stories.* New York: Viking, 1990.

____. *The Jaguar Smile: A Nicaraguan Journey.* New York: Viking, 1987.

____. *Midnight's Children: A Novel.* New York: Knopf, 1981.

____. *The Satanic Verses.* New York: Viking, 1989.

____. *Shame.* New York: Knopf, 1983.

Schulman, Sarah. *After Delores.* New York: Dutton, 1989.

_____. *Girls, Visions, and Everything*. Seattle: Seal Press, 1986.

_____. *People in Trouble*. New York: Dutton, 1990.

_____. *The Sophie Horowitz Story*. Tallahassee: Naiad Press, 1984.

Shammas, Anton. *Arabesques*. Translated by Vivian Eden. New York: Harper and Row, 1988.

Shulman, Alix Kates. *Burning Questions: A Novel*. New York: Knopf, 1978.

_____. *In Every Woman's Life: A Novel*. New York: Knopf, 1987.

_____. *Memoirs of an Ex-Prom Queen*. New York: Knopf, 1972.

_____. *On the Stroll*. New York: Knopf, 1981.

Silko, Leslie Marmon. *Almanac of the Dead*. New York: Simon and Schuster, 1991.

_____. *Ceremony*. New York: Viking, 1977.

_____. *Storyteller*. New York: Seaver Books, 1981.

Tillman, Lynne. *Absence Makes the Heart*. London: Serpent's Tail, 1990.

_____. *Haunted Houses*. New York: Poseidon Press, 1987.

_____. *Living with Contradictions*. New York: Top Stories, 1982.

_____. *Madame Realism*. New York: 1984.

_____. *Motion Sickness*. New York: Poseidon Press, 1991.

_____. *Weird Fucks*. New York: Bikini Girl, 1980.

Valenzuela, Luisa. *Clara: Thirteen Short Stories and a Novel*. Translated by Hortense Carpentier and Jorge Castello. New York: Harcourt Brace Jovanovich, 1976.

_____. *He Who Searches*. Translated by Helen Lane. Elmwood Park, Ill.: Dalkey Archive Pres, 1988.

_____. *The Lizard's Tail: A Novel*. Translated by Gregory Rabassa. New York: Farrar, Straus and Giroux, 1983.

_____. *Open Door*. Translated by Hortense Carpentier et al. San Francisco: North Point Press, 1988.

_____. *Other Weapons*. Translated by Deborah Bonner. Hanover, N.H.: Ediciones del Norte, 1985.

_____. *Strange Things Happen Here*. Translated by Helen Lane. New York: Harcourt Brace Jovanovich, 1979.

Walker, Alice. *The Color Purple*. New York: Harcourt Brace Jovanovich, 1982.

_____. *In Love and Trouble: Stories of Black Women*. New York: Harcourt Brace Jovanovich, 1973.

_____. *In Search of Our Mothers' Gardens: Womanist Prose*. New York: Harcourt Brace Jovanovich, 1983.

_____. *Living by the Word: Selected Writings, 1973-1987*. New York: Harcourt Brace Jovanovich, 1988.

_____. *Meridian*. New York: Harcourt Brace Jovanovich, 1976.

_____. *The Temple of My Familiar*. New York: Harcourt Brace Jovanovich, 1989.

_____. *You Can't Keep a Good Woman Down*. New York: Harcourt Brace Jovanovich, 1981.

Wallace, Michele. *Black Macho and the Myth of the Superwoman*. 1979; New York: Verso, 1990.

_____. *Invisibility Blues: From Pop to Theory*. New York: Verso, 1990.

Wicomb, Zoë. *You Can't Get Lost in Cape Town*. New York: Pantheon, 1987.

Wolf, Christa. *Accident: A Day's News*. Translated by Heike Schwarzbauer and Rick Takvorian. New York: Farrar, Straus and Giroux, 1989.

_____. *Cassandra: A Novel and Four Essays*. Translated by Jan van Heurck. New York: Farrar, Straus and Giroux, 1984.

_____. *No Place on Earth*. New York: Farrar, Straus and Giroux, 1982.

_____. *Patterns of Childhood*. Translated by Ursule Molinaro and Hedwig Rappolt. New York: Farrar, Straus and Giroux, 1980.

_____. *The Quest for Christa T.* Translated by Christopher Middleton. New York: Farrar, Straus and Giroux, 1970.

_____. *Selected Essays*. New York: Farrar, Straus and Giroux, 1992.